Software Engineering from Scratch

A Comprehensive Introduction Using Scala

Jason Lee Hodges

Apress®

Software Engineering from Scratch

Jason Lee Hodges
Draper, UT, USA

ISBN-13 (pbk): 978-1-4842-5205-5   ISBN-13 (electronic): 978-1-4842-5206-2
https://doi.org/10.1007/978-1-4842-5206-2

Managing Director, Apress Media LLC: Welmoed Spahr
Acquisitions Editor: Louise Corrigan
Development Editor: James Markham
Coordinating Editor: Nancy Chen

Cover designed by eStudioCalamar

Distributed to the book trade worldwide by Springer Science+Business Media New York, 233 Spring Street, 6th Floor, New York, NY 10013. Phone 1-800-SPRINGER, fax (201) 348-4505, e-mail orders-ny@springer-sbm.com, or visit www.springeronline.com. Apress Media, LLC is a California LLC and the sole member (owner) is Springer Science + Business Media Finance Inc (SSBM Finance Inc). SSBM Finance Inc is a **Delaware** corporation.

For information on translations, please e-mail rights@apress.com, or visit http://www.apress.com/rights-permissions.

Apress titles may be purchased in bulk for academic, corporate, or promotional use. eBook versions and licenses are also available for most titles. For more information, reference our Print and eBook Bulk Sales web page at http://www.apress.com/bulk-sales.

Any source code or other supplementary material referenced by the author in this book is available to readers on GitHub via the book's product page, located at www.apress.com/9781484252055. For more detailed information, please visit http://www.apress.com/source-code.

Printed on acid-free paper

For Hunter and Jax

During the writing of this book, my children asked me why I chose a nebula for the cover. I asked them, "Do you know what a nebula is?" They quickly and unequivocally boasted, "Of course, it's where stars are born!" To which I replied, "Exactly."

I hope that by reading this book a few stars are born.

Table of Contents

About the Author ....**xi**

About the Technical Reviewer ....**xiii**

Chapter 1: Introduction...1

Brief History of Programming 2

Why Scala? 8

Summary..10

Chapter 2: Installing Everything You Need 11

Installing Java JDK..11

Installing JDK on Windows 12

Installing JDK on MacOS 12

Installing JDK on Linux 14

Installing Scala...15

Installing Scala on Windows..15

Installing Scala on MacOS...16

Installing Scala on Linux...17

Summary..17

Chapter 3: Contextual Knowledge 19

Command-Line Operating Systems 19

File Systems 21

Navigation..22

Language Syntax and Semantics...27

Summary...30

Chapter 4: Expressions and Variables 31

Basic Expressions 32

Advanced Expressions 38

    Arithmetic Operators 44

    Comparison Operators..46

    Logical Operators 48

Variables 50

Summary...53

Chapter 5: Basic Data Types 55

Numeric Types 56

Booleans 60

Groups of Data 62

    Lists 63

    Maps..67

Characters and Strings 70

    String Manipulation 72

Summary...78

Chapter 6: Control Flow 81

Scripting...82

Conditional Statements...88

Pattern Matching 92

Loops 95

    While Loop 95

    Do/While Loop 97

    For Loop..100

Exception Handling 103

Summary.. 108

Chapter 7: Functions 109

Function Definition 110

Calling a Function 115

Benefits.. 117

    Abstraction 118

    Modularity 123

Application 125

Summary.. 128

Chapter 8: Classes 129

Encapsulation 130

Object Reference.. 135

Case Classes.. 141

Companion Objects 144

Application 145

Summary.. 148

Chapter 9: Dependency Management 151

Compiler.. 152

Scala Object... 154

Packages.. 155

Imports.. 157

Standard Library 160

Application 162

Summary.. 169

Chapter 10: Programming Paradigms 171

Procedural Programming 173

Object-Oriented Programming 176

    Inheritance 177

    Polymorphism...180

    Interfaces and Abstract Classes 185

Functional Programming...191

    Higher-Order Functions 194

    Putting It All Together 205

Summary...207

Chapter 11: What Is Software Engineering? 209

Efficiency and Optimization 212

Testing...217

Architecture Planning...224

Software Deployment...226

Summary...228

Chapter 12: Data Structures 231

Arrays...232

Linked Lists...234

Queues and Stacks 238

Hash Table...242

Trees 246

Sets...250

Maps 253

Performance Reference 255

Summary...256

Chapter 13: Algorithms 257

Greedy Algorithms..258

Divide and Conquer 261

Merge Sort...263

Binary Search 269

Graph Traversal Algorithms 274

Depth First Search...281

Breadth First Search..285

Dynamic Programming 287

Levenshtein Distance 288

Summary..292

Chapter 14: Design Patterns..293

Creational Patterns 294

Structural Patterns...297

Behavioral Patterns..301

Summary..304

Chapter 15: Further Study 305

Database Administration...305

Data Engineering..307

Data Science..309

Embedded Systems 310

Distributed Systems...311

Web Development..313

Conclusion 314

Index...317

About the Author

Jason Lee Hodges is currently a Software Engineering Lead at a high-growth unicorn technology start-up. He started programming when he was 11 years old and currently codes in Python, Java, Scala, Kotlin, TypeScript, and Rust on a daily basis. He believes Scala is the ultimate teaching language and that anyone who is willing to put in the work can learn to be a software engineer. You can reach Jason on Twitter @jasonleehodges.

About the Technical Reviewer

Toby Jee is a Software Programmer currently located in Sydney, Australia. He loves Linux and open source projects. He programs mainly in Java, JavaScript, TypeScript, and Python. In his spare time, Toby enjoys walkabouts, reading, and playing guitar.

CHAPTER 1

Introduction

Perhaps second only to witnessing the birth of a child, in my opinion there is no experience closer to pure creation than through the arduous efforts and subsequent yield of software engineering. In regard to such efforts, I have found that, in many cases, the amount of fulfillment perceived by an individual is directly proportional to the level of difficulty that they were required to overcome. That is to say, the harder something is, the greater the feeling of accomplishment once you succeed. There is no doubt that software engineering is a difficult discipline to learn and its limits are never-ending. But there is nothing more fruitlessly frustrating than spending tireless hours of energy learning something just to find out that its applications are limited.

That's how I have felt on several occasions when wading through the bottomless lakes of software engineering topics over time. Granted, no topic on its own was useless – I was always able to extrapolate the theme and apply it in another area. However, the aim of this book is to spare you the misery of learning software engineering in a myriad of different ways that ultimately leaves the job of distilling the information usefully up to you. The following chapters will gently guide you through the landscape of computer science and software engineering methodologies and paradigms so that, once completed, you will have a holistic view of what is fundamentally relevant without wasting any time on what is not.

© Jason Lee Hodges 2019
J. L. Hodges, *Software Engineering from Scratch*,
https://doi.org/10.1007/978-1-4842-5206-2_1

That being said, the study of software engineering takes a good amount of practice and self-discipline. It is advised that you read this book with a group and follow along together, hold each other accountable, help each other get unstuck, code with the examples (don't just read them), and go through all of the exercises. It is important that by the end of each chapter you can accomplish the easy stuff in your sleep without needing to look it up. If you progress through each chapter as such, by the end of this book you should feel confident enough in the software engineering skills you've gained to comfortably write simple programs in an efficient, performant, and scalable manner.

I have found that the most effective way to learn to be a software engineer is to start with a baseline of context. So, in this chapter you will be presented with an abridged history of programming in order to build this context. After which you will be briefly introduced to the Scala programming language and why it is the ultimate teaching language.

Brief History of Programming

In order to properly introduce software engineering, it is necessary to first define programming and how it was derived. So, what is programming and what is code? A program, in its most basic form, is a set of instructions that tells a machine what to do. That program is written using code which is a series of language constructs or symbols that are written to form meaning to the machine. It is extremely important to understand that, despite the complexity of modern software engineering, all programs are made up of a series of very basic instructions that when combined together create increasingly more complex functionality.

To demonstrate this, let's create a mental model of what a computer is and how it works. If you take the outer shell off of any computer and look inside, you will see a whole lot of wires and chips plugged into components that are soldered onto a variety of green silicon boards. But just like the complexity of software, the hardware can be boiled down to a series of basic components as well. For the purposes of this introduction, we'll boil down a computer to a simple, small, green silicon board and that's it. Not very useful yet. Next, let's add to this mental model of a computer the notion that a computer really only interprets a basic program's instructions in the form of whether or not a transistor on our green silicon board should allow electricity to flow through it or not. So, let's put a transistor on our board. Effectively, the transistor is an on/off switch. A very basic program would give the machine a series of combinations of "on" and "off" instructions in an attempt to accomplish something. Perhaps, for the sake of example, allowing electricity to flow through a transistor would turn on a tiny light bulb. So next, we'll add a light bulb to our model computer. By providing a series of on/off instructions, a programmer could communicate with that light in Morse Code, thereby providing meaning or application to their program. But, given a basic silicon electrical board with a transistor and a light bulb, how does the programmer provide the instructions to the machine?

Early historical programmers created a mechanism that they added to these electrical boards that consumed a spool of narrow paper with holes punched into it – these were known as punched tape. The paper was fed into the mechanism and it rolled the tape through it in a constant speed much like you see a printer operating today. As the paper tape went through the mechanism, the hole punches in the paper told the machine whether or not to allow electricity to pass through the transistor. Well, how did it do that? In our Morse Code model, let's think of the tape as being able to conduct electricity (perhaps our tape is made of a thin copper sheet). We could then pass the tape through our transistor, complete an electrical circuit, and turn the light bulb on. If there is a hole in our electrical conducting tape, then it won't complete the circuit, and the light bulb turns off. If we know how fast the gears of the input mechanism consume the tape and thereby complete the circuit, then we can punch enough holes in the tape to create a complete message in Morse Code with our basic machine. In fact, during the 1800s some telegraph operators used a similar method to send Morse Code messages.

As technology advanced, programmers went from manually punching holes to having machines store the on/off instructions on a disk instead of punched tape. But if there is no more punched tape and only instructions on disk, then how does the programmer tell the machine what instructions to store? This is when the code part of programming actually starts. In our Morse Code example, we physically decided whether or not electricity would flow through the transistor by providing it a mechanism to do so. Instead of physically creating something, programmers had to develop a symbol to represent on and a symbol to represent off, thereby effectively creating the bed rock of coding that we use today. The concepts surrounding said symbols, coding, and the idea for the modern computer came from many early mathematicians. One especially influential mathematician from the 1940s was named Alan Turing and many of his ideas percolated all throughout computer science, including "Turing Tests" (a test to grade artificial intelligence) and "Turing Machines" (which is essentially the computers we know today). Because early computing held its roots in mathematics, many of the first pieces of software tended to focus on mathematical applications, like your basic calculator. Because of that, the symbols that were used early on were numbers.

The symbol decided on for "on" became the number 1 and the symbol decided on for "off" became the number 0. This type of code is known as binary, which is a mathematical number system that dates back at least as early as 16th century Europe, long before the first computer was ever invented. Conversely, the number system that we were taught in elementary school was a ten-based (or decimal) system, where you count from 0 to 9 and then when you hit 10 you start back over at 0 in the ones spot and you add a 1 in the tens spot. Because 0 and 1 were used for "on" and "off," early programmers were able to use a two-based (binary) system to represent other numbers. So you count 0, and then 1, and when you get to what we think of as 2, you start back over at 0 and add a 1 in front – just like in a ten-based system but you restart at 2 instead of 10 and you only ever use ones and zeros. Given this, the binary representation of basic decimal system numbers could be translated as shown in Table 1-1.

Table 1-1. *A representation of decimal numbers in binary*

Decimal	Binary
0	0
1	1
2	10
3	11
4	100
5	101
6	110
7	111
8	1000
9	1001
10	1010

Using binary to represent on and off electrical signals allowed for the ever-increasing complexity of mathematical equations to be carried out. But all binary was at its core (at least in this context of computer science) was an abstraction for on and off. So the next level abstraction from representing numbers in binary is representing alphabetical characters in binary. Ultimately, after a series of abstractions, programs were created that could interpret alphabetical characters and convert them to binary so that the machine could then interpret them as on/off instructions. The act of converting alphabetical characters to its binary representation is called assembling, and the programs that are written to do the conversion are called assemblers.

Once machines were able to understand alphabetical characters through assembly down to binary, combining alphabetical characters into words that then had further meaning or perhaps contained several steps worth of binary instructions in one word could be created. This was the basis for the first programming languages. Languages that are assembled down to binary are referred to as Assembly Language and are specific to the hardware architecture and operating system that a programmer is writing the program for. This represented challenges as assembly machine code written for one machine could not necessarily be used on a machine with a different architecture. "High-level" languages were developed in an attempt to tackle this challenge.

Assembly Language is often referred to as a "low-level" language since it is the least amount of abstractions away from the actual hardware. A one-step further abstraction from a low-level language is a "high-level" language in which the same code can be compiled down to different architectures and executed across different types of machines. The program used to complete the conversion of a high-level language to machine code is typically referred to as a compiler. A compiler and an assembler are very similar in that they both take symbolic representations of logic (code) and convert them to binary machine code for computer hardware to execute. In actuality all assemblers are also considered compilers, but not all compilers are assemblers. Compilers usually have broader functionality that allows for writing symbols or languages in a much more abstracted, expressive, and powerful way, which is why they can be used for high-level languages. Assemblers, on the other hand, typically have a very narrow set of instructions to draw from in order to optimize for speed which is why they can only be used with lower-level languages.

One of the first programming languages that used a compiler was Fortran which was used to program IBM mainframes in the 1950s. Common predecessors that shortly followed and are still used today include Lisp and COBOL. Dozens of similar languages also popped up in the decades to follow. In the 1970s, however, came the emergence of C which is considered the most widely used programming language of all time. Many programming languages that followed C draw heavy influence from its standards and style, including Scala. Languages that draw influence or inspiration from C are known as the C family of languages, and they include but may not be limited to

- C++

- C#

- Objective-C

- JavaScript

- Java (and its Java Virtual Machine variants like Scala, Kotlin, Clojure, and Groovy)

- Python

- Perl

So, if C is the most used programming language of all time, then why am I introducing you to software engineering in a different language? The basic answer is that introducing smaller concepts that are heavily abstracted away from the actual machine and working your way backward through the levels of abstraction is much easier than working with a less abstracted language like C. Does that mean that Scala is the most abstracted language then? Many would argue that it is not. Why, then, is Scala the ultimate teaching language for software engineering?

Why Scala?

Scala has not been the traditional language taught in most schools when it comes to introducing software engineering or programming. Most of the time when a developer is introduced to Scala, it is assumed that they have some programming experience or are at least familiar with the concepts introduced from other languages. What is unique about this book is that it will build up all of the fundamentals of software engineering in Scala assuming that you've never been introduced to programming or software engineering before.

That being said, it is important to note that this is not a book about Scala. The concepts taught in this book are not meant to demonstrate idiomatic Scala programming. Rather, the objective is to teach you software engineering concepts in the most digestible manner possible in an extremely flexible language that no other language can match. It is also relevant to point out that many of the topics in this book have entire books written about them. The intention of this book is not to cover these topics exhaustively, but rather mildly introduce them to you in a refined and curated fashion.

Often you might observe that introductory courses to programming might be taught in Python – especially courses that are intended for non-computer science majors who still need programming skills like scientists and statisticians. Some schools start with Python as an easy introduction because it reads a lot like English, is a concise and expressive language, and has many real-world applications. Its huge downside is that it is not a very good language if your application is reliant on strong performance. Because of the way Python was created, it's code runs extremely slow compared to other languages. So, oftentimes, schools will take some of the basic concepts you learned in Python and then teach you Java as the next step. There are whole courses that are aimed at translating what you learned between the two languages. Java is extremely fast, in comparison to Python, so that solves that particular problem, but it is also a very verbose language and is only intended to fit into a very specific software engineering paradigm. So why isn't there a happy medium you might ask? That's where Scala comes in.

The name "Scala" is derived from the expression "Scalable Language." It was developed by Martin Odersky in the early 2000s in an attempt to create a language that could *scale* to fit different use cases and grow with you as a developer or company. Because of this intent, along with the architecture on which it was created, Scala fits into several software engineering paradigms and therefor lends itself capable of teaching all the different paradigms in one language rather than bouncing back and forth between languages. This creates the benefit of allowing a developer to focus on learning new concepts rather than the mental overhead of learning the new syntax (the rules that govern the combination of symbols in a programming language – more on that to come later) of a language simply to demonstrate a concept that is only available in that language.

Because Scala fits into so many paradigms, you will often find criticisms of it as a language, suggesting that Scala is "*everything and the kitchen sink*" in one language. Others will say that it is hard to learn, or that it has a really long ramp-up time. While that is true – it can, in fact, be very complex because of all of the different things it can do and all of the different paradigms it can conform to – if you digest Scala in isolated partitions until you understand each concept before moving on to the next concept, it can add efficiency to your software engineering education in the long run. Additionally, if you learn Scala first, you will be very well positioned to transfer your knowledge and experience over to all the other languages (especially C family languages) as you will have learned concepts that are inherent to all of them, which will make you especially valuable as an engineer. Alternatively, if you were to go the traditional route and work through each paradigm one language at a time, it would take you much longer to achieve the same amount of value as an engineer.

Another reason why Scala is a good language to use as an introduction to software engineering is that it can be written in a very concise way – similar to Python but with the performance of Java. A concept that may take five to ten lines of code in other languages may only take 1 or 2 lines of code to demonstrate in Scala. Scale that out to an entire program and you could be saving hundreds or thousands of lines of code for a single application. This provides the benefit of getting the concept across to a new developer more quickly and also allows them to try it and understand it faster as they move throughout the concepts without sacrificing the runtime performance of the code.

Finally, Scala has been seeing an uptick in relevance in concurrency, latency-sensitive, big data, and machine learning/artificial intelligence projects lately. Having a core understanding of the language and all of the accompanying software engineering concepts will position a developer rather favorably when starting to dive into and learn more about these topics. These trends will continue to grow and dominate the software engineering industry in the near future and an engineer who doesn't need to get caught up to speed on concepts that weren't covered in their language or paradigm will be ahead of the game.

Because of all of these things, in my opinion Scala is the ultimate teaching language, and you should be incredibly excited to start learning software engineering using Scala.

Summary

In this chapter, you were briefly introduced to what a computer is and how a program works with a computer to provide applicable functionality. To demonstrate this functionality, the benefit of using Scala as an introductory programming language was established. In the next chapter, we'll get your coding environment set up and ready to start programming.

CHAPTER 2

Installing Everything You Need

Okay, so now that you are excited about all of the different software engineering concepts that you can learn with Scala, the first thing you will need to do is install… Java. Wait, what? It may seem a bit misleading, but the Java Development Kit (JDK) is required for Scala since the Scala programming language is built off of the Java Virtual Machine (JVM). So, you will need to ensure that it is installed as a dependency before installing Scala.

Installing Java JDK

As of the time of this writing, you will need to ensure that you have the Java Development Kit or JDK version 1.8 or higher. You can check to see if you already have it installed by opening up a command line (in Windows cmd. exe or in macOS or Linux open up a terminal). From there, type the code listed on the first line in Listing 2-1, which will return to you on the second line the version of Java you have installed.

Listing 2-1. Command to check if the Java JDK is installed on your system

```
> javac -version
javac1.8.0_171
```

© Jason Lee Hodges 2019
J. L. Hodges, *Software Engineering from Scratch*,
https://doi.org/10.1007/978-1-4842-5206-2_2

If you receive an error, then you don't have the JDK installed, and you will need to install it before moving on to installing Scala. If you do have it installed, you can skip ahead to the installing Scala section. The steps to install Java vary slightly by operating system.

Installing JDK on Windows

If you are running a Windows operating system, you will need to navigate to the following Oracle web site to download and install the most recent JDK for Windows and run through the installer wizard.

`www.oracle.com/technetwork/java/javase/downloads/index.html`

There should be a button that says "Download" with a reference to either the Oracle JDK or the Java Platform JDK (both will take you to the same page). From there, you will see a list of different operating systems for which you can download the JDK. Choose the download for Windows. Once the download is complete, you can open up the installer executable file and walk through the wizard. You should be able to choose all of the default installation configurations (unless you feel strongly otherwise).

You can verify that the installation worked correctly by clicking your start menu and search for `cmd` to open up a command-line terminal. From there, type in `javac -version` as you did at the beginning of this chapter. If a version number is returned, the installation worked correctly. If you encounter an error, then the installation did not work correctly and you will need to retrace your steps to ensure that you did not miss anything.

Installing JDK on MacOS

If you are on a MacOS system, the easiest way to install the JDK is using Homebrew, which is a command-line package installer. You can visit `https://brew.sh` for simple installation instructions. At the time of this writing, the installation instructions for Homebrew are simply to open up a terminal (you can hit command + space bar and search for "terminal") and type in the command shown in Listing 2-2.

Listing 2-2. Terminal command to install the Homebrew package manager

```
/usr/bin/ruby -e "$(curl -fsSL https://raw.githubusercontent.com/
Homebrew/install/master/install)"
```

This command will prompt you to hit Enter/Return in order to confirm that it will install a number of directories on your computer. It will then ask you for your system password. Once that has been entered, it will automatically install everything you need to use the Homebrew package manager. This package manager can install most programs that you will need for development purposes on a Mac so it is a useful thing to have as a software engineer. You can browse some of the packages you can install with Homebrew by navigating to https://formulae.brew.sh. Verify that you have Homebrew installed correctly by typing in the command in Listing 2-3. If a version number is returned, then it was successfully installed.

Listing 2-3. Check that Homebrew was installed successfully

```
>brew --version
Homebrew 1.8.3
```

Once Homebrew is installed, all you need to do to install the JDK is type the two commands in Listing 2-4. The first command will update all the packages that Homebrew has a reference to on your computer. The second command actually does the installation.

Listing 2-4. Install the Java JDK using Homebrew

```
> brew update
> brew cask install java
```

You can verify that the installation worked correctly by typing in `javac -version` as you did at the beginning of this chapter. If a version number is returned, the installation worked correctly. If you encounter an error, then the installation did not work correctly and you will need to retrace your steps to ensure that you did not miss anything.

Installing JDK on Linux

For Linux-based operating systems (like Ubuntu or Debian), you can install Java through the built-in package manager apt-get. This package manager is very similar to Homebrew if you read through the section for MacOS-based systems. Most development-based packages that you might need to install as a software engineer can be managed through apt-get on a Linux machine, so it is a useful tool to be aware of.

To install the Java JDK on Linux, simply open a terminal (click your Home button and search for terminal) and type in the commands in Listing 2-5. The first command will update the package manager to ensure you have the latest package references. The second command actually does the installation. The first word, `sudo`, stands for "Super User Do" and allows you administrator rights to the command that is about to be executed. It will prompt you for your administrator password.

Listing 2-5. Commands to install JDK on Linux

```
> sudo apt-get update
> sudo apt-get install default-jdk
```

You can verify that the installation worked correctly by typing in `javac -version` as you did at the beginning of this chapter. If a version number is returned, the installation worked correctly. If you encounter an error, then the installation did not work correctly and you will need to retrace your steps to ensure that you did not miss anything.

Installing Scala

Once you have the Java JDK installed on your computer, you can move on to installing Scala which is the programming language that we will be using to demonstrate the various software engineering paradigms in this book. You can check if it is already installed by typing the command in Listing 2-6 into a command prompt or terminal.

Listing 2-6. Check if Scala is installed

```
> scala -version
Scala code runner version 2.12.7 - Copyright 2002-2018,
LAMP/EPFL and Lightbend, Inc.
```

If the command returns a version number, then you already have Scala installed. We will be using version 2.12, the latest stable version of Scala, for the examples in this book. If you already have Scala installed, you can skip ahead to the next chapter. Conversely, if you received an error from the command in Listing 2-6, you will need to install Scala. As usual the steps vary slightly depending on what operating system you are using.

Installing Scala on Windows

To install Scala on Windows, you will need to navigate to the following Scala language web site and download the package binaries.

```
www.scala-lang.org/download/
```

You will notice at first that the web site will direct you to install Scala by downloading an IDE (Integrated Development Environment) or by downloading SBT (Simple Build Tool). Those topics will be covered later in this book, but for now we do not want to install them.

15

Instead, navigate to the bottom of the page where there are several binary packages available to download for all operating systems under the "Other Resources" section. Pick the download that matches your version of Windows. At the time of this writing, the appropriate link will be titled "scala-2.12.7.msi" which will download a .msi installer package that you can open up to walk through a wizard installation. You should be able to select all the defaults as you walk through the wizard. When it is done installing, verify that the installation was successful by repeating the command in Listing 2-6. If you receive a version number, then you have successfully installed Scala and you are ready to get programming.

Installing Scala on MacOS

To install Scala on a Mac, you can use the same package installer that you used to install Java, Homebrew. If you already had Java installed and did not need to install the Homebrew package manager, go back to the section in this chapter that covered installing Java for Mac and follow the instructions to install Homebrew. Once you have confirmed that Homebrew is installed on your Mac, you can run the command in Listing 2-7 to install Scala.

Listing 2-7. Command to install Scala on Mac

```
> brew install scala@2.12
```

This will run through a series of installation steps including updating Homebrew for any new package references and downloading the latest version of the Scala install package. From there, it will automatically install Scala on your machine. When it is done installing, verify that the installation was successful by repeating the command in Listing 2-6. If you receive a version number, then you have successfully installed Scala and you are ready to get programming.

Installing Scala on Linux

To install Scala on the Linux operating system, you can use the same package manager you used to install Java. Use the commands in Listing 2-8 to install Scala on your machine. You will be prompted for your machine's administrator password due to the use of the sudo command.

Listing 2-8. Command to install Scala on Linux

```
> sudo wget https://downloads.lightbend.com/scala/2.12.7/
  scala-2.12.7.deb
> sudo dpkg -i scala-2.12.7.deb
> sudo apt-get update
> sudo apt-get install scala
```

You may also be asked to confirm the use of disk space on your computer. Type Y and hit Enter to confirm. This will download the most recent version of Scala and automatically install it on your machine. When it is done installing, verify that the installation was successful by repeating the command in Listing 2-6. If you receive a version number, then you have successfully installed Scala and you are ready to get programming.

Summary

In this chapter, you successfully installed both the Java JDK and Scala. You learned that the Java JDK is a prerequisite for Scala since the Scala programming language is built off of the JVM. You will learn more about that in the coming chapters. Additionally, if you are using either a Mac or Linux operating system, you learned about package managers and how simple and convenient they can be. You will likely use package managers a great deal throughout your career as a software engineer.

In the next chapter, you will be introduced to some prerequisite knowledge that will be extremely important context to build before you actually start programming. First, you will be introduced to command-line-based operating systems followed by a brief introduction to the linguistic concepts of syntax and semantics.

CHAPTER 3

Contextual Knowledge

In order to learn any type of programming, you must be comfortable with two main topics. First, the operating system that you will be programming on, its origins, and common usages. Second, the concepts of languages as a whole – spoken, written, and symbolic or coded. Without this prerequisite context, some of the instructions in the coming chapters will be difficult to follow. So, before we attempt to learn anything in Scala, let's briefly dive in and gain a deeper understanding of these topics as they will build a strong foundation for your software engineering career.

Command-Line Operating Systems

When you start up your computer today, you will likely see a Windows or Apple logo. Sometimes you might see some start-up scripts running by the screen really fast and you have no idea what they are and you likely never will need to know. As long as the operating system gets you to your desktop so that you can click on icons and run applications, that's all you need to see. But behind your desktop, running in the background, as alluded to by those start-up scripts, is just a simple command-line operating system that has been built up with incrementally increasing complexity over time. How the operating system works and how it came to work that way

© Jason Lee Hodges 2019
J. L. Hodges, *Software Engineering from Scratch*,
https://doi.org/10.1007/978-1-4842-5206-2_3

are hidden from you so that you don't have to worry about it. You can simply browse the Internet, write a program or a book, or generate some other type of content. You can be productive on a computer by building off of a piece of code that was written by others and, as long as it works for you as intended, you will never need to know how it was created. This is a concept known as abstraction. There are several abstractions in this book, including a lot of concepts that could have been covered in the first chapter that will be glossed over in order to focus only on what's important in the context of software engineering in Scala. That being said, in order to write programs in their most basic form, it will be useful to peel back the layers of abstraction on an operating system to understand how it works.

Your desktop has elements that can be clicked on, dragged, or modified in different ways. The way you interact with your desktop is known as input. The way the computer responds to your input is known as output. Input and output (I/O) are the building blocks of an operating system. In fact, the very first operating systems were simple text input and text output. There was no graphical user interface (GUI) – no pictures, no mouse cursor, no icons, no windows or graphics of any kind. Just a command line waiting for input, ready to respond with output. In this way, the first operating systems were not unlike a basic calculator, albeit perhaps with more input keys.

More specifically, the process the operating system would go through to interact with user input was a Read, Evaluate, Print, and Loop cycle. This is also known as REPL and it is one way that you can interact with a computer to write software (more on that in the coming chapters). The "Read" step is simply the computer waiting for input from the user. Once the user types something into the command line and hits enter or return, the operating system reads in the input and stores it in memory. The next step is an "Evaluation" of the input. Typically, the user would expect the computer to do something with their input. In the case of a simple calculator, the user input of "2 + 2" would need to be evaluated to an answer of 4. Once the computer has determined that the output should be 4, what's next? That's where "Print" comes in. It is not enough for the computer to know that 4 is the answer; it must also let the user know that it evaluated their input and the answer is 4. So the operating system must print the answer out to the screen as output. You will often see this referred to as "printing to the console." The console is just another word for the output terminal or command-line screen. Finally, the computer "Loops" back to the start where it again waits for user input to read.

So, what type of input is the computer expecting? Probably the most intimidating thing about working with a command-line-based operating system is knowing by heart what commands to enter into the "Read" step of a REPL in order to get anything done. Rest assured, you do not need to memorize everything in order to get things done with the command line. By gaining a simple understanding of the way the file system of an operating system works and how to navigate that file system, you should have the majority of what you will need as a software engineer when working from the terminal.

File Systems

One of the most common evaluations a user might ask an operating system to do is store data of some kind. This might be pictures of your family, a research paper, or some music. In the case of software engineering, the data that will often be stored is simply a file that contains a programmer's code that needs to be executed at a later time. As you likely have experienced, as your data storage gets bigger and bigger, it becomes more and more important to have a system of organization to navigate to the files that you want to find. That's where the file system comes in. Most, if not all, operating systems have some type of file system for managing and organizing content.

Current Windows operating systems run off of a file system called NTFS which stands for New Technology File System (as opposed to the old system that was called FAT32, which was a 32-bit File Allocation Table).

Both Apple computers and Linux-based operating systems run on the Unix File System. Both NTFS and Unix file systems support similar terminal input commands for navigating, storing, and moving data around on a computer. This will be important as you start to write software so that you can quickly and easily access the programs that you write without needing a graphical user interface. The reason you don't want to rely on the GUI is so that you can write programs that can access and interact with other programs or files. This is much easier to accomplish if you can write a simple file system command that you can pass to the operating system to execute for you.

The most important thing for you to understand about the file system on a command-line operating system is that you can navigate through it similar to how you would on a graphical user interface. In the GUI you open up windows and double-click on folders to see the sub-folders and files that they contain. The same can also be accomplished directly from the command line using input commands rather than using a mouse cursor.

Navigation

The digital file systems that operating systems use were modeled after a traditional, physical, filing cabinet system with folders and files. In order to access a file, you must first open the folder that the file resides in. But in a digital filing system, you can't see the physical folders from the command line, so how do you know what folder to open?

The first input command you will learn is `ls` (for Unix) and `dir` (for NTFS) which stand for "list" and "directory," respectively. Both of these commands list all of the contents of the directory or folder that you are currently in. It is important to note that folders can contain other folders. Given that, there can be infinitely many levels of nested folders to navigate through, but each directory or folder can list out its contents as well once you open them. So, once you've decided on a sub-folder to open from the list of folder contents that the `ls` or `dir` command returns, how do you open that sub-folder?

The next important command is the same for both Unix and NTFS file systems and that is cd, which stands for "change directory." The cd command should be following by something called an input parameter. In this case, the input parameter is the name of the directory that you want to open. Listing 3-1 provides an example of listing the contents of a directory and then changing the directory to a sub-folder.

Listing 3-1. Listing the contents of a directory and then changing directory from a command-line interface

```
> ls
Desktop
Documents
Downloads
Pictures
example.log
install.sh
> cd Documents
/Documents> ls
example.doc
rough_draft.txt
/Documents> cd ..
>
```

Note   For command-line examples in this book, the folders in each directory will be in plain text, while the files are denoted in italics. How they are formatted on your file system is going to depend on the settings of your particular shell or terminal. This example starts from a home directory. Oftentimes in a Windows or NTFS file system, you will start out in a hard drive directory like your C:\ drive. But for the sake of unified examples, this book will use the Unix commands throughout.

From the home directory in this example, if you input ls, you will see the folders labeled "Desktop," "Documents," "Downloads," and "Pictures." You will also see two files, one labeled "example.log" and one labeled "install.sh." In this example, let's assume you want to access a file from your documents folder. To change directories and go into that documents folder, you would type in cd Documents and the file system would then change to the "Documents" directory. You'll notice that the input prompt will now show you that you are in the "Documents" directory, denoted by /Documents>. From there, you can list the contents of that directory again using ls. That command shows you that the Documents directory contains two files named "example.doc" and "rough_draft.txt." Finally, assume that you changed your mind because you couldn't find the file you wanted and you wanted to go back up to your home directory. The command you would use for that is cd .. . The two periods tell the file system to go back up one directory. This is the same for both types of file systems.

If you know the entire path of the folder you want to go to in a nested file structure, you can also cd into a full path as demonstrated in Listing 3-2.

Listing 3-2. Changing directly into a nested directory

```
> cd Downloads/StockTickers/data/2018/Q1
/Downloads/StockTickers/data/2018/Q1> cd ../..
/Downloads/StockTickers/data>
```

Just as you can navigate several layers deep in one command, you can also go back up several levels in one command. By typing in ../.. you've told the file system to go back up twice given the twice instantiation of the double period operator. The opposite of the double period operator is the single period operator which basically tells the file system that you would like to access a file or folder that is relative to the current directory (as opposed to the parent directory as denoted by the double period). This is useful when writing a program that needs to access other files in the same directory, but you are not yet sure which directory the program will be installed on or saved to. You will see examples of that later on in this book.

You can open a file in a text editor program by typing in the command for the editor that you prefer, followed by a space and then the file name (the file name being the input parameter). If the file name that you entered does not exist in the current directory, it will create one for you. In Unix, a popular editor that comes with most operating systems is nano. On a Windows operating system, you can use the command edit to open the MS-DOS Editor. Both of these will open the file for editing in a text editor. Each of these programs will have their own commands for creating text files that falls outside the scope of this chapter.

To create a folder in the current working directory, you can type in mkdir followed by the folder name that you want to create as an input parameter. Both file systems will accept this command the same way. To remove a folder in Unix, you would type in rm -rf foldername which will delete the folder and all of its contents if you have the appropriate permissions to do so. You can also precede this command with the sudo keyword to give yourself super user access (you will be prompted for your administrator password). On Windows you would type in rmdir foldername to obtain the same behavior. To delete a file instead of a folder, the command is rm filename.txt on Unix and del /f filename.txt on Windows. Listing 3-3 demonstrates these commands.

Listing 3-3. Commands to create and remove files and folders. Note after the "rm filename.txt" command, the "ls" command returns a blank line to denote that the folder is now empty

```
> ls
Documents
> mkdir foldername
> ls
Documents
foldername
```

```
> cd foldername
/foldername> nano filename.txt
/foldername> ls
filename.txt
/foldername> rm filename.txt
/foldername> ls

/foldername> cd ..
> rm -rf foldername
> ls
Documents
```

That should give you a pretty solid base understanding of how to navigate between folder structures from the command line, how to create and remove folders and files, and how to point to relative directories. These are commands that you should memorize. All other command-line-based commands can be easily looked up on the Internet if you ever need to use them, depending on what it is you are trying to do. But for now, let's stick to the minimum necessary amount of commands to maintain the digestibility of the concepts. Once you feel confident with these commands, you can move on to understanding more about language constructs as a whole. All of this will be useful context when writing your own software later in this book.

EXERCISE 3-1

From the command line, create a file system–based representation of your family tree starting with a single relative. Try to go back as far as you can – a great, great, grandparent would be excellent. Each folder should be labeled with the names of the parents of the family, and there should be a folder for each child within that household. Navigate between the levels of folders to create sub-folders. Try to build this out as far as you can so that creating folders and moving between them becomes like second nature.

Once you've created the entire family tree, try the following exercises:

1. See if you can create a file in each of the child folders that contains the birthday of that particular child.

2. Remove some of the individual files you just created.

3. Once you've deleted a few files, delete an empty sub-folder.

4. Delete a folder that contains files.

5. Remove a folder that contains sub-folders.

Language Syntax and Semantics

Programming languages, just like spoken languages, have a set of rules that govern what is an acceptable pattern of lexeme combinations. A lexeme is simply a part of speech (like a noun or a verb) used in the construction of an interpretable code unit or sentence (in the case of spoken languages). When a compiler or a human encounters a code unit or a sentence and parses through it to extract the meaning, this is called lexical analysis. The main difference between the lexical analysis that a human performs and the analysis that a compiler performs is that the human brain can easily interpret improper grammar such as slang, sarcasm, or simple mistakes and extrapolate the connotative meaning behind what was said nonetheless. Conversely, a computer's compiler can only do exactly what it is told according to the rules defined by the language. Any deviation from the predefined grammar rules can cause either an error in the compiler or a behavior other than what was connotatively expected.

Consider the following quote from a comic published in 1997 depicting cavemen inventing language. To the human brain, it is easy to interpret what the connotative meaning of the sentence is without it following the actual grammar rules of the English language. However, without following exact grammar rules, a computer would not be able to understand the meaning of this sentence.

> *Words down got we've good pretty... Should now invent we syntax!*
>
> —Bob Thaves, 1997

Alternatively, the sentence might have said, "We have." Syntactically that sentence would be correct. It has a subject and a verb in the correct order with the correct punctuation. A computer would not throw a compiler error trying to parse this syntax. But what does it mean? What do we have? Why does it matter? What is it that you are trying to communicate? It's hard to derive any context from those two simple words. Computers can often compile correctly with proper syntax and yet fail to execute as expected due to a lack of meaning derived from a "sentence" of code.

The study of languages and their grammar, which includes rules like punctuation, parts of speech, and their order, is called linguistics. The study of linguistics becomes very important for those who are interested in creating their own programming languages as much of the subject areas overlap. Within linguistics, the governing rules of a language are referred to as a language's syntax.

Referring back to the Thaves quote, even though we can infer the meaning behind what the caveman is trying to say, the order of his words is syntactically incorrect. English syntax would dictate the he should have structured the sentence starting with a noun, and then a verb, followed by a direct object, and so on. The correct syntax for this sentence should have been, "We've got words down pretty good. Now we should invent syntax!" The meaning has not changed in this corrected sentence, but the order of the words is now consistent with what has been agreed upon in English as the correct way to state the idea.

The connotative meaning derived from this properly formatted or syntactically correct sentence is called semantics. As demonstrated earlier, it is possible to have a syntactically correct sentence that is semantically meaningless. These concepts apply equally as well to coded or symbolic language as they do to spoken or written language. For our purposes, it is extremely important that all sentences or code units are both syntactically correct and semantically meaningful as the computer will not be able to interpret your code otherwise. Understanding both syntax and semantics will be very important in your software engineering journey as it will help you best diagnose where potential errors or unexpected behaviors are occurring in your software.

EXERCISE 3-2

Answer the following questions to the best of your ability. Choose the option that best answers the question.

1. Which of the following sentences has a syntax error?

   A) computer science is the study of computation

   B) $a^2 + b^2$ equals c squared

   C) Software engineering

   D) All of the above.

2. Which of the following sentences has the most semantic meaning?

   A) Where did you learn?

   B) Albeit underwhelming, the study of superfluous references is of the utmost anxieties.

   C) "Turing Tests" were named after Alan Turing who came up with the idea for measuring artificial intelligence.

   D) All of the above.

Summary

In this chapter, you've learned the contextual foundation that you will need in order to build your software engineering skill set. Do not move on from this chapter until you feel like you can do the exercises from this chapter in your sleep. You should be able to create and delete files and folders and navigate up and down a tree of files in a file system from the command line with ease. You should also have a thorough understanding of the difference between syntax and semantics and their corresponding impact on spoken and coded languages. In the next chapter, you will begin to get to know the Scala language using mathematical expressions and variable assignments, similar to the work that early computer scientists started with.

CHAPTER 4

Expressions and Variables

The ancient Chinese philosopher, Lao Tzu, once said, "The journey of a thousand miles begins with a single step." Recognizing that there is a long way to go in your journey toward learning software engineering, this chapter may certainly be considered your first step as you begin to venture into the Scala language. And while taking that first step is indeed a momentous and commendable occasion, ensuring that you are headed in the appropriate direction is also a critical consideration.

There is an archetypal and yet naive notion within the industry that the best way to learn how to program is to pick a problem that you are trying to solve and write an application to solve it. By relating what you are learning to something with practical application, this method keeps fledgling developers engaged and consciously reinforces the concepts learned. However, what if the problem that you really want to solve relates to streaming a virtual reality environment across the globe in real time? Learning the vast quantities of methods and paradigms necessary to solve that problem would be like drinking from a fire hose. The counterargument might be to simply pick a reasonable sized problem to solve as an alternative. But what does that mean to a beginner? How would a beginner know what a reasonable sized problem is without already having the programming knowledge necessary to accomplish the task?

© Jason Lee Hodges 2019
J. L. Hodges, *Software Engineering from Scratch*,
https://doi.org/10.1007/978-1-4842-5206-2_4

Given this paradoxical conundrum, it would stand to reason that the primary focus for your departure on this metaphorical journey should be ensuring that the concepts you learn first are easily digestible. For that reason, the programming constructs that we will start with in this book will be related to arithmetic, since that will provide a common basis of knowledge from which to draw upon. So, does that mean you need to be really good at math? By no means. The arithmetic that will be used in this book will be very basic, so do not be intimidated. Also, the remainder of the book will not have nearly as much math as this chapter as we start to move on to more concrete concepts. So, if you are not a fan of math, just stick with it as these foundational concepts are crucial. That being said, in this chapter we will first cover basic mathematical expressions followed by variable assignments and substitution, similar to concepts you might have learned in a pre-algebra class.

Basic Expressions

The most basic building block of software engineering is the expression. An expression, in both computer science and mathematics, is the combination of symbols that when evaluated will produce a fixed result. In Scala, everything can be distilled down to a series of expressions. Understanding this will become incredibly valuable in the future as you learn to test and debug your code because you will be able to isolate individual expressions from the overall program for separate evaluation and assessment. Let's program a few basic expressions in Scala to help further demonstrate what they are and why they are useful.

In order to do that, it's imperative to understand your Scala environment and its behavior. To help you understand, we will first walk through a couple of examples that produce expected results and how best for you to interpret those results. After that, we will walk through a few unexpected results so that you can learn how to get around road blocks with basic expressions before moving on to more complex expressions.

Open up your terminal and type in the command scala. This will open up the Scala REPL, which is Scala's own Integrated Development Environment (IDE) for evaluating code. Just like the commands you learned in the previous chapter, the Scala REPL will wait for code to be put into the REPL, evaluate that code, print out a result, and then loop back to listen for more input. Code that can be evaluated in a REPL without first going through a compiler is said to be interpreted because the computer is interpreting the code on the fly rather than evaluating it all up front and translating it into machine code. The mechanism that interprets the code on the fly for the machine to understand is called an interpreter. Interpreted code is extremely useful when demonstrating simple expressions and invaluable to those who are learning to code as you get real-time feedback on what you are typing. Let's start with the most basic mathematical expression you probably remember learning, 2+2, which is demonstrated in Listing 4-1.

Listing 4-1. The Scala REPL and a basic mathematical expression

```
> scala
Welcome to Scala 2.12.7 (Java Hotspot(TM) 64-Bit Server VM,
Java 1.8.0_181). Type in expressions for evaluation. Or try
:help.

scala> 2 + 2
res0: Int = 4

scala>
```

After typing in 2 + 2 and hitting enter, the interpreter will evaluate the expression and return to you the answer 4, much like a calculator. Any syntactically valid expression will follow this same pattern within the Scala REPL. Unlike a calculator, you'll notice a couple of extra things in the "Print" step of the interpreter.

First, there is the symbol res0. The res symbol stands for "result" and the 0 is an ordered unique identifier (also known as an index) that denotes that this is the first result in the REPL session. A session is an individual Scala REPL that is open for a unit of time. Subsequent results in the session will increment that number by one for each interpreted expression. When you close your terminal or quit the Scala REPL (by typing in :quit), that will end your session and the number will start back over at 0 for future sessions. You might wonder, if it's the first result, then why is the unique identifier a zero and not a one? Influenced by binary among other things, most incremental counting indexes in computer science start at zero.

Second, there is the symbol Int which stands for Integer. If you remember from your mathematics education, an integer is any whole number. The symbol is just the interpreter telling you that it has inferred the type of the evaluated expression result and that type is an integer. We will cover more on the different types in later chapters, but for now you can be content to understand that Scala is inferring types for you.

Let's move on to another expressions; this time let's do some multiplication. It would be intuitive to assume that the syntax for a multiplication expression in Scala would be something like 3 x 4. However, as demonstrated by Listing 4-2, entering in that expression will yield an error.

Listing 4-2. Example of a multiplication expression with invalid syntax

```
scala> 2 x 3
<console>:12: error: value x is not a member of Int
       2 x 3
         ^

scala>
```

You'll notice that the interpreter has printed out three lines of response as a result of the input expression. The first line provides an error message in an attempt to help us understand why we did not get the result we expected and how we might go about debugging it. Because we haven't covered members or types, you should not be expected to understand the meaning of the error message at this point. The second line reprints your original expression so that the third line can point out where the interpreter encountered the error (as denoted by the caret ^ symbol). The caret and the error message seem to be pointing us to the x in the expression. Intuition would suggest that it seems to be implying that we have a syntax error. As we covered in the previous chapter, if a sentence or code block is combined in the wrong order or with the wrong punctuation, the underlying meaning might change or have no meaning at all. Computers cannot interpret code unless it is written exactly as specified by the syntax rules of the language.

You might wonder then, what is proper syntax in Scala? There are a few strange symbols that we should be using for correct syntax instead of what you might be used to with standard mathematical arithmetic. But similar to mathematics, Scala has some rules that govern proper syntax. Expressions tend to have a combination of operators and operands that, when combined in a proper sequence, can be evaluated. In the expression 2 x 3, the operands are the 2 and the 3, and the operator is the multiplication sign. Operands are the objects in expressions that are operated on. Operators are the symbols that represent particular operations like addition, subtractions, division, and so on. However, a valid expression does not necessarily need an operator. Simply typing in the number 2 in the Scala REPL and hitting enter will yield a valid expression, returning the result as Int = 2. Conversely, an operator without an object to operate on is not valid syntax. Listing 4-3 demonstrates the proper syntax for multiplication.

Listing 4-3. Example of valid multiplication expression

```
scala> 2 * 3
res2: Int = 6
```

Note You might notice that in the listings in this chapter there are spaces separating the operators and the operands for each expression. These spaces are known as "whitespace" in programming. In some languages, most notably Python, whitespace is an important part of the syntax and meaning is derived from their use. In Scala, however, the whitespace has no meaning to the interpreter or the compiler and is therefore ignored in simple expressions like these. Deciding whether or not to have extra whitespace in your code is a personal preference, but most organizations will prefer you to be consistent with their coding style.

Another simple expression that you might try is division. The proper syntax for division requires two numbers representing the operands and a division symbol of / in the middle as the operator. Listing 4-4 represents two examples of proper syntax of a division expression in Scala.

Listing 4-4. Examples of valid division expressions

```
scala> 3 / 3
res3: Int = 1

scala> 4 / 5
res4: Int = 0
```

You might look at the second example and question whether or not it is indeed proper syntax given the answer. After all, 4 / 5 on a standard calculator evaluates to 0.8. This is the quintessential example of the difference between a syntax error and a semantic error in computer science. The syntax is absolutely correct – it has two operands separated by a symbol that represents an appropriate operator. Yet, we did not get the result we wanted. When the meaning of your expression and therefor the result is not what you intended, there is sure to be a semantic error somewhere. It just so happens that with semantic errors, Scala does not return any error results back to you in the terminal window because it assumes that, since what you typed in as input was a syntactically valid expression, it is exactly what you meant to type.

So, what is the semantic error in this case? This example was intended to demonstrate integer division. Because both operands are integers, the Scala interpreter has determined that the expression result must also be an integer. In integer division, the fractional remainder of the result is dropped, leaving you with just the whole number or integer. In this case because the standard result would be 0.8, it just rounds down to 0. If you were to do integer division on the expression 6 / 5, you would get a result of 1 because the remainder of 0.2 would be dropped. If you do want to keep the remainder, you must have at least one operand that is not an integer in order for the interpreter to infer that the result should not be an integer and therefor use standard division instead of integer division. Listing 4-5 demonstrates how that might be accomplished.

Listing 4-5. Examples of division expressions with non-integers

```
scala> 4.0 / 5
res5: Double = 0.8

scala> 6 / 5.0
res6: Double = 1.2
```

You'll notice that although 4.0 and 5.0 are, in fact, whole number since they do not have any remainders in the decimal position, by adding the decimal and the zero, it helps the Scala interpreter know that you intended for the type of these operands to be decimals that can accept remainders. The type of the result of these expressions is a `Double`, which we will cover in more detail in later chapters. For now, all you need to know is that a `Double` type can accept partial decimals where integers cannot.

Now that you've seen a few examples of basic expressions with different outcomes, we can move on to more advanced expressions to demonstrate the broader set of syntax rules surrounding Scala expressions.

Advanced Expressions

In order to best represent advanced expressions in Scala, I have found it useful to use popular mathematical formulas that most people are familiar with. The formulas that will be used for the remainder of this chapter in the examples and exercises will be the basic linear equation, Einstein's theory of relativity, and the Pythagorean Theorem. If you are not familiar with these equations, it might be useful for you to go look them up, but we will cover their definitions briefly as well.

Perhaps the easiest expression to start with syntactically would be the standard linear equation, which is `y = mx + b`. This equation is used to determine the coordinates of a point on a line that exists on a two-dimensional graph given the slope of the line and the point at which the line crosses the vertical axis, known as the Y intercept. The point is represented as `(x,y)` which corresponds to the variables of the same label within the equation. The slope of the line is represented by the variable `m`, and the Y intercept is represented by the variable `b`. Figure 4-1 shows a representation of this equation.

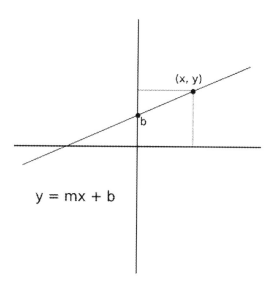

Figure 4-1. *A visual representation of the linear equation y = mx + b*

To solve this equation in Scala, let's assume that we know that the slope of a line is 0.5 and that the Y intercept is 3. With that knowledge we can determine the x and y values for any point on the line as long as we know one of the two coordinates of the point. Let's assume for the sake of this example that we know the x coordinate to be 8. From there, we can solve for y. Listing 4-6 shows how you would write the expression to solve for y in the Scala REPL.

Listing 4-6. A representation of the linear equation expression

```
Scala> 0.5 * 8 + 3
res7: Double = 7.0
```

So, what we've discovered as a result of this expression is that on this particular line, when the X coordinate is 8, the Y coordinate is 7. In this example, you can see that the result type is a Double since we used a fractional operand in the expression. You might also notice that for this particular expression there are multiple operators and they are evaluated from left to right. You can imagine an even more advanced scenario where you might need to chain several more operations together in this manner. We'll start to see such examples later on in the chapter, but for now just ensure that you understand how to use the information gained to solve a simple linear equation.

EXERCISE 4-1

Given what you've just learned, try solving the linear equation a few more times to solidify the example in your mind using the following questions:

1. All other factors being the same, if the X coordinate is 3.2, what is the Y coordinate?

2. If the slope changed to 2 and the X coordinate is 4, what is the Y coordinate? What is the type of the result?

3. Keeping the slope at 2, if the Y coordinate is 5, what is the X coordinate (this will take a bit of algebra to re-arrange the formula)?

Once you feel comfortable writing expressions with multiple operators, we can move on to the formula that expresses Einstein's theory of special relativity. This is a particularly fascinating theory which is a wonderful physics topic on its own, but for our purposes we will focus only on the formula used to express the theory, which is known as the mass-energy equivalence formula. That formula is $E = mc^2$ where E represents the kinetic energy of a particular body of mass m, multiplied by the speed of light squared c^2. If we know that the universal physical constant of the speed of light in a vacuum is 299,792,458 meters per second, we can deduce the kinetic energy (in joules) of a body of mass (let's say 10 kg) using the expression in Listing 4-7.

Listing 4-7. A representation of Einstein's mass-energy equivalence formula

```scala
scala> 10*Math.pow(299792458,2)
res8: Double = 8.9875517873681766E17
```

In this expression, the answer is shown in scientific notation. You might very well be used to seeing scientific notation expressed in terms of $8.9875517873681766 \times 10^{17}$ joules. All you need to know in Scala is that the "x 10" part is replaced with an "E" and even though the 17 does not appear to look like it is an exponent, you can safely assume that it is. Knowing how scientific notation is expressed in the Scala REPL is important, but more important than that is the demonstration of exponent syntax in this example. In this exponent expression, the speed of light constant is the operand and the operators are Math.pow (which tells Scala you want to raise your operand to a certain power), the parentheses, the comma, and the 2, which is the power you want to raise your operand to. If you wanted to raise an operand to the power of 3, you would simply use something like Math.pow(2,3) which is the equivalent of 2^3 and would yield an answer of 8.0.

It is worthy to note that Scala expressions follow the same order of operations syntax as standard mathematical rules. So, in the mass-energy equivalence equation, the exponent is evaluated first followed by the multiplication. As a reminder, the order of operations are

1. Evaluate expressions within parentheses first and simplify the terms inside them.

2. Evaluate all exponents.

3. Evaluate multiplication or division. If an expression contains both, evaluate left to right.

4. Evaluate addition or subtraction. If an expression contains both, evaluate left to right.

EXERCISE 4-2

Take a moment to see if you can extrapolate the information you've gained so far to represent the following expression in Scala:

$$(4^2 + 3)(2^2 - 4)$$

Note that the two sets of parentheses could represent factors in a polynomial equation. As you code your answer, consider the order of operations in which Scala will evaluate your expression.

Keeping this refresher in mind, let's move on to the Pythagorean Theorem. This expression uses the lengths of two sides of a right triangle to determine the length of the third side. The theorem provides that the two sides that form the right angle of the triangle, a and b, are equal to the third side c, known as the hypotenuse, if their lengths are all squared. Figure 4-2 shows an example of the premise of this equation.

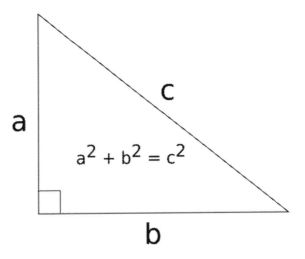

Figure 4-2. *A representation of the Pythagorean Theorem $a^2 + b^2 = c^2$*

Based on this representation, if we knew the lengths of a and b, we could determine the length of c. So, for the sake of example with Scala, let's say that the length of a is 4 and the length of b is 6. The equation to determine the length of c would thus be the square root of $4^2 + 6^2$. Listing 4-8 demonstrates a representation of this expression.

Listing 4-8. Literal expression of the Pythagorean Theorem

```scala
scala> Math.sqrt(Math.pow(4,2) + Math.pow(6,2))
res9: Double = 7.21102550927978
```

Notice the new syntax to denote the square root in a similar fashion to the exponent syntax, Math.sqrt. It will simply take the square root of anything inside its parentheses. An imperative observation to note here is that expressions can contain other expressions just as in mathematics. This notion allows for ever-increasing complexity of expressions. It's also a useful concept to grasp when attempting to debug an expression. If the answer you received seemed less than intuitive, you could simple pull the individual expressions out of the larger expression and evaluate them independently to ensure everything is operating as you would have expected. In evaluating this expression, given the order of operations rules, the exponents of 4^2 and 6^2 are evaluated first, then the terms inside the square root parentheses are simplified by adding them together, and finally the square root is taken from the result giving us the answer of approximately 7.211.

EXERCISE 4-3

Given what you've learned about the Pythagorean Theorem, see if you can solve the following questions:

1. What is the hypotenuse of a right triangle if a = 7 and b = 9?

2. Given a right triangle with a base side equal to 3 and its hypotenuse equal to 30, what is the area of the triangle?

Hint: To solve this, you will need to understand what the length of the third side is as the formula to solve for the area of the triangle is 1/2*base*height.

Now that you have seen a few examples of complex expressions, the next step is to gain a better understanding of the rest of the Scala operators that are possible. These can be grouped into three categories including arithmetic operators, comparison operators, and logical operators. After you have absorbed the universe of operators, you will be introduced to variables which will further expound upon the vast capabilities of expressiveness that is available in the Scala language.

Arithmetic Operators

You've already seen the majority of the arithmetic operators in Scala – basic operators like addition, multiplication, and division. Subtraction is a very basic operator that works exactly as you would expect. There's also a modulo operator that you have not yet seen that returns the remainder of the division of two operands. Listing 4-9 presents an example of the modulo and subtraction operators.

Listing 4-9. An example of the subtraction and modulo operators

```
Scala> (12 - 1) % 3
res10: Int = 2
```

Notice that the subtraction occurs first as the expression inside the parentheses obtains the evaluation priority. Parentheses are considered grouping operators in this scenario. Next, the modulo evaluates that 11 divided by 3 would yield the integer 3 with a remainder of 2, and thus it returns the integer 2 as the final result. The modulo operator is extremely useful when trying to evaluate whether a certain number is considered even or odd because any number that is divided by 2 with no remainder is even and any number that has a remainder is odd. It would be prudent to make a mental note of this fact as it will likely come in handy in your career as a software engineer.

The remaining arithmetic operators that need to be covered in this section belong to the Math package in the Scala standard library. You do not need to understand what a package is at this point; just note that you've seen this package before when using Math.pow and Math.sqrt. The Math package contains implementations of several mathematical concepts that you've likely encountered in your education. This includes things like rounding, logarithms, and absolute value, among other things. The population of basic arithmetic operations that you should likely know are listed in Table 4-1 for reference.

Table 4-1. *A list of arithmetic operators*

Operator	Name	Description
+	Addition	Returns the sum of the operands on either side.
-	Subtraction	Returns the difference between the operands on either side.
*	Multiplication	Returns the product of the operands on either side.
/	Division	Returns the quotient of the operands on either side.
( )	Parentheses	Groups expressions for prioritized evaluation.
Math.pow(n,m)	Exponent	Returns the evaluation of n raised to the m power.

(*continued*)

Table 4-1. (*continued*)

Operator	Name	Description
Math.sqrt(*n*)	Square root	Returns the square root of *n*.
Math.abs(*n*)	Absolute value	Returns the absolute value of expression *n*.
Math.round(*n*)	Rounding	Returns the closest integer of the result of expression *n*.
Math.log(*n*)	Logarithm	Returns the natural logarithm of the result of expression *n*.

Comparison Operators

Just like in arithmetic, comparison operators evaluate expressions that concern equality. Each comparison operator is surrounded by two operands, one on either side, and always evaluates to either true or false rather than a concrete value. Table 4-2 lists each of these comparison operators in Scala.

Table 4-2. *A list of comparison operators*

Operator	Name	Description
>	Greater than	Expression on the left is greater than the expression on the right.
<	Less than	Expression on the left is less than the expression on the right.
>=	Greater than or equal to	Expression on the left is greater than or equal to the expression on the right.
<=	Less than or equal to	Expression on the left is less than or equal to the expression on the right.
==	Equal	Both expressions are equal.
!=	Not equal	The two expressions are not equal.

You might have seen the first four operators in a math class in relation to the concepts of comparison sentences or inequality equations. The last two tie directly to testing the equality of the operands in which they describe. Listing 4-10 showcases some examples of their use to further illustrate the construct.

Listing 4-10. Examples of comparison operators

```scala
scala> (2 + 2) > 3
res11: Boolean = true

scala> Math.sqrt(9) <= 2
res12: Boolean = false

scala> 8 >= Math.pow(2,3)
res13: Boolean = true

scala> 5 == Math.abs(-5)
res14: Boolean = true

scala> Math.round(4.5) == 4
res15: Boolean = false

scala> 12 / 5 != 2.4
res16: Boolean = true

scala> 5 * 3 != (5 + 5 + 5)
res17: Boolean = false
```

Look through each of these expressions carefully. As you can see, some of the arithmetic operations from the previous section have been added in to help express these inequality equations. You might also notice the type of the response is Boolean. We will cover types in later chapters, but for now all you need to know is that Scala has inferred the type of the response as a true/false value called Boolean. Some of these might not be terribly intuitive at first. Ensure that you comprehend why each of these returned the evaluated response before moving forward. If you don't understand, go back and review the chapter again before moving on to logical operators.

Logical Operators

There are only three logical operators that need to be covered in the Scala language. Logical operators will be used extensively in future chapters as we begin to cover control flow and Boolean types. For now, let's just cover a few examples of how logical operators evaluate particular expressions. All of these operators relate to whether the expression they are evaluating has either a *true* or *false* value. A description of each of the three logical operators is listed in Table 4-3.

Table 4-3. *A list of logical operators*

Operator	Name	Description
&&	And	Evaluates whether the operands on either side are both true and returns a true value if so; otherwise, it returns false.
||	Or	Evaluates whether either operand that surrounds it is true and returns a true value if so. If both operands are false, it returns false.
!	Not	Evaluates the operand that it immediately precedes to the opposite of its true/false value.

These logical operators become incredibly useful when combined with the comparison operators that were covered in the previous section. They can be combined within nested expressions to create infinitely complex expressions. Listing 4-11 provides an example of some basic expressions with logical operators and some complex expressions that you might want to spend some time understanding.

Listing 4-11. Examples of logical operators

```scala
scala> 4 > 5 && 7 < 8
res18: Boolean = false

scala>  !(4 > 5) && 7 < 8
res19: Boolean = true

scala> 4 > 5 || 7 < 8
res20: Boolean = true

scala> 4 > 5 || 7 > 8
res21: Boolean = false
```

The first expression in this example evaluates to false because in order for the expression as a whole to evaluate to true, both sides of the operator must also be true. Because 4 is not greater than 5, the left side of the operator evaluates to false and the expression as a whole is therefore false. In the second expression, you'll notice that 4 > 5 is put inside parentheses so that it will first be evaluated before the Not operator is applied to it. By applying the Not operator, the false expression on the left of the And operator flips from false to true, therefore making the expression as a whole true. In the last two expressions, only one side of the Or operator needs to be true for the expression as a whole to evaluate to true. The first Or expression has one true value and is therefore true, and the second Or expression has false expressions on both sides of the operator so the overall expression value is false.

The combination of these logical operators along with comparison operators and arithmetic operators can yield some extraordinarily complex expressions, as you might have guessed. In such complex expressions, reading and understanding the equation often becomes unwieldy. For this reason, among a plethora of others, the next section will introduce you to variables which allow for abstracting out pieces of the expression and storing their evaluated result for later use. This provides the benefit of being able to easily break up an expression into smaller, more digestible parts and also allows for the reuse of an expression evaluation.

Variables

Just like in your early math classes, programming has a concept of a variable that allows for storing a dynamic result or value in a symbol. Many math students tend to be intimidated by the variety of symbols that get introduced to their arithmetic tool set and mentally check out as soon as they see a letter in an equation. However, variables actually make programming much easier as their existence prevents expressions from infinitely chaining together.

Scala has two variable types that you will need to be familiar with. The first is denoted by the keyword val and the second is denoted by the keyword var. The difference between the two has to do with a term known as mutability. Mutability is the concept that determines whether a variable can be changed once it has been assigned. The val variable cannot be changed once it has been assigned and is therefore said to be immutable. Conversely, the var variable *can* be reassigned and is therefore considered mutable. Why there are two variable types and which one you should use is a topic that will be discussed later on in the book. For now, I want you to keep your focus on the usefulness that variables bring to expressions.

The way you assign a variable in Scala is by typing in the keyword that represents which type of variable you wish to use, followed by the variable name that you want to store the value in and then the single equal sign. Do not confuse the single equal sign with the double equal sign that is used to evaluate equality (which you were introduced to in the previous section regarding comparison operators). They might seem like similar operators in your mind, but they do vastly different things and their confusion is the source of many bugs for new developers. As for the symbol or name that you wish to assign a value to, a valid variable name can be any combination of numbers, letters (both uppercase and lowercase – the variable names are case sensitive), and special characters as long as they don't conflict with an existing reserved keyword or operator. Once you have assigned an expression result to a variable name, Scala reserves an address in the computer's short-term memory (you might know it as RAM or random access memory) for later use in the existing Scala session. Once the session is closed, the variables will be cleared from memory. Listing 4-12 depicts a resurrection of the example we used when expressing the Pythagorean Theorem, but this time individual values have been replaced with variables to illustrate the fact that variables in programming, just like math, can be used as drop-in substitutes.

Listing 4-12. The Pythagorean Theorem with variables introduced as substitutes

```
scala> var a = 4
a: Int = 4

scala> var b = 6
b: Int = 6

scala> Math.sqrt(Math.pow(a,2) + Math.pow(b,2))
res22: Double = 7.211102550927978
```

Note   Something in Listing 4-12 may seem different to you. Notice that the responses for variable assignment do not include the res symbol anymore but rather the symbol in which you assigned them. You might be enticed to deduce, then, that the results of the expressions you have been evaluating up to this point have been stored in the computer's memory as variables with the res keyword. If that is something that crossed your mind, you'll be delighted to find out that it is in fact true. You can reuse any of your previous expression results using the keyword that it returns. Take a moment to give this a try in your REPL by combining previous expression results into new expressions.

It would be prudent to point out that Listing 4-12 does not on its own prove a lot of value-add in the expression besides a simple drop in replacement of an individual term. Listing 4-13 illustrates how you can break up expressions into sub-expressions to simplify a problem and store the variables for reuse.

Listing 4-13. Sub-expressions stored as variables

```
scala> var a2 = Math.pow(a,2)
a2: Double = 16.0

scala> var b2 = Math.pow(b,2)
b2: Double = 36.0

scala> Math.sqrt(a2 + b2)
res23: Double = 7.211102550927978
```

As you can see, not only is there the added benefit of extracting expressions for simplification and readability, but you can also see the results of the sub-expression as they are assigned. As stated before, this will be incredibly useful for you in the future as you begin to break up complex problems into smaller pieces for debugging purposes.

Now that you have an understanding of variables and the concept of an assignment operator, there are a few more operators that you can take a look at before moving on to basic data types in the next chapter. Table 4-4 provides an introduction to a variety of new assignment operators. An example of one of these assignment operators is also depicted in Listing 4-14 to help illustrate their definition.

Table 4-4. *A list of assignment operators*

Operator	Name	Description
=	Variable assignment	Sets an expression result equal to a variable. Not to be confused with the == comparison operator.
+=	Increment	Increments the value of a variable and reassigns the variable to the incremented result.
-=	Decrement	Decrements the value of a variable and reassigns the variable to the decremented result.
/=	Divide and reassign	Divides the value of a variable and reassigns the variable to the result of the division.
*=	Multiply and reassign	Multiplies the value of a variable and reassigns the variable to the result of the multiplication.

Listing 4-14. Demonstration of various assignment operators

```scala
scala> var c = 7
c: Int = 7

scala> c += 3
scala> c
res24: Int = 10
```

Summary

In this chapter, you were introduced to the Scala REPL and you were able to do some actual coding, albeit mostly mathematical. You were introduced to the concept of expressions, both mathematical and their Scala equivalent, and you got to know some of the basic Scala syntax surrounding operators and operands. These concepts were reinforced by applying them to a basic linear equation, Einstein's mass-energy equivalence formula, and the Pythagorean Theorem. Finally, you were shown how these expressions can be stored in a computer's short-term memory for later reuse using variable assignment.

In the next chapter, we'll move away from all the numbers and do some interesting things with text and groups of data. You'll also be introduced to different basic data types and learn a few reasons why they are important. As usual, make sure that you can do all of the basic concepts in this chapter in your sleep before moving on.

CHAPTER 5

Basic Data Types

It is often an impulsive tendency among programming students to dismiss data types as a less than impactful topic. After all, Scala is inferring the type for each expression or variable for you, and since there are so many other topics to learn, why spend the upfront time on a seemingly minor topic, right? Not only that, but in many introductory computer science languages, the type system is neglected entirely. Why, then, is it important to understand the difference between data types?

Like a benevolent creator, what you code defines the rules of the world in which your program operates. Should your software allow for the representation of a half human or a negative human? Or would it make more sense for the representation of a population's census to be calculated with positive integers only? Will your program have a form of population control by defining a max number of humans that can be represented within the software? Can they have text-based names or will they all be represented as numbers like some post-apocalyptic dystopian society? How might families be defined? If your software is in charge of distributing medication to these families, at what level of precision should the amount of medication be rounded? As a creator, having control over such decisions becomes an incredible responsibility, especially as the impact of your software grows.

In the previous chapter, you were shown an example of a semantic error. These kinds of errors occur when the computer interprets an expression in a manner that you, the programmer and creator, did not anticipate. The reason the result of the expression is incorrect is that you

J. L. Hodges, *Software Engineering from Scratch*,
https://doi.org/10.1007/978-1-4842-5206-2_5

allowed Scala to interpret the type of the expression as needing to be an integer. If this error occurred when calculating medication dosages for a family, the impact could be incredibly costly. This is the exact reason why types are so important. If you know and understand types, you can avoid potentially catastrophic semantic errors in your code. Scala, unlike many introductory programming languages, allows you to define the types of your variables and expressions upfront, if you desire, instead of simply asking it to infer the types for you. It is this method of control that allows you the power to create exceptionally precise and optimally performant software.

In this chapter, you will be introduced to the basic data types of the Scala language that are necessary to garner such control. You will also learn some of the properties and behaviors of each data type as well as how to assign these types to variables. We will start with the numeric types and how they all relate within the Scala type system. After that you will be briefly introduced to Boolean types, followed by groups of data. Finally, we will finish off with text-based data and string manipulations.

Numeric Types

There are several different types of numeric data in computer science. You might wonder why all numbers aren't represented the same way, or why there needs to be a delineation between integers vs. rational numbers. Besides simply determining precise methods of control, the computer needs to know how much memory it needs to reserve for the given type of data. A very large number is going to take up more memory than a small number, and an integer will take up different amounts of memory than a rational number. Dynamically typed languages (which are languages that don't allow you to define a type for your variables) tend to either be conservative and reserve more memory than is necessary or do type conversions on the fly, when necessary, in order to account for needing more memory than was initially allocated. And while that is convenient, it also costs an enormous performance penalty on your program and relegates control away from you and gives it to the interpreter. The beauty of Scala is that it gives you the choice as to whether you want to let the language infer the type, whether you want to define the type, or if you want to choose among some varying "in-between" options.

One such "in-between" option is known as the AnyVal type. AnyVal is a super-type of all the primitive data types, meaning that when you specify a type for your mathematical expression or variable, any number type that you define is also considered an AnyVal type. This is known as type class inheritance. A real-world example of this is the fact that all squares are rectangles but not all rectangles are squares. A rectangle would be the super-type in this example, and the square would inherit the type of rectangle while also being more specific about its own properties (thereby being a sub-type). Listing 5-1 provides an example of how you might assign the type AnyVal to a variable.

Listing 5-1. Assigning the AnyVal type to a variable

```
scala> var x: AnyVal = 5
x: AnyVal = 5

scala> var y: AnyVal = 6.0
y: AnyVal = 6.0
```

As you can see from this example, the way to assign a type to a variable is by typing a colon after the variable name, typing out the name of the type, and then following that up with the normal assignment operation. You'll notice that the type of the evaluated expression is AnyVal. If you had not explicitly assigned a type, Scala would have inferred the type of the first expression as an Integer and the second expression as a Double. But the AnyVal type can accept both types of numbers, therefore acting as a kind of "in-between" or general type. The problem with defining general types is, just like a rectangle has less specific properties than a square, Scala knows less about what you are trying to do with a general type variable and therefore allows less operations. Scala knows that the AnyVal might be some type of number and that it should not accept any non-primitive data types (like lists and objects which we will get to later) for this particular variable. But because you have not been specific about what kind of number the variable is, how should it handle division? It will not know whether to handle integer division or what to do with any potential remainders. It will also not know how much memory it should allocate as the result of an expression that adds two AnyVals. The same is also true for other mathematical operations. So, if you are going to do any mathematical operations with the AnyVal type, you will end up needing to convert the variable to a more specific data type. Table 5-1 lists all the specific numeric types that AnyVal can be converted to and their properties.

Table 5-1. *A list of numeric sub-types of the AnyVal super-type*

Type Name	Description
Short	A 16-bit whole number with value ranging from −32768 to 32767.
Int	A 32-bit whole number with value ranging from −2147483648 to 2147483647.
Long	A 64-bit whole number with value ranging from −9223372036854775808 to 9223372036854775807.
Float	A 32-bit rational number.
Double	A 64-bit rational number.

As you can see, the main difference between the numeric types is how big of a value they can hold, which subsequently determines how much memory the computer should allocate for a variable of that type. If you know that the variable will only store a number within a very small range, it would be optimal for you to define that variable with the corresponding type that fits that range. This is incredibly important when programming for embedded systems or small devices that have very limited memory and need to be heavily optimized for performance. That being said, most computers have a significant amount of memory these days, so sticking to Integers and Doubles usually works out just fine if you're not sure what range your number will fall into. To further illustrate the difference between the sizes of data that your numbers can fall into, Listing 5-2 demonstrates the same expression evaluated as a Float and also as a Double.

Listing 5-2. An expression evaluated and stored with different data types

```scala
scala> var x: Float = 2f/3f
x: Float = 0.6666667

scala> var y: Double = 2.0/3.0
y: Double = 0.6666666666666666
```

There are two things to notice about the differences between these expressions. The first is the type casting that occurs which allows Scala to understand the literal values in which you are trying to divide. Just like adding a decimal at the end of an integer tells Scala that the type of the numeric literal you are evaluating is a Double, adding an f to the end of a number tells it you intend the type of the literal value to be a Float. You could have stored these values as variables first in order to explicitly set the type, but this is an example of how you would set the type for numbers using an inline expression. The corresponding type casting characters for Double and Long are D and L, respectively, although the D is often omitted in favor of setting the type with a decimal.

The second thing to notice is the number of decimal places that this infinite fraction is allowed to store and what occurs at the last digit in terms of rounding. The `Double` type stores double the amount of decimal places (hence the name). Alternatively, because it can only store half the number of decimal places, the `Float` type rounds at a much lower level of precision. This type of rounding behavior could have a big impact on your code if you are dealing with use cases that have extreme fractional sensitivity (like our example of the medication dosages) so you will need be aware of this upfront.

Note   There is not an inline shorthand expression for setting a value as a `Short` data type. However, you can attempt to convert any data type into another data type by using the `.asInstanceOf` function. Functions as a whole will be covered later in the book, but for now you can try casting an Integer to a `Short` using the code `1.asInstanceOf[Short]`.

If you are still confused as to which numeric data type you should use at any given time, don't worry. As a rule of thumb, if you know your number will always be a whole number, use an `Integer`; otherwise, use a `Double`.

Booleans

In addition to the five numeric data types, there is another important type that is a sub-type of `AnyVal` that was not listed in Table 5-1. You have seen this data type before in the section that described comparison operators, however. That data type is the `Boolean`. A `Boolean` value is simply a way to store the notion of "on" or "off", 0 or 1, true or false (just like the examples of binary in the first chapter). Some languages store Boolean values in the binary 0 or 1 format, but Scala uses the true/false format. Listing 5-3 shows an example of explicitly setting a variable to a Boolean value and also how expressions can be evaluated to a Boolean value using comparison operators.

Listing 5-3. Examples of a Boolean assignment and a Boolean expression

```
scala> var z: Boolean = true
z: Boolean = true

scala> var f: Boolean = 2 == 3
f: Boolean = false

scala> !true
res1: Boolean = false

scala> (!false || 3 != 3) && ((5+3) == 8 && true)
res2: Boolean = true
```

Notice the final expression uses the parentheses operator to group nested comparisons. Take a moment to understand how the expression evaluated to true since understanding Boolean expressions of this type will become extremely important in the next chapter when evaluating control flow. Within the first group of parentheses, the left half of the Or operation uses a Not operator (the exclamation point) which turns the false value into true. Even though the second operator of "3 does not equal 3" is false, because the expression is an Or, only one of the two sides needs to be true for the overall expression to be true. So, you can simplify the first grouped expression to true.

Listing 5-4. Simplifying a nested expression

```
scala> true && ((5+3) == 8 && true)
res3: Boolean = true

scala> true && (true && true)
res4: Boolean = true

scala> true && true
res5: Boolean = true
```

Listing 5-4 continues to simplify the expression progressively to show you how you might further break down this nested expression of comparisons and Booleans. Any And comparison operator will need both sides to evaluate to true in order for the overall expression to be true. As you can see, as the expression continues to be simplified, every expression ultimately equates to true. Make sure you fully understand how to simplify and evaluate Boolean expressions before moving on.

EXERCISE 5-1

Evaluate the following Boolean expressions without using the Scala REPL:

1) !((18 - 3 == 15) && 7 / 2 != 3) || (false && (3+1) != 4)

2) !(1 > 3 && (false && 5 <= 25 / 5))

3) (Math.abs(Math.pow(4,-2)) == 16 && true)

Groups of Data

Now that you've had a general overview of a few different basic data types, the next concept to understand is how to group pieces of data together. This could be either literal data values themselves or their stored variable names. The main thing to grasp about these groups of data is that instead of the computer allocating one slot of memory for a single data value, it is allocating several locations in memory and linking them together in a fashion such that you can refer to them as a single entity. A nice analogy would be to think of the basic data types you have learned so far as individuals and a group of data as a family made up of individuals. The two main groups of data that you need to be aware of initially are called lists and maps.

Lists

Lists have various forms and implementations depending on the language that you are using. You may hear several languages referring to a group of data known as Arrays which, for the purpose of learning this data type, you can think of as the same thing as a List (we will dive more into implementation details of this when we cover data structures later on in the book). Simply put, Lists or Arrays are just a collection of data items.

As an example of such a collection, we could think of directions from one location to another location as a group of data. Each data point would contain the distance that needs to be traveled and then whether you need to turn left or right. To put this in terms of data types that have been demonstrated thus far in this book only, let's use a Boolean value to determine which direction to turn. True will mean that you need to turn right, and false will mean that you do not need to turn right (and therefor you should turn left). Listing 5-5 illustrates this example with a Scala List.

Listing 5-5. The instantiation of a Scala list

```
scala> var right = true
right: Boolean = true

scala> var left = false
left: Boolean = false

scala> var directions = List(5,right,6,left,3,left)
directions: List[AnyVal] = List(5, true, 6, false, 3, false)
```

This example demonstrates that the appropriate syntax to create a list in Scala is to use the List keyword, followed by parentheses that contain a comma-separated list of data. Note that the inferred type of the directions variable is a List[AnyVal]. What that means is that the variable type is a List that can contain any data type that is a sub-type of the AnyVal type, which makes sense since all of the data types that we have learned so far (and subsequently used in our list) have the AnyVal type as their super-type. If you were to instantiate a variable like var x: List[Int], then the values you put into that list must all be integers or Scala will throw an error.

The way data in a list is organized is by an ordered index, meaning that each position within the list has a corresponding value that marks its place, much like a street address for a house. If you want to extract just one value from the list, you would provide its index value to a set of parentheses following the list's variable name. The indexes start at 0 and increment up for each item added to the list. A representation of the indexes for our example list is illustrated in Table 5-2.

Table 5-2. *An illustration of the auto-incrementing index position of a List*

Index	0	1	2	3	4	5
Value	5	true	6	false	3	false

If you want to add a new item to this list, you would type the list variable name, followed by the :+ operator, and then the item you wish to add. It's worthy to note that the item you wish to add could be yet another list, as groups of data can be nested. You can also combine two lists, if you wish, using the ++ operator. This is known as list concatenation. Examples of these List operators are shown in Listing 5-6.

Listing 5-6. Examples of various operators that apply to Lists

```
scala> var first = directions(0)
first: AnyVal = 5

scala> var last = directions(5)
last: AnyVal = false

scala> directions :+ 6
res0: List[AnyVal] = List(5, true, 6, false, 3, false, 6)

scala> directions :+ List(1,2,3)
res1: List[Any] = List(5, true, 6, false, 3, false, List(1, 2, 3))

scala> directions ++ List(1,2,3)
res2: List[AnyVal] = List(5, true, 6, false, 3, false, 1, 2, 3)
```

Notice that the type of res1 is a List[Any] rather than a List[AnyVal]. Why might that be? Well, the data type List is not a sub-type of the AnyVal type even though it contains only AnyVal types. Groups of data are sub-types of the AnyRef data type. And both AnyVal and AnyRef data types are sub-types of the Any type (which all types ultimately roll up to). So, because res1 is assigned to a List that contains both AnyVal types and a List, which is an AnyRef type, the variable must be assigned to the most generic ancestor that all items in the list share, which in this case is the Any type.

You might also notice that these operators do not directly affect the list, but rather evaluate like an expression that returns a result. The expression that evaluates to res2 is not impacted by the expression that evaluates to res1 because the directions list has not been altered by these operators. Operations like these that don't affect the value stored in the underlying variable are said to be immutable operations. If you wanted to have these immutable operations build on one another, you would need to store the result of each expression in a new variable and then perform the next operation on the new variable. You would then continue this pattern of storing each new expression result in a new variable and performing the next operation on each new variable.

Besides these expression operators, there are a few extra pieces of useful syntax that are commonly used on Lists that you should be aware of. The first is known as a slice which can return to you a piece of the list. It takes a starting index (inclusive) and an ending index (which is not included) and returns a List with all the values in between. The second is called length that returns to you the integer value of the number of items in the list. If you wanted to take a slice halfway through the list until the end of the list, you could do so by first knowing the length of the list. Finally, there is contains which will return a Boolean value that represents whether or not the value you provided exists in the list. You can observe these in action in Listing 5-7.

Listing 5-7. Additional List methods

```scala
scala> directions.slice(1,3)
res3: List[AnyVal] = List(true, 6)

scala> directions.length
res4: Int = 6

scala> directions.slice(directions.length/2, directions.length)
res5: List[AnyVal] = List(false, 3, false)

scala> directions.contains(9)
res6: Boolean = false
```

There are several other methods and operators that apply to Lists and list-like data structures, but this will give you a solid start. The important piece here is understanding that grouping data in order by an index position is a common data type that you will use extensively in software engineering.

Maps

Maps are a very similar data type to Lists, but instead of the data within the group being organized by index position, data in a map is organized by an unordered key/value pair. You as the developer get to define the key used to access the data you are looking for instead of relying on knowing its index value. An analogous concept would be looking up a word in a dictionary to find its definition. The word in this scenario is the key and the definition is the value. In fact, the map data type in Python is known as a dictionary for this reason.

The syntax to instantiate a new map is to first use the Map keyword, followed by parentheses that contain a comma-separated list of key/value pairs. The key/value pairs are separated by the -> operator. Keys can be any literal value that you have learned so far and also text values, denoted with double quotation marks as you will see in the next section. It is worthy to note that, just like you wouldn't see the same word listed twice in the dictionary, there can be no duplicate keys in a map. An example of creating a map and accessing its values using a key is presented in Listing 5-8.

Listing 5-8. Creating a Map of key/value pairs

```scala
scala> var numbers = Map("one" -> 1, "two" -> 2)
numbers: scala.collection.immutable.Map[String,Int] = Map(one
-> 1, two -> 2)

scala> numbers("one")
res7: Int = 1

scala> numbers("two")
res8: Int = 2
```

Notice that, similar to a list, the resulting Map type takes in data types in brackets that define what an acceptable key type might be and what an acceptable value type might be. In this example the resulting map type is

Map[String,Int], meaning all the keys must be of type String (text data) and all the values must be of type Int.

Just like lists, the map data type can be nested with lists or even other maps. To add a new key/value pair to a map, you use the + operator followed by parentheses containing a comma-separated list of pairs to add. To concatenate two maps together, you can use the ++ operator. Again, just like lists, these operations are immutable, meaning they do not affect the source data but instead evaluate to a result that contains new Maps that can be stored however you like. Examples of these immutable operators can be seen in Listing 5-9.

Listing 5-9. Immutable map operations

```
scala> numbers = numbers + ("three" -> 3, "four" -> 4)
numbers: scala.collection.immutable.Map[String,Int] = Map(one
-> 1, two -> 2, three -> 3, four -> 4)

scala> var moreNumbers = Map("five" -> 5, "six" -> 6)
moreNumbers: scala.collection.immutable.Map[String,Int] =
Map(five -> 5, six -> 6)

scala> numbers = numbers ++ moreNumbers
numbers: scala.collection.immutable.Map[String,Int] = Map(four
-> 4, three -> 3, two -> 2, six -> 6, five -> 5, one -> 1)

scala> var nested = numbers + ("nest" -> List(1,2,3))
nested: scala.collection.immutable.Map[String,Any] = Map(four
-> 4, nest -> List(1, 2, 3), three -> 3, two -> 2, six -> 6,
five -> 5, one -> 1)
```

As you can see, the first expression adds the "three" and "four" keys to the numbers map and then reassigns the original variable numbers to the result of the expression. This is only possible because numbers was instantiated as a var variable type, meaning it is mutable and can be changed. Otherwise, the result of the expression would need to be stored in a new variable. The second expression creates a new map called moreNumbers so that the third expression can demonstrate the concatenation of two Maps together, again reassigning the numbers variable to the result of the expression. You'll notice that the result of the concatenation does not appear to be in order. As stated earlier, Maps contain unordered key/value pairs. So when expressions are evaluated, there is no guarantee that the result will resemble the original order. The reasons why this is the case will be covered more later when covering data structures, but for now just know that you do not need to care about the order since you access the variables from their key directly and not their ordered position within the Map. Finally, the fourth expression demonstrates how a Map can take a list as a value. Notice the resulting map type is a Map[String,Any] rather than a Map[String,Int] since a list is not a integer.

In addition to adding new key/value pairs and concatenation, Maps have a few other methods that can be called that will be useful for you to know. The first is the keys method that returns a list of all the keys in the Map. The second is the values method that returns a list of all the values in the Map. The third is a size method which, similar to the length method of a list, returns an integer representing the number of items in the Map. And finally there is the contains function in which you provide a key to the parentheses of the method, and it will return whether or not that key exists within the Map. Examples of these methods are exhibited in Listing 5-10.

Listing 5-10. Additional Map methods

```scala
scala> numbers.keys
res9: Iterable[String] = Set(four, three, two, six, five, one)

scala> numbers.values
res10: Iterable[Int] = MapLike.DefaultValuesIterable(4, 3, 2,
6, 5, 1)
```

```
scala> numbers.size
res11: Int = 6

scala> numbers.contains("seven")
res12: Boolean = false
```

Just like Lists, Maps have several other useful methods that you will use later on, but the important concept to grasp here is that a Map is a collection of unordered key/value pairs that can be accessed based on the key.

EXERCISE 5-2

Create a Map that contains other maps as the values to your keys. See if you can figure out how to assign the value of a nested key within your Map of Maps to a variable.

Characters and Strings

You briefly saw a String data type in the last section. Strings are text-based data represented by a series of alphabetic, numeric, or special characters encased within double quotation marks. That should seem somewhat intuitive to you. But perhaps less obvious is the fact that a String data type is actually just a collection or group of individual characters. Thus, strings mimic a lot of the same properties of the group data types that you just saw. Both groups and strings are sub-types of the AnyRef data type. But, you might ask, if a String type is a collection of characters, then what is a character?

Characters are individual letters, numbers, or special characters that are encased in single quotes and are represented by the Char data type. They are different from groups of letters in that they can only occupy a single byte of the computer's memory. Because Char is a primitive data type just like all of the numeric data types and the Boolean data type, it is a sub-type of the AnyVal type. Any data type that is a group of data must be a sub-type of the AnyRef type. Therefor, if you tried to assign a Char variable two letters or if you tried to assign it with double quotes instead of single quotes, Scala would throw an error. The only way to represent text that is more than one character is through the String data type which, aptly named, strings together individual characters. Listing 5-11 provides an example of assigning both a String and a Char data type.

Listing 5-11. Assigning Characters and Strings

```scala
scala> var c: Char = 'a'
c: Char = a

scala> var s: String = "Text data"
s: String = Text data

scala> '1' == 1
res13: Boolean = false

scala> "1" == 1
res14: Boolean = false

scala> "1" == '1'
res15: Boolean = false
```

It is important to note that the literal character '1' and the literal integer 1 are not equal. The first is a text-based character that has the properties and methods that all text-based characters have. The second is an actual number that can be used in arithmetic calculations. The same is also true for the literal string "1"; it is not equal to the integer 1 or the character '1'. To further demonstrate their difference, imagine subtracting "1" from "a". What might the result be? As you might have guessed, that would throw an error as it would have no semantic meaning. Contrast that with subtracting two integers, which intuitively makes sense. Perhaps unexpectedly though, Scala does allow you to add Strings together. That operation is similar to joining two groups of data as you have seen before. Listing 5-12 illustrates such an attempt.

Listing 5-12. String and Character operators

```scala
scala> "1" + "a"
res16: String = 1a

scala> "5" + 5
res17: String = 55
```

As you can see, adding two Strings just concatenates the strings together. Adding a String to an Int, however, might yield unexpected results. A cursory observer might suspect that the expression "5" + 5 should evaluate to 10. However, because one of the data types is a String, Scala coerces the other data type to a String and concatenates them together, since a String cannot be used in actual arithmetic. This is why understanding data types is so important. Imagine that a string-based representation of a number sneaks its way into your program through an inadvertent bug and you evaluate a dosage of medication (to use our previous example) to be 55 instead of 10. That would be potentially catastrophic. If you do find a string representation of data in your code that you want to evaluate to a number, you would simply call the toInt method on it to cast it to an integer. So, in this example, the corrected expression of "5".toInt + 5 would evaluate to the expected result of 10.

String Manipulation

You've already seen an example of concatenating two strings together. But, just like other groups of data, strings have several other useful methods that you will want to know for everyday coding. These methods will become extremely important when you start to work with data that comes from other programs or sources that you don't have control over as the data will likely not be in the format that you need it. These methods will allow you to cleanse it prior to any necessary processing.

The first set of methods that you'll need to know involves the case of the string. The toUpperCase method converts all the characters in the string to uppercase, and the toLowerCase method converts all the characters in the string to lowercase. These are most often used when comparing two strings to ensure that the comparison is not case sensitive. That being said, there is also an equalsIgnoreCase method that accomplishes this same goal. Examples of these methods are shown in Listing 5-13.

Listing 5-13. String methods involving case

```scala
scala> var VaderQuote = "No, I am your Father."
VaderQuote: String = No, I am your Father.

scala> VaderQuote.toUpperCase
res18: String = NO, I AM YOUR FATHER.

scala> VaderQuote.toLowerCase
res19: String = no, i am your father.

scala> VaderQuote == VaderQuote.toLowerCase
res20: Boolean = false

scala> VaderQuote.equalsIgnoreCase("nO, I Am yOuR fAtHer.")
res21: Boolean = true
```

Besides case sensitivity, another scenario that might come up when using the equals comparison operator with strings is the existence of extra whitespace or extra margin characters like quotes, parentheses, or brackets in a string. These extra unwanted characters will result in an equals comparison operator evaluating to false. Extra whitespace can be removed by calling the trim method on a string, and extra margin characters can be removed by calling stripPrefix or stripSuffix on a string and provide the character that you need to remove from the start and the end. Examples of these methods are shown in Listing 5-14.

Listing 5-14. Examples of trim, stripPrefix, and stripSuffix methods on strings

```
scala> " hello world ".trim == "hello world"
res22: Boolean = true

scala> "[hello world]"
.stripPrefix("[").stripSuffix("]")
res23: String = hello world
```

Another strategy that you could use to remove characters from a string is to use the replace method. The replace method takes two arguments. The first argument is used to scan the string and find matches for sub-strings that you want to replace. The second argument is what you want to replace the sub-string with. So, in the example in Listing 5-14 instead of stripping the prefix and suffix, we could have called .replace("[", "") which would replace the bracket with an empty string and accomplish the same task. Listing 5-15 shows a few more examples of this functionality.

Listing 5-15. Examples of the replace method

```
scala> "Hello John".replace("John", "Jane")
res24:String = Hello Jane

scala> "I like to eat apples and bananas".replace("a", "o")
res25: String = I like to eot opples ond bononos
```

The next method you will need to use quite often is called a template string. A template string is an easy way in Scala to accomplish the task of string interpolation, which is a process wherein the language scans strings for variables or expressions and replaces them with their evaluated form. Almost every programming language has some form of string interpolation, but they have varying implementations.

The syntax to use a template string is to simply put an s in front of the quotes of the string that you want to use. Then within the quote you can add a $ in front of a variable name or you can use curly brackets along with the $ as an alternative if you need to evaluate an expression, like so: ${ x }. If you need to use a quotation mark or other special characters within your string, you can use triple quotes to ensure that Scala doesn't interpret the quote inside your string as the end of the string. You can observe these methods in action in Listing 5-16.

Listing 5-16. String interpolation

```
scala> """Vader said, "No, I am your father.""""
res26: String = Vader said, "No, I am your father."

scala> var number = "four"
number: String = four

scala> var numbers = Map("one" -> 1, "two" -> 2, "three" -> 3,
"four" -> 4)
 numbers: scala.collection.immutable.Map[String,Int] = Map(one
-> 1, two -> 2, three -> 3, four -> 4)

scala> s"""The numeric representation of "$number" is ${
numbers(number) }."""
res27: String = The numeric representation of "four" is 4.
```

You can see how string interpolation might be useful if you needed to create this same string for each of the key/value pairs in this numbers map. You would not need to rewrite the whole string every time, rather you could just replace the value of the number variable and then re-evaluate the template string expression. Try evaluating this same expression for each key/value pair to cement this concept in your mind.

> **Note**   It is really easy to reuse a previous line of code from the terminal or the REPL. In both cases you can simply push the up arrow continuously on your keyboard and it will cycle through previously executed commands. This might be useful in this string interpolation example so that you don't have to re-type the expression each time you change the value of the number variable.

Another common task you may need to accomplish with string manipulation is extracting just a piece of a string. Just as you can slice a list, you can also slice a string. Just like a list, each character of a string has an index position starting with 0. You can also use the indexOf method to find the index position of the start of a sub-string if you don't know the index that you need to pass to the slice function. Listing 5-17 demonstrates this functionality.

Listing 5-17. String slicing using the indexOf method

```scala
scala> var quote = "Great Scott!"
quote: String Great Scott!

scala> quote.slice(0,3)
res28: String = Gre

scala> quote.slice(quote.indexOf("Scott"), quote.length)
res29: String = Scott!
```

Take a close look at the last expression. You'll notice that strings also have the length method, just like lists, which tells you how many characters there are in the string. As usual, if you don't understand the expression, you can pull sub-expressions out of it to evaluate in the REPL and simplify it in your mind. It is useful to note that if Scala cannot find the index of a sub-string in your string, then it will return an index of −1, meaning not found. This could be useful in combination with a comparison operator if you are simply trying to see if a sub-string exists within a given string. Another method you could use to solve the same use case is called contains. Contains simplifies the need to write out a comparison operator to get the Boolean value of the expression. Listing 5-18 represents both options.

Listing 5-18. Checking for the existence of a sub-string in a string

```scala
scala> quote.indexOf("Scott") >= 0
res30: Boolean = true

scala> quote.indexOf("Marty") >= 0
res31: Boolean = false

scala> quote.contains("Scott")
res32: Boolean = true

scala> quote.contains("Marty")
res33: Boolean = false
```

The final two methods that are going to be extremely useful are the split and mkString methods (which are opposites of each other). Their use will be markedly demonstrable when dealing with data from other sources, since often the data is presented to you in a continuous string format that you need to be able to parse through in order to use. Once you have processed it according to your needs, you may often need to return it back to the source in a single continuous string format just as you received it, so you will need to put it back. The split method allows you to split a single string of data into a collection of data that has been separated by a certain character (most often this is a comma in the case of csv files, but it is not uncommon to see a tab or a pipe character either). A character that separates data in this way is called a delimiter, and data that contains a delimiter is called delimited data. The mkString method can be performed on a collection of data to put it back into a continuous string delimited with whatever character you like. Listing 5-19 demonstrates how you might take a comma-delimited string and turn it into a pipe delimited string using these two methods.

Listing 5-19. Converting comma delimited data into pipe delimited data

```
scala> var csv = "Married,Male,28,6ft,170 lbs."
csv: String = Married,Male,28,6ft,170 lbs.

scala> var parsed = csv.split(",")
parsed: Array[String] = Array(Married, Male, 28, 6ft, 170 lbs.)

scala> var psv = parsed.mkString("|")
psv: String = Married|Male|28|6ft|170 lbs.
```

As you can see, there are many useful methods for manipulating strings in Scala. You might not fully understand the applications for all of these methods right now, but they will become more apparent in future examples once more functionality of the Scala language has been exposed to you. For now, just ensure that you have memorized each function. When you are introduced to future examples and exercises, having to look up the syntax for these simple functions will start to slow you down when you could be focusing on the new concept instead. If you need to, write these methods down on flash cards and drill them with a peer.

Summary

In this chapter, you were introduced to the basic types of data and how they relate within the Scala type system. A diagram of all of their relationships from the official Scala documentation is presented in Figure 5-1 for reference. We also discussed why controlling data types in your program is important, even for introductory programming students. As you become more experienced, you will learn when to allow Scala to infer your types for you as it is a convenience that allows for greater productivity. While you are learning, though, it is important to intentionally control your data types. In this chapter, you were also shown some key methods that each data type implements and some examples on how and when to use them. Finally, you were given a large list of methods that string types can use for manipulating text-based data.

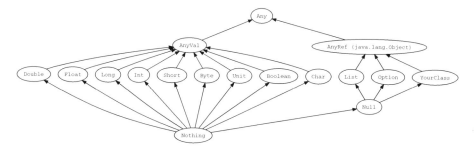

Figure 5-1. *The unified type system from the Scala documentation*

In the next chapter, you will be introduced to the various topics surrounding control flow. The difficulty level in the code and its subsequent capabilities will begin to increase dramatically. That being said, if you know string manipulation and comparison operators thoroughly, you will be extremely well positioned to comprehend the material in a fervent manner.

CHAPTER 6

Control Flow

The Salesforce Tower is the tallest building in San Francisco and the second tallest building west of the Mississippi River. Its grandeur was made possible by the over 18 hours' worth of work and 49 million pounds of concrete it took to pour its foundation. Without such intense effort and substance, such a spectacular building would be vulnerable to earthquakes, sinking, and swaying that could ultimately cause the building to collapse.

Up to this point you have only been writing and evaluating expressions in the Scala REPL. Just like the foundation of the Salesforce Tower, this has been in an effort to establish the strongest base possible for your software engineering education. Without such effort, you might encounter gaps in your understanding when introduced to complex concepts. That being said, at this point we have established enough context that you should be ready to actually start writing simple programs.

In this chapter, you will be introduced to Scala scripts and how to execute them from the command line. That will be followed by conditional statements and pattern matching. From there, we will cover the concept of loops that will allow you to repeat code. You will likely find this extremely useful for task automation. Finally, you will be shown how to handle errors in your code to keep the program from crashing unnecessarily. All of this will be framed using an example of a model operating system.

© Jason Lee Hodges 2019
J. L. Hodges, *Software Engineering from Scratch,*
https://doi.org/10.1007/978-1-4842-5206-2_6

Scripting

So far, you have only been executing code directly in the Scala REPL for the interpreter to read and evaluate. And while it's easy enough to copy and paste or rewrite small snippets of code from the command line, as programs get larger and have more opportunities for errors, it becomes increasingly more tedious to encounter errors when the code is evaluated at runtime. Running code exclusively from the REPL also makes it difficult to store and execute programs at a later time. Scala scripts allow you to write your Scala code in any code or text editor that you want and execute them from the command line at a later time when you are ready. Using this scripting strategy, you can plan out a small program from start to finish before ever evaluating a line of code, writing each line as a set of instructions like a recipe that will produce a final result. This makes it easy to change your mind, delete a line of code, or refactor a step in the process. Also, once you have code that you can refer back to, you can share that code with your colleagues so they can execute it or contribute to it.

To get started, download or open your text editor of choice. This could be a simple Notepad on a Windows machine that takes in plain text, or it could be a more full-featured Integrated Development Environment or Code Editor. One of the main advantages of using an IDE is it will often highlight syntax for you to let you know when you've made a mistake before you've even executed the code. This leads to a better, more productive developer experience. There is a large range of features that comes with each IDE, and choosing the one that you feel most comfortable with might seem daunting. For a beginner, it is recommended to use a code editor that has a light feature set and a simple user interface to minimize the number of things you need to learn in order to get up and running quickly. Examples of these might be programs like VS Code, Sublime, or Atom text editors (all of which should have some form of Scala Plugin to assist with syntax highlighting of the Scala language). Other more professional and heavy featured options include IntelliJ IDEA and Eclipse.

While the choice is ultimately up to you, I prefer VS Code for lightweight development as it has a very active community of plugins and support.

Once you've chosen a text editor, you can open it up and write a simple line of Scala code in a new document. For the sake of example, let's use the expression 2 + 2. Save this document with the file name `example_script.sc` to your computer somewhere. The `.sc` represents the file extension necessary for your computer to interpret the file as a Scala script. Next, open up a terminal and navigate to the location where you saved your Scala script. VS Code has a native terminal that, when opened, will take you directly to the location of the current working directory which is really nice additional feature. From there, type in the command `scala -nowarn example_script.sc`. This will execute your script and ignore any potential warnings that the compiler might have about your code. You can execute any Scala script this same way by providing the script name or script file path that you want to run as an argument to the `scala` command. It may take a moment for your code to be compiled and executed (which will speed up the next time you run the script), after which... nothing will happen. Congratulations! You just wrote and executed your first Scala program. However, your terminal simply returned back to input mode waiting for another command. So what happened? Why didn't we see the result of our expression?

Unlike the REPL, an executed Scala program will only print feedback to the console or terminal if the code you write tells it to. You might wonder why that is. Some programs might have a lot going on for any given command or user input. A program might request data from the Internet, reformat it, save a temporary file to your computer, split that file up into several other files, and store it to several database systems, for example. If each of those actions required some output to be printed to the console, the user might get overwhelmed by the response to their input command. It is also not very efficient to print to the console for every command as each print is an extra instruction that the computer has to process.

By eliminating mandatory print commands, you have the ability to control the user experience and the efficiency of your program.

Up to this point, the Scala REPL has been handling the input, output, evaluation, and looping for you, so you wouldn't necessarily have a choice as to whether or not each expression evaluation gets printed to the console. Outside of the REPL when working with a Scala script, you as the developer have the control as to whether or not the evaluation step of the REPL process needs to print anything back to the console for the user to see. The best way to demonstrate this concept is to build our own REPL process. Just like the windows command prompt or the Mac terminal or bash shell, we can create our own command-line tool that has a REPL process. Our example shell, like a command-line operating system, will take user input in the form of predefined commands, evaluate the input, print out only what we want the user to see, and then loop back to wait for more user input. First, let's examine controlling what gets printed to the console.

There are two functions that can accomplish this task, `print` and `println`. The former prints any String method that you provide to its parentheses and the later prints any String in the same fashion but then adds a new line character to the end of the String so that the next terminal output will be printed on a new line. To demonstrate the difference in their functionality, Listing 6-1 shows both the example_script.sc and its executed output.

Listing 6-1. Scala printing functions

example_script.sc
```
print(2 + 2)
println("Same Line")
println("New Line")
```

Terminal Output
```
4Same Line
New Line
```

Notice that because the print functions only take strings as arguments, the result of the expression 2 + 2 is coerced into a string and printed next to the "Same Line" string since it did not add a new line character to the end of the resulting string "4". Alternatively, because the "Same Line" string was passed to the println function, a new line character was printed to the console so that the "New Line" string would end up on a new line. Also, because the "New Line" string was passed to a println function, any output that follows will also be on a new line.

Note   A new line character is a ASCII standard character that denotes the end of one line and the start of the next line. It is not a visible character in console output, but if you were to write it yourself in code, it would look like \n. You might also see the return carriage character that returns the cursor to the beginning of the same line \r or the tab character \t which represents the amount of space the tab key would occupy if you pressed it on the keyboard. If you like, you can manually add the new line character to the strings you wish to print instead of using the println function. However, it is common practice to just use the println function.

Now that you've seen how to code the print portion of the REPL process, how do you take user input? The function you can use to accomplish obtaining user input is the readLine() function. The readLine function takes a string in its parentheses that it can use as the text prompt that is printed to the terminal to let the user know that it is awaiting input. Once the user types something in that line and hits enter, Scala will take in whatever they typed as a string and the readLine function will evaluate it to a literal value as an expression. From there, you can store it as a variable or pass it to the print functions to echo back to the user exactly what they typed. Consider Listing 6-2 which shows a simple "times three" program that takes in user input, multiplies it by 3, and returns the output to the user.

Listing 6-2. Demonstration of the readLine functionality

times_three.sc
```
println(readLine("Enter a number: ").toInt * 3)
```

Terminal Output
```
Enter a number: 3
9
```

Notice that, because the number that the user typed in is coerced by Scala into a String, this script explicitly converts the user input into an integer to ensure that the program behaves exactly how it is intended to run. If the user had entered a string value that cannot be converted to an integer, the program would have thrown an error rather than return an incorrect answer (which would have been a string concatenated three times, which for this particular expression would have resulted in the string "333").

EXERCISE 6-1

See if you can write your own Scala script that reads in user input and prints out user output according to the following specifications:

1. Prompt the user for the height in feet of a building and store the response in a variable named "height."

2. Prompt the user for the width of the building and store that in a variable named "width."

3. Prompt the user for the length of the building and store that in a variable named "length."

4. Print a message back to the user describing the cubic volume of the building by multiplying height, width, and length together.

It might be useful to remind yourself when looking at this times_ three.sc script in the future why you had to type in the .toInt method and what the expression would evaluate to if you didn't. And even if you are confident that you would remember why you did write it that way, it might still be useful to leave a note for other developers to understand your logic. The way to do that in a Scala script is to leave a "comment." A code comment is a line or block of code that you can write in your scripts that is not executed by the computer; it is completely ignored. It's only purpose is to document whatever the developer wants to write to remind themselves or other developers something in particular about the code. You often see comments left in scripts to describe particularly complicated implementation logic or reminders to come back and change something about the code in the future. The syntax for a single line of comments is the double slash operator //. If you need more than one line for your comment, you can either put a double slash at the beginning of each line or you can use a block comment operator which begins with the start block comment operator /* followed by your comment spanning several lines before ending with the close block comment operator */. Examples of these operators are illustrated in Listing 6-3 for reference.

Listing 6-3. Example of code comments

times_three.sc
```
// Added the toInt method to convert input to Int
println(readLine("Enter a number: ").toInt * 3)

/* If the toInt method were not added the string representation
of the user input would just be concatenated together three
times */
```

This example will execute exactly the same as it did before, but it now has documentation added to it for future reference making it easier to collaborate. It is, however, a best practice to ensure that you are not adding a comment for every line of code, especially if that code is reasonably well understood by most developers. It is usually only important to add comments to leave reminders about particularly complicated blocks of code that might be difficult to read or interpret or to leave a "to-do" item for yourself or others to implement at a later time.

Conditional Statements

Up to this point, both in the REPL and in Scala scripts, you have only seen simple examples of straight-line programs. Straight-line programs are programs that run through a set of linear instructions from start to finish evaluating each non-comment instruction exactly once. Knowing that, you might easily glean that your programs would have a difficult time doing anything reasonably complex as a straight-line program without writing a considerable amount of code. In order to create more complex programs that can perform dynamic logic evaluations, you must create what is called a branching program. A branching program uses conditional operators to evaluate optional branches in your program. Unlike a straight-line program where all code is executed once, conditional branches in your code are only evaluated if the conditional operator that precedes the branch evaluates to true. If it does not evaluate to true, the branch is skipped entirely. Alternatively, if the conditional operator evaluates to false, your program can execute a different branch. You can think of the conditional operator as a gatekeeper to the different branches in your code. In this way, your code can act similar to a "choose your own adventure" type story. Code branches that are preceded by a conditional operator are referred to as conditional statements or sometimes if/then/else statements.

To write a conditional statement, you first type the if keyword, followed by a set of parentheses. Within the parentheses, you pass your conditional expression that will evaluate to either true or false. After the parentheses, the conditional statement takes a pair of curly braces that denotes the code branch that you would like to be executed if the conditional operation returns true. Any code that is within the curly braces will be considered part of this branch, also known as the scope of the if statement or the "then" statement. Some languages even use the keyword then to denote the scope. All code within the "then" branch should be indented to allow future developers to easily read the scope of the if statement without needing to first find where the first and last curly brace are. This is not enforced by the Scala language, but it is considered a best practice in order to ensure that collaborating developers are writing clean, readable, and easily modifiable code. If the conditional expression of this statement does not evaluate to true, the code branch will not execute at all. Scala will simply skip over anything contained within the if statement's scope. Optionally, after the curly braces you can use the else keyword followed by another pair of curly braces to denote a separate branch that *will* execute if the condition is false. Both the if code branch and the else code branch can contain nested if statements as well to compound the branching logic. Listing 6-4 provides an example of this new branching syntax using a new Scala script that we will call nebula.sc. In our nebula.sc script, we will start to build out our mock operating system shell.

Listing 6-4. Example of a conditional statement

nebula.sc

```
var command = readLine("Provide Command: ")
if(command.contains("+")) {
      println(s"Addition command: ${command}")
}
else {
      println("Cannot evaluate command.")
}
```

```
if(command.contains("-")) {
      println(s"Subtraction command: ${command}")
}
else {
      if(command.contains("help")) {
            println("Help command")
      }
      else {
            println("Cannot evaluate command.")
      }
}

if(false) println("A") else if(true) println("B")
```

Terminal Output
```
Provide Command: 2 + 2
Addition command: 2 + 2
Cannot evaluate command.
B
```

Walking through this particular code, you can see that the first thing that we do is prompt the user to input a command. We store that input in the variable command. In this example, we are assuming that the user has typed 2 + 2 as their input, as shown in the terminal output section of the code listing. The next thing that we do is write our first conditional statement that evaluates whether the input string that the user provided contains the sub-string "+". Since 2 + 2 does contain the sub-string "+", the code branch contained within its curly braces executes and provides the output string "Addition command: 2 + 2". You'll notice that because the if statement evaluated to true, the else code branch is ignored by Scala.

In the second conditional statement, we are checking to see if the user input contains the "-" sub-string. Because it does not, the condition evaluates to false and the branch that contains the code `println(s"Subtraction command: ${command}")` is ignored. Because the condition is false, Scala moves on to the else code branch which happens to contain a nested if statement. That statement checks to see if the user input contains the sub-string `"help"`. Because the user input in our example does not contain that sub-string, the nested if statement's code branch does not execute and Scala moves on to the nested else statement. That nested else statement prints out the string `"Cannot evaluate command"`. Try running this same code with different user inputs to see how the output of the code changes similar to a "choose your own adventure" book.

In the last conditional statement, you'll notice that it does not use any curly braces. This is considered inline shorthand for very simple expressions that can fit on a single line of your code. For reference, other languages have a concept called a ternary operator to provide this same logic of an inline conditional statement. For larger, more complicated expressions, it is a best practice to enclose your code branch in curly braces and provide proper indentation to show the nested nature of your code branch.

Hopefully you can see how conditional statements provide your programs the power to make dynamic decisions on the fly during the program's runtime to allow a user's input to customize the user experience. Listing 6-5 provides another example with an ice cream recommendation engine that has several if statements chained together to help solidify the concept in your mind.

Listing 6-5. Examples of conditional statements

```
var choice = readLine("What flavor of ice cream do you like? ")

if(choice.equalsIgnoreCase("chocolate")) {
    println("Rocky Road")
}
```

```
if(choice.equalsIgnoreCase("vanilla")) {
     println("French Vanilla")
}
if(choice.equalsIgnoreCase("fruity")) {
     println("Strawberry")
}
```

In this example, you can see an example of where the equalsIgnoreCase method is useful when comparing user input, since you don't know what case they might have used. You can also see from this example that the else branch of each if statement is completely optional and is not used. You can chain together a series of if branches like this that only execute if the desired condition is met. You can see how this strategy might become a bit verbose over time if you need to evaluate a large set of conditions. For those scenarios, using the concept of pattern matching is a best practice.

Pattern Matching

Instead of chaining together if statements, a more concise syntax is called pattern matching where Scala looks to match a very particular pattern that you are evaluating for. If Scala finds a match, it will execute the code related to that pattern as denoted by the => operator. Some languages call this type of code a switch statement. A new version of the previous ice cream example refactored as a pattern matching statement is provided in Listing 6-6.

Listing 6-6. An example of pattern matching

```
var choice = readLine("What flavor of ice cream do you like? ")
println(choice.toLowerCase match{
    case "chocolate" => "Rocky Road"
    case "vanilla" => "French Vanilla"
```

```
    case "fruity" => "Strawberry"
    case _ => "Unknown Flavor"
})
```

Notice that the keyword to start the pattern matching expression is match followed by a pair of curly braces that captures the different cases or scenarios that you are trying to match on. The match keyword is used after the string or string variable that you are testing your match scenarios on. In this example, we are handling case sensitivity by converting the string variable to use all lowercase and then ensuring that each case condition is also lowercase. Each case condition within the match scope is indented as a best practice. When a condition is met, the code written after the arrow operator => is evaluated and returned as the result of the overall pattern matching expression. In this example, we are not evaluating any expressions just returning the literal value provided as the result of the match expression, which is then printed out to the console since the entire match expression is contained within a println function. You might have also noticed the underscore character in the last scenario. The underscore in Scala acts as a wildcard and in this particular expression it is the "catch all" condition in case none of the provided conditions are met. In some languages this is called the default case. Hopefully you can see how refactoring the code in this way is more clean and concise. Let's refactor the code in our example operating system to use this new methodology in Listing 6-7.

Listing 6-7. Nebula script refactored for pattern matching

```
println("Welcome to the Nebula Operating System (NOS)!
Version 1.0.0")
var command = readLine("NOS> ")
println(command match {
    case c if c.contains("+") => s"Addition command: ${command}"
    case c if c.contains("-") => s"Subtraction command: ${command}"
```

```
  case c if c.equalsIgnoreCase("help") => "Help Command"
  case _ => s"${command} is not a known command."
})
```

You'll notice some additional syntax in this example. The pattern matching expression captures the input of the command variable as a new variable c that can then be checked with a condition using the if keyword. If that condition evaluates to true, then the pattern is considered a match and its corresponding expression will be returned. Otherwise, Scala will continue checking other patterns for matches. It is worthy to note that in a pattern matching expression, the first condition that matches the pattern will be returned by the expression, even if the input being checked for patterns might match multiple patterns in the expression. Thus, it is important to consider the order of the conditions when you write them (which is why the catch all/wildcard variable is last).

EXERCISE 6-2

Write your own pattern matching expression that returns the square footage that a piece of furniture would occupy in a building based on user input.

1. Capture the user input in a variable named "request."

2. Create a case that will match if the request contains the sub-string "desk." If the case matches, return the string "15 square feet."

3. Create a case that will match if the request contains the sub-string "chair." If the case matches, return the string "4 square feet."

4. Create a default case to handle unknown requests.

At this point our Nebula shell program takes in three potential commands and returns output if those commands match a pattern. If none of those patterns match, the default case prints out feedback to the user that the command they typed was unknown. This operates fairly similarly to our description of the REPL process except that after the program receives the user input and prints out the corresponding output, the program ends. We need a way to loop back to the beginning of the script and await more user input to truly wrap up our REPL shell.

Loops

A loop is a method of control flow within your program that allows for the continual execution of a particular block of code until a defined condition is met. If that defined condition is never met, you may be trapped in an infinite loop that can cripple your computer, so you must always ensure that the condition that you define has the ability to be exited. In the event that you execute a script that gets stuck in an infinite loop, you can always hit `Ctrl + C` to kill your program and return back to the command prompt. There are three different types of loops that you will need to understand in software engineering: the while loop, the do/while loop, and the for loop.

While Loop

The while loop is defined by using the `while` keyword at any point in your code followed by a set of parentheses that contain the exiting condition. Following the parentheses, you provide the block of code that you want to be executed repeatedly. Just like conditional statements, you can provide the repeatable code inline without any curly braces or wrap the code block in curly braces and indent your code. Also like conditional statements, loops can be nested with other loops.

While loops are especially useful when you don't know how many times you want the loop to execute, like in our Nebula OS example shell where we want to continue looping back in the REPL pattern until the user decides to shut down the program. Listing 6-8 illustrates how we would add a while loop to our program to continually loop back and ask for new user input. You'll notice that there is a new command in the pattern matching scenarios that looks for the "shutdown" keyword.

Listing 6-8. Demonstration of a while loop

```scala
println("Welcome to the Nebula Operating System (NOS)!
Version 1.0.1")
while (true) {
    var command = readLine("NOS> ")
    command match {
        case c if c.contains("+") => println(s"Addition
        command: ${command}")
        case c if c.contains("-") => println(s"Subtraction
        command: ${command}")
        case c if c.equalsIgnoreCase("help") => println("Help
        Command")
        case c if c.equalsIgnoreCase("shutdown") => scala.util.
        control.Breaks.break
        case _ => println(s"${command} is not a known
        command.")
    }
}
```

In this example, we've simply wrapped the entire code in the scope of the while loop using the curly braces. You'll notice that the condition provided to the while loop is simply true. That means this code loop will execute infinitely until it is shut down. In order to ensure that the loop can be exited gracefully, the shutdown command uses a method from Scala's utilities library called break. The break will exit out of the while loop, and the program will move on to the next line of code to execute. Because there is no additional code to execute after the while loop in this example, the program will terminate.

If you execute this scala script, you will notice that each time you enter in user input for the prompt NOS> your shell will evaluate the code, print out a response, and then loop back and prompt you again with another NOS> text string. When you are done testing each command in the pattern matching scenarios, you can type "shutdown" to execute the break. You'll notice that Scala will print out a response of scala.util.control. BreakControl as a result of that break. To avoid that scenario, let's initialize a variable outside of the scope of the loop so that we can change the exit condition of the loop. At the same time, we can look at an example of refactoring our code as a do/while loop instead of simply a while loop.

Do/While Loop

A do/while loop operates the exact same way as a while loop, except it uses the keyword do first, followed by curly braces surrounding the repeatable code block, and finally ending with the while keyword and its exit condition. The functional difference of the do/while loop is that the code block in the scope of the do statement is always executed at least once. Conversely, the normal while loop might have a condition that never evaluates to true and the code block is skipped entirely. If that happened in the event of a do/while loop, the code block would print exactly once instead of being skipped. An example of this scenario is demonstrated in Listing 6-9.

Listing 6-9. While and do/while loops with an always false condition

```
scala> while(false) println("Hello World")

scala> do println("Hello World") while(false)
Hello World

scala> do { var x = 1 } while (false)

scala> println(x)
<console>:12: error: not found: value x
```

Something to note about the scope of both conditional statements and loop statements is that variables defined inside their scope cannot be accessed outside of their scope, as demonstrated in the error in this example. Because of that, when we refactor our Nebula shell to use a do/while loop, we must initialize the command variable outside of the while loop's scope in order to check its value in the exit condition. You'll see an example of this and also an explicit message provided by the shutdown command in Listing 6-10.

Listing 6-10. Refactoring the Nebula OS script to use a do/while loop

```
println("Welcome to the Nebula Operating System (NOS)!
Version 1.0.2")
var command = ""
do {
    command = readLine("NOS> ")
    command match {
        case c if c.contains("+") => println(s"Addition
        command: ${command}")
        case c if c.contains("-") => println(s"Subtraction
        command: ${command}")
```

```
    case c if c.equalsIgnoreCase("help") => println("Help
    Command")
    case c if c.equalsIgnoreCase("shutdown") =>
    println("Shutting down...")
    case _ => println(s"${command} is not a known command.")
  }
}
while (!command.equalsIgnoreCase("shutdown"))
```

As you can see, the mutable variable command is assigned an empty string to start with outside of the do/while loop, followed by a repeating code block that reassigns the value of command each time it goes through the loop. Only after the reassignment and any executed command is the exit condition evaluated. That exit condition checks to see if the command variable has been assigned the string "shutdown", and if it has, then the conditional statement evaluates to false and it exits the loop. If the command variable is assigned anything other than "shutdown", the condition will evaluate to true and it will continue to loop. If you execute this version of the code and type in the "shutdown" command, your program will print "Shutting down..." to the console instead of scala.util.control.BreakControl and then the program will terminate.

This strategy of using a variable outside of the scope of the loop (known as a global variable) can be used in what is called the accumulator pattern. A pattern in software engineering is a repeatable strategy used to accomplish a particular task (you will learn more about that in the chapter on design patterns). In the accumulator pattern, the global variable is what is known as the accumulator. The accumulator is updated during each pass through the loop. In this way, the accumulator acts as the variable to be passed to the loop's exit condition, and only when the accumulator has been updated to the appropriate condition does the loop exit. For example, if you want to repeat the same line of code a set number of times, you could do so using the accumulator pattern presented in Listing 6-11.

Listing 6-11. Demonstration of the accumulator pattern with a
while loop

```scala
var i = 0
while(i < 3) {
        println(s"This is iteration #${i}")
        i += 1
}
```

Terminal Output
```
This is iteration #0
This is iteration #1
This is iteration #2
```

In this example the accumulator was initialized with a value of 0 and the
while loop's exit condition checks whether the accumulator is less than 3.
By reassigning the accumulator to its previous value plus one (as denoted
by the += operator) each time the loop executes, you will guarantee that the
while condition will eventually exit and you can determine the set number
of times you want the code to execute (which is three times in this example).
If you had accidentally used the - = operator to continually decrement
the accumulator by 1, the value of the accumulator would extend into the
negatives and never be greater than 3, thereby trapping your code in an
infinite loop. This accumulator pattern can be used in several scenarios
where you need absolute control over the variables and conditions.
However, it is so common to use it in the same way as the previous example
that the for loop was created to streamline the syntax.

For Loop

The for loop can be called anywhere in your Scala code using the for
keyword followed by a set of parentheses that take special syntax to
replicate the accumulator pattern. First, you provide the name of an

accumulator variable that you wish to initialize. Then you use the
<- operator, followed by a group of data. Groups of data in Scala are
considered iterable, and as such a for loop can iterate through each
individual item within the group and assign its literal value to the
accumulator variable. You can create the group of data inline with the for
loop or ahead of time as a variable. Listing 6-12 shows a refactoring of our
accumulator pattern using the for loop to demonstrate this methodology.

Listing 6-12. Accumulator pattern refactored as a for loop

```
for(i <- Range(0,3)) println(s"This is iteration #${i}")
```

Terminal Output
```
This is iteration #0
This is iteration #1
This is iteration #2
```

The way you would translate this syntax in English would be to say,
"For an accumulator variable i in the range of 0 to 3 execute the following
code." You can see how the syntax is much less verbose in this example;
however, this type of loop requires that you know exactly how many
iterations need to occur. Just like while loops and conditional statements,
the for loop executes a repeatable block of code following its parentheses.
The code can be inline (as is demonstrated in this example) or it can
be contained in a code block wrapped in curly braces. In this example,
the way the for loop is told how many times to execute is not by using a
conditional operator, but rather by iterating through a Range, which is a
group of integer values that is generated using a start value and an end
value. With each iteration, the value of the individual integer is assigned to
the accumulator variable, and when each value has been assigned exactly
one time, the for loop exits. Listing 6-13 demonstrates how you might use
a for loop to iterate through other groups of data, either initialized inline or
beforehand and stored as a variable.

Listing 6-13. For loop examples with different groups of data

```
var ints = Range(0,4)

var shows = Map("Friends" -> List("Ross", "Rachel", "Joey"),
"Big Bang Theory" -> List("Leonard", "Sheldon", "Penny"))

for(i <- ints) println(s"This is iteration #${i}")
for(i <- List("football", "basketball", "baseball"))
println(s"I like ${i}.")
for((show, characters) <- shows) {
      for(character <- characters) {
            println(s"${character} is in ${show}.")
      }
}
```

Terminal Output
```
This is iteration #0
This is iteration #1
This is iteration #2
This is iteration #3
I like football.
I like basketball.
I like baseball.
Ross is in Friends.
Rachel is in Friends.
Joey is in Friends.
Leonard is in Big Bang Theory.
Sheldon is in Big Bang Theory.
Penny is in Big Bang Theory.
```

Notice that in the last for loop the Map group of data is destructured into two accumulator variables. The first accumulator variable, show, represents the key of the map. The second accumulator value, characters, represents the value for each key. By assigning both the key and the value to a variable in the for loop, we can access their values in the scope of the for loop. You'll also notice that the for loop scope contains a nested for loop that then uses that characters variable, which contains a list of characters for each show, as an iterator to assign a new accumulator variable the individual names of each character. This allows the nested for loop to print out a statement for each character in each show.

EXERCISE 6-3

Many language paradigms use the index value of items in a List to access the data within a for loop. See if you can use the length property of the list to initialize a Range that will iterate through each of the sports in the list in Listing 6-13 and print the same string using the index.

By now, you should be able to see the power of both conditional statements and loops. Using these two constructs, you could brute force your way to solving very complex problems and heavily repetitive problems with relatively little code. But what happens if unexpected user input finds its way into your code that doesn't fit with the operations you are trying to perform? Often you will find that your script will crash when encountering these scenarios when really you would prefer to skip bad user input or handle the bad user input in some way similar to the default case in our operating system example. This can be accomplished using an error handling syntax known as the try/catch operators.

Exception Handling

An exception is an error event that occurs during the execution of a program that disrupts the instructions sent to the computer for processing. If not handled, an exception will halt the progress of the program. This is often referred to as the program "throwing an exception."

The method used to handle an exception so that it does not halt your code is called a try/catch block. You can use the try keyword anywhere in your code followed by curly braces that contain the code you wish to try to execute. If an error occurs while executing code in the scope of the try code block, instead of crashing the program, the try block stops the execution of instructions and immediately skips to the catch code block which catches the error and allows you to do something with it. The catch keyword and a set of curly braces immediately follow the scope of the try block. Within the curly braces of the catch block, you can execute a pattern match to check for different exception types and you can handle each exception type differently. The most generic exception type is Throwable and it contains several sub-types. An example of a try/catch block is demonstrated in Listing 6-14.

Listing 6-14. Example of a try/catch block

```
try {
    throw new Exception()
}
catch {
    case _: IllegalArgumentException => println("Illegal
    argument provided.")
    case _: Throwable => println("An error occurred.")
}
```

This example exemplifies how to manually throw an exception within the try block as well as how to pattern match within the catch block. In the last pattern matching example, we stored the value of the string that we were matching into the variable c. In this example, we do not necessarily need to store the value of the error that we are matching on; we just need to ensure we are matching it by its data type. Because of this, we are using the underscore wildcard character to tell Scala to catch anything that is of the following type but don't worry about giving its value a variable name. When you execute this example, the script will print out "An error occurred." because it matches on the generic Throwable type (of which Exception is a sub-type). If you change the try block to say throw new IllegalArgumentException(), then the catch block will print out "Illegal argument provided." instead since the pattern will match on that type. Again, be conscious of the order of your pattern matching as the first pattern that matches will be executed. It is thus a best practice to have the most specific exception to match on at the top and the most generic exception at the bottom.

If we look back on our Nebula Operating System, we'll see that there is not really an opportunity to use this new try/catch logic anywhere in our code. Right now, anything that the user types in will either match one of the commands or default to the catch all case. That being said, we are not really doing anything special with any of the commands either. At this point, we can start to implement some additional logic for each command so that we can do some interesting things with our operating system and handle any exceptions to our logic using the try/catch functionality.

The first thing that we can do is actually try to process an addition command if the user is trying to add two numbers. You might recall from the topic of syntax that when parsing a set of lexeme for meaning, a compiler or interpreter will perform a process called lexical analysis. What that means is that it looks at each word in the sentence and tries to figure out what to do with it. In order to look at each word individually, it must first convert a string of characters into individual words or tokens. This is a process known as tokenization. There are several ways to tokenize a string command, but for the sake of simplicity, we are simply going to parse/tokenize each command by separating the string assuming a space character delimiter. If you remember from the section on string manipulation, we can do that using the split function. Listing 6-15 shows how we can accomplish this and wrap the code in a try/catch in case we get bad user input. The ellipsis is provided to show that the code has been abbreviated to only show the block that we are interested in changing.

Listing 6-15. Example of tokenization and a try/catch block

nebula.sc

```
...
case c if c.contains("+") => {
    var tokens = c.split(" ")
    var plusIndex = tokens.indexOf("+")
    try {
        println(tokens(plusIndex-1).toDouble +
        tokens(plusIndex+1).toDouble)
    }
    catch {
        case _ : Throwable => println("An error occurred trying
        to process an addition command.")
    }
}
...
```

This code shows that in the case where the command contains a "+" character we can take the command and split it into a list of strings or tokens and store that list in our tokens variable. Then, we check what the index of the plus operator is within that array and store that in the plusIndex variable. Once we have those two things, we can attempt to add any two numbers that occur before and after the plus character in our list of tokens using their indexes, which are derived by taking the plusIndex and subtracting and adding 1 from it for the number before the plus and after the plus respectively. From there, we can print the result of the addition expression to the screen. In this example we are explicitly attempting to convert any number provided as a string by the user into a Double type. If this fails because the user input a string before or after the "+" character that cannot be converted to a Double, the catch block will catch our error and allow our while loop to keep listening for additional user input rather than crashing. If the user only provides a "+" character or only gives the shell a number on one side of the "+" character, the catch block will catch the corresponding error. Also, if the user does not provide spaces between the tokens in their command, an error will also be thrown as the tokenization process will fail to split the command into the appropriate list and the catch block will catch the error. All of these exceptions are handled the same way in our example by simply printing "An error occurred trying to process an addition command" to the screen. If you like, you can handle each of these exceptions in a different way if you allow the code to execute without a try/catch block and observe what error is thrown. Then you can pattern match on the specific exceptions that are thrown and tailor the message to the user to give them additional information as to what went wrong.

EXERCISE 6-4

1. Observe what happens when adding more than three tokens to a command. How might you handle the behavior differently?

2. Using the example provided for the addition command, implement the same tokenization logic for the subtraction command. Before adding the try/catch block, observe the program crashing when providing a bad input command. Then implement the try/catch logic to preserve the REPL session when bad input is provided.

3. Customize the help command to provide the user with specific instructions on how to use the addition and subtraction commands.

Summary

In this chapter, you learned how to execute a Scala script which allows you to store code for collaboration and execution at a later time. In these scripts you learned how to take in user input, print output, and leave code comments where necessary. You also learned several control flow processes for managing complex logic in your scripts. These control flow methods included conditional statements, pattern matching, loops, and exception handling. You also started building your own operating system shell using a Scala script. In the next chapter, we will continue to build out this operating system using an abstraction construct known as functions.

CHAPTER 7

Functions

Famous science fiction writer, Arthur C. Clarke, once wrote that any sufficiently advanced technology is indistinguishable from magic. If such a technology is indeed considered magic, its software engineers would most assuredly be viewed as its magicians. You might be familiar with some of the prototypical tricks that a magician might perform. Often their repertoire would include spectacular acts of spontaneous materialization or object transformation, through means of a magical black top hat as a medium, sprinkled with the citation of a few magic words. To extend the magical analogy, in software engineering, the magical black top hat would be considered a function and the function's name might be deemed the magic word.

Functions in programming are simply special expressions that can take input and return output. In this way they are much like the magic black top hat. Perhaps a handkerchief might go into the hat and "Presto Change-o!" a dove will come back out. What happened inside the hat is obfuscated from the audience. All they need to know is that, given a handkerchief as an input, a dove will be produced as an output. The suppression of the material details of what happened in the black hat is called abstraction. You might often hear the concept of abstraction referred to as a "black box" since you cannot see what's happening inside. Functions abstract the implementation details from your code and wrap them up into a function name so that you do not have to worry about re-implementing previously written code each time you need to use the function. The reusability of

© Jason Lee Hodges 2019
J. L. Hodges, *Software Engineering from Scratch*,
https://doi.org/10.1007/978-1-4842-5206-2_7

a function is one way to create a concept known as modularity in your code, by segregating common pieces of functionality into function code. Modularity and abstraction are the two main purposes of functions.

There are several built-in functions in the Scala language that you have seen already such as `println` and `readLine`. However, you can also define your own functions. In this chapter, you will be introduced to the creation of custom functions, how to use a custom function, and some of the benefits of using functions in your code. You will also see how to apply this new functionality to our example operating system.

Function Definition

Functions can be created in Scala using the `def` keyword that stands for "definition." Creating a function is said to be defining a function. You might also hear it referred to as declaring a function. The `def` keyword is followed by the name of the function or the magic word that you wish to use to produce a given output. It is a best practice to use camel case when naming a function (capitalizing each word in a phrase except the first word and excluding any spaces, i.e., `blackHat`). After the function name is provided, Scala will look for parentheses that take in parameters much like the `println` and `readLine` functions. Within the parentheses, you provide a comma-separated list of input parameter names and their data types. The input parameter names can then be used later in the scope of the function much like a variable placeholder. After the parentheses you can optionally provide a colon and then the data type of the value that will be returned. If you do not provide the return type, Scala will infer it for you, but as mentioned previously, it is a good practice to always define your types for better control and optimization. After the return type, you provide an equal sign and a pair of curly braces that hold the scope of the function. Figure 7-1 illustrates our magic hat example as a reference.

Input   **Output**

Function

Figure 7-1. *Illustration of the input and output capabilities of a function*

Within the scope or body of the function definition, you provide the implementation details of what you want the function to do with the given input. You can manipulate the input parameters in any way you like. When you have completed the function's implementation details, you use the return keyword to return a value back as output from the function. If you do not use the return keyword, Scala will infer that the evaluated expression in the last line of your function body should be the returned value. Figure 7-2 shows an example of how we might define a basic function and also provides a breakdown of each part of the syntax for our magic black hat example.

111

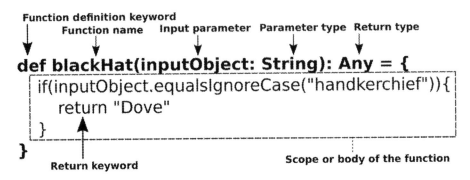

Figure 7-2. *Definition and key pieces of function syntax*

Listing 7-1 provides the unmarked code version of this same example written in an examples.sc Scala script that you can execute to ensure that the compiler correctly recognizes the syntax. You'll notice that, just as control flow constructs maintain scope independent variable assignment, variables assigned within a function's scope cannot be accessed outside of the function. In other words, the variables defined within the function body are said to have a local scope. You can also think of the input parameters as variables with a scope that is local to the function.

Listing 7-1. Blackhat function definition

examples.sc
```
def blackHat(inputObject: String): Any = {
   if(inputObject.equalsIgnoreCase("handkerchief")) {
       return "Dove"
   }
}
```

It should be noted that as soon as a branch of code in your function reaches a return statement, the rest of the code within the function will cease to execute. As soon as the function returns an output, the function's process is complete. To illustrate this concept, Listing 7-2 demonstrates an example where two return statements are provided.

Listing 7-2. Function with multiple return statements

examples.sc
```
def magician(name: String): String = {
    if(name.equalsIgnoreCase("David")){
        return "David Copperfield"
    }
    return "Harry Houdini"
}
```

In this example, if the input string parameter name is "David," the function will return the string "David Copperfield" and ignore the second return statement. If the string does not equal "David," the conditional branch will be ignored and the final line will be executed returning "Harry Houdini." In this function, the return keyword could be removed before the string "Harry Houdini" as Scala would imply that the last line is the expression that should be returned as long as it matches the return type that is defined in the first line of the function definition. However, as a best practice while you are starting out, it is better to explicitly provide return statements.

Worthy of note is the fact that functions are not required to have parameters at all, and if they do have parameters, they can be made to be optional. If there are no parameters, Scala still requires parentheses; they will simply contain no characters in between. If you wish to make the parameters optional, you must provide a default value by succeeding the parameter type with an equal sign and a literal value that represents what you want the default value to be. By providing a default value, Scala will implicitly understand that if the value is not provided, it should use the default value provided in the function definition and you can handle any subsequent default logic surrounding that parameter in your corresponding function body. Listing 7-3 provides examples of functions with no parameters and functions with both optional and required parameters.

Listing 7-3. Functions with no parameters and default parameters

```
def generateDove() = {
    "Dove"
}

def generateBirds(numOfBirds: Int, typeOfBird: String = "Dove") = {
    s"${typeOfBird} " * numOfBirds
}
```

Notice in this example that the return keyword and the return type have been removed for the sake of demonstrating implicit return options. The first function, which has no parameters, will always return the string "Dove" as an output. The second function takes an integer as its first parameter that is required (since no default value is provided to it) to tell the function how many birds to generate. The second parameter is an optional parameter. If no parameter is provided, the function will return a string that contains the number of "Doves" required by the numOfBirds parameter delimited by a space character. If a different string is provided to the typeOfBird parameter, the function will return that string multiplied by the numOfBirds instead of the default "Dove" string. Both of these functions implicitly return a String even though no return type was specified. But, functions can also effectively return nothing as demonstrated by Listing 7-4.

Listing 7-4. Function that does not return a value

```
def presto(): Unit = {
    println("Poof!")
}
```

Observe that although this function is an example of a function that does not return a value, a return type is specified. That return type is Unit which is essentially a stand in data type for "Nothing." It tells Scala that the function is not expected to return a value at all. You might hear other languages might refer to this type as void. So, if this function does not return a value, then what is its purpose? Functions with no return type typically exist to perform some type of "side effect." You will learn more about side effects in the chapter that describes the functional programming paradigm, but for now just know that functions with no return value perform an action in your code that does not require a response from your expression. In this example that action is a println function that prints out a string value to the console. Other examples of functions that might not require a return type might include functions that save a file to your computer or write data to a database. But even in those scenarios it is often useful to receive a return value back from the function indicating whether or not the function was successful. Thus, it is a best practice to always have a function return some type of value if possible.

Calling a Function

Now that you know how to define your own custom function, you can now use it as many times as you like in your code. Using a function in your code is known as "calling" a function. You might also hear it referred to as invoking a function or executing a function. A function call is said to "take" arguments. An argument is the value that you provide to the function as an input to satisfy its parameter definition. Arguments and parameters are often confused for one another. Just remember that the locally scoped variable that is created when defining the function is the parameter and the value given to the function at the time that it is called in your code is the argument. Providing arguments to a function call is known as "passing" the arguments to the function. Arguments can be literal values, expressions, or variables. Examples of these different argument usages and the syntax for calling various functions are provided in Listing 7-5 using the functions defined in Listing 7-3.

Listing 7-5. Syntax for calling functions and passing arguments

examples.sc
```
var birds1 = generateBirds(1)
var birds2 = generateBirds(1 + 1, "Finch")
var three = 3
var birds3 = generateBirds(three, generateDove())
var birdList = List(birds1, birds2, birds3)

for(bird <- birdList) println(bird)
```

Terminal Output:
```
Dove
Finch Finch
Dove Dove Dove
```

As you can see, the first function call only passes an argument to the function for the required parameter. Because only one argument is provided and the second parameter is optional, there is no need to add a comma and pass another argument to the function; Scala will simply assume that the literal value for that second parameter should be the default value of "Dove." In the second function invocation, instead of passing a literal value for the first argument, an expression is passed. That expression will evaluate to 2 in order to satisfy the integer type requirement from the function definition. You can also see that a second argument is provided in the parentheses to explicitly set the type of bird that is going to be generated as "Finch." The third function execution uses a variable to pass to the required parameter. That variable, three, evaluates to the integer 3 to satisfy the requirement from the function definition. After that a function is passed for the second parameter. That function call is a function that does not take any arguments, but notice that it still requires that you provide the parentheses in order to invoke the function execution. That function returns a value of "Dove" that is then passed as the second parameter to the function. You would be wise to observe that the second parameter would have evaluated to "Dove" even if you did not pass the generateDove() function to it as the second argument. However, it was used in this case to explicitly demonstrate that functions can be passed as arguments assuming that their return value will satisfy the parameter type required by the function definition that they are being passed to. The last few lines of code simply wrap the variables up in a list so that it is easily to loop through them with a for loop and print their evaluated values out to the console for the user to see. You just as easily could have called the functions directly in the instantiation of the list and avoided the three variable assignments. Listing 7-6 demonstrates that refactor.

Listing 7-6. Functions called directly in the instantiation of a list

```
var birdList = List(generateBirds(1), generateBirds(1 + 1,
"Finch"), generateBirds(three, generateDove()))
for(bird <- birdList) println(bird)
```

This example will yield the same exact terminal output as Listing 7-5. As you might deduce, this demonstrates that custom functions evaluate to their return value just like expressions do and can be used throughout your code anywhere where an expression could be used. This yields several extremely valuable benefits that continually recur throughout the common paradigms in computer science.

Benefits

Functions in programming provide two demonstrable key benefits that will be illustrated in the coming code listings. The first is the concept of abstraction that obfuscates implementation details and reduces code duplication. The second is modularity or decomposition which breaks your code into logically separated pieces for greater organization and

117

readability. Both abstraction and modularity provide the added benefit of being easily tested which provides for the long-term maintainability of your code base.

Abstraction

In the 2006 film *The Prestige,* two 19th-century rival magicians write entries in their diaries that include details about how to perform their tricks. In order to ensure that no one can read their diaries and discover their magical methods, they ensure that every entry is encoded as a cipher. An example of a ciphered message is presented in Listing 7-7 along with the implementation details surrounding how to decipher the message.

Listing 7-7. A ciphered message and its corresponding decoding algorithm

```
var cipher = new StringBuilder("Ue:h5jf6& Wit Set d6'r!cfjet6,!
vli3dn9lp!cs5uetdt9ds5jf 7swa!een66pcb Eepcen5ffdd.ds!ctT6gi,
9eda!dwte5s3!i:kd4kkdd!aey55pcbue9!vbu%vtatew4!aei6.uce
Fag5koeas69 Waj5isbd!cbe7nw.te!asd4ywau66hdajd4nwahce.b5")

var shiftedEncoding = List.newBuilder[Int]
for(i <- Range(0, cipher.length)){
    if(i % 2 == 0){
        shiftedEncoding += i
    }
}
var positionalEncoding = List.newBuilder[Int]
for(i <- Range(0, cipher.length)){
    if(i % 3 == 0){
        positionalEncoding += i
    }
}
```

```
for(i <- Range(0,cipher.length)){
    if(shiftedEncoding.result().contains(i)){
        cipher(i) = (cipher(i)-1).asInstanceOf[Char]
    }
}
var message = ""
for(i <- Range(0,cipher.length)){
    if(positionalEncoding.result().contains(i)){
        message += cipher(i)
    }
}
println(message)
```

There are a couple of new concepts here that you haven't seen yet, but despite the fact that this implementation could have been solved in a much more elegant way, I wanted to stick to the concepts you already know for this example as much as possible. The two main things you haven't seen are the StringBuilder and the newBuilder function that is a member of the List data structure. These will likely make more sense to you later on in the book. However, for now all you need to know is that they are necessary to ensure that the cipher string and the two lists of encoding integers can be mutated.

The first line of code defines a new variable called cipher that uses the string builder to create a garbled sequence of characters in a string. The characters in this string will need to be modified in order to decipher the message and, in order to modify the individual characters, a string builder was necessary. Next, two variables are defined, shiftedEncoding and positionalEncoding. Both variables are assigned to a list builder that creates a mutable list that can easily be added to using the += operator. Next, both of the lists run through a for loop that spans the same length as the cipher and adds any numbers that match a modulo operation to the list. For the shiftedEncoding list, the modulo is checking to see if the position is divisible by 2, and for the `positionEncoding` list, the modulo is checking to see if the position is divisible by 3. After these two for loops end, each list contains the positions from the cipher that match the modulo condition. So `shiftedEncoding` will contain 0, 2, 4, 6, and so on, and `positionEncoding` will include 0, 3, 6, 9, and so on. You'll notice that the steps that were taken for both lists were almost exactly the same besides which integer to use when creating the conditional statement with the modulo operator. Any time you see code that is repetitive it should trigger an alert in your head that there is an opportunity for abstraction. Repeated code is what is known as a "code smell," which is the notion that a bad practice is being used in code that is in need of obvious refactoring. A common mnemonic device in programming is DRY, which stands for "Don't Repeat Yourself." That being said, it's pretty obvious that we can refactor this cipher code using functional abstraction; however, let's finish walking through the deciphering algorithm first.

After the two encoding lists are created, the code runs through the length of the cipher in a for loop again and checks to see if each position in the cipher exists in the `shiftedEncoding` list. If it does exist, the character in the string at that position is shifted back one spot in the alphabet (hence the need for the `StringBuilder`). So, if there is a `'b'` at that position, it will be mutated into an `'a'`; if it's a `'z'`, it will be mutated into a `'y'`; and so on. Because of the nature of the modulo 2 in the creation of the `shiftedEncoding` list, every other character in the cipher will be shifted back one letter in the alphabet.

Finally, a `message` variable is defined and set to an empty string. Then we loop through the length of cipher yet again and pull out any character that has a position that exists in the `positionalEncoding` list and add it to the message string. Essentially, after every other character has been shifted, every third character is then selected to be in the final message. After the loop has been completed and the `message` variable has added every third character, the `message` variable is printed to the console to unveil the complete deciphered message. Try running this code on your own to discover what the secret message is. Listing 7-8 illustrates how we might pull some of the common code out of this linear procedural program and create a function to demonstrate abstraction (the cipher string has been replaced with an ellipsis for brevity).

Listing 7-8. Deciphering algorithm refactored to abstract common functionality into a function

```
...

def findPositions(mod: Int): List[Int] = {
    var listBuilder = List.newBuilder[Int]
    for(i <- Range(0, cipher.length)){
        if(i % mod == 0){
            listBuilder += i
        }
    }
    return listBuilder.result()
}

var shiftedEncoding = findPositions(2)
var positionalEncoding = findPositions(3)
for(i <- Range(0,cipher.length)){
    if(shiftedEncoding.contains(i)){
        cipher(i) = (cipher(i)-1).asInstanceOf[Char]
    }
}
var message = ""
for(i <- Range(0,cipher.length)){
    if(positionalEncoding.contains(i)){
        message += cipher(i)
    }
}
println(message)
```

Notice that the common functionality has been removed from beneath the creation of the two encoding variables and written one time in the body of a function called findPositions. The findPositions function takes one argument which is the integer that you want to use in the conditional statement with the modulo. It creates a list and fills it with integers that match the modulo operation. Now that the function is declared, you could reuse this function over and over again throughout your code and only have to write the definition once. By calling it, you could generate a list that is every 4th integer, every 5th integer, and so on. Also, once you know what input you have to provide to the function and what it will return, you can completely forget about what it does to create that return value. All you need to care about is that you can pass it an integer and it will return a list of integers. Other developers will also be able to use your function in their code without ever needing to fully understand the implementation details in the body of the function. Based on that, you should be able to recognize the benefit of this type of reusability that is inherent with an abstracted piece of code.

Once the repeated code has been abstracted, you can see that the function is called twice when assigning values to the two encoding variables, each with a different argument being passed to the function. You might also notice that the result() function that was being called on the encoding lists when checking if the position is contained in them has been removed from the conditional statement and added into the function in the return statement.

EXERCISE 7-1

See if you can identify any additional repeated code in Listing 7-7 that can be abstracted into functions without changing the final result of this program.

Modularity

In the introduction to that same 2006 film, it is stated that every magic trick has three parts. First is the pledge, where the magician shows you something ordinary. Next is the turn, where the magician makes that something ordinary do something extraordinary. And finally the prestige, where the magician makes the extraordinary thing return to its ordinary state. These three parts or modules are individual pieces that *compose* an overall *composition*: the magic trick. Breaking down the trick into its component pieces is called decomposition, which is a key advantage to using functions and allows a programmer to organize their code for long-term maintainability. If your program is the overall magic trick, then breaking it down into three functions called pledge(), turn(), and prestige() is the perfect example of decomposing code for modularity.

Modularity is the notion that a component of code can be isolated and extracted from its program and reused in any other program as an individual module. By isolating code to an individual module, the code can be easily tested. You can give it several inputs with the expectation that you know what the outputs should be. Then, independent of the rest of your program, you can test whether the expected outputs were actually received. This is critical in creating and maintaining large systems over long periods of time. We will cover this in more detail in the chapter on testing. In our magic trick components example, if future magic trick programs needed to reuse the same pledge, turn, or prestige component, that function could be extracted and reused very easily with no extra work necessary. Thus, it could be said that creating modular components is a key strategy in writing DRY code.

So, if our cipher code has been refactored to use a function that demonstrates abstraction, could it also be said that the same function demonstrates modularity? To answer that, we must examine the code to determine whether or not the code is isolated from the rest of the program. Could we extract this code out of our cipher program and put it in another program and achieve working, testable code? The answer is no, because the function itself uses a variable, cipher, that is defined in the global scope of the program. A completely isolated and modular function uses only the inputs given to it or defined itself in order to calculate its output. Listing 7-9 demonstrates how we might refactor our cipher code to make our findPosition() function modular.

Listing 7-9. Cipher code refactored to demonstrate modularity

```
var cipher = new StringBuilder("Ue:h5jf6& Wit Set d6'r!cfjet6,!
vli3dn9lp!cs5uetdt9ds5jf 7swa!een66pcb Eepcen5ffdd.ds!ctT6gi,
9eda!dwte5s3!i:kd4kkdd!aey55pcbue9!vbu%vtatew4!aei6.uce
Fag5koeas69 Waj5isbd!cbe7nw.te!asd4ywau66hdajd4nwahce.b5")

def findPositions(mod: Int, encryptedMessage: StringBuilder):
List[Int] = {
    var listBuilder = List.newBuilder[Int]
    for(i <- Range(0, encryptedMessage.length)){
        if(i % mod == 0){
            listBuilder += i
        }
    }
    return listBuilder.result()
}

var shiftedEncoding = findPositions(2, cipher)
var positionalEncoding = findPositions(3, cipher)
...
```

Notice that the definition of the findPosition() function now includes a parameter called encryptedMessage that is used to take in whatever message you are looking to find positions on. Then the for loop uses that parameter instead of the global variable cipher to determine the length of the loop. Finally, you'll notice that when the functions are called, the `cipher` variable is passed to the function as the second argument to obtain the same functionality that previously existed. But now the function operates independently and modularly. If you took the `findPositions()` function out of this program and put it in another program, it could be used to find positions for any message that was built with a `StringBuilder` and required a list of positions as an output.

Application

Now that you know how to define and call a function, let's refactor our Nebula Operating System to allow for the use of this great new tool. In our last example of this command-line shell, we started to actually build out functionality surrounding potential commands that match a certain pattern based on user input. In order to better organize the code, let's abstract the code block that executes the addition command and place it in a function. An example of that refactor can be observed in Listing 7-10.

Listing 7-10. The Nebula OS shell refactored to abstract the addition command into a function

```
def addCommand(userInput: String) {
    var tokens = userInput.split(" ")
    var plusIndex = tokens.indexOf("+")
    try {
        println(tokens(plusIndex-1).toDouble +
        tokens(plusIndex+1).toDouble)
    }
    catch {
        case _ : Throwable => println("An error occurred trying
        to process an addition command.")
    }
}
```

```
println("Welcome to the Nebula Operating System (NOS)!
Version 1.0.3")
var command = ""
do {
    command = readLine("NOS> ")
    command match {
        case c if c.contains("+") => addCommand(c)
        case c if c.contains("-") => println(s"Subtraction
        command: ${command}")
        case c if c.equalsIgnoreCase("help") => println("Help
        Command")
        case c if c.equalsIgnoreCase("shutdown") =>
        println("Shutting down...")
        case _ => println(s"${command} is not a known command.")
    }
}
while (!command.equalsIgnoreCase("shutdown"))
```

As you can see, by moving the code logic into its own function, it cleans up the pattern matching expression. All the match expression needs to know is that if the user input contains a "+" then it can pass that command along to the addCommand() function and it will handle the rest. By doing this, we can further clean up the other match conditions to make that code block even more concise and delegate the execution of each command to function code blocks. There might also be commonalities between these functions that can be further abstracted.

EXERCISE 7-2

Create a function for each of the following requirements:

1. Given a number as an input, return a Boolean that denotes whether or not that number is an even number.

2. Given a first name and a last name, return a string that is considered the full name of an individual.

3. Given a width and a height of a rectangle, return the area of that rectangle.

4. Given a list as input, return the first element of that list.

5. Given a list as input, return the last element of that list.

6. Given a list of words, return the largest word.

7. Given a list of words, return the length of the smallest word.

8. Given a list of integers, return the sum of all integers.

Complete the following exercises related to the Nebula OS shell:

1. Create a function for each pattern matching condition.

2. Identify the common functionality between the addition and subtraction functions and abstract it further so there is no repeated code.

Summary

In this chapter, you learned how to define a function with both optional and required parameters and a return value. You also learned how to call that function by passing arguments to satisfy the function's defined parameters. The benefits of using functions include reusability, ease of testing for long-term maintenance, "black-box" abstraction, and extractable modularity. In the next chapter, you will learn another strategy used quite extensively to satisfy the necessity for modular code in software engineering known as classes.

CHAPTER 8

Classes

During the industrial revolution, Eli Whitney, while striving to produce and fulfill an order of 10,000 muskets for the US military, invented the manufacturing concept of interchangeable parts. His interchangeable parts were components of the weapon that were so near identical that they would fit into any assembly of that same type of weapon. This made it possible to mass produce individual parts with huge productivity gains and assemble the weapons at a later time as necessary. Prior to this methodology, weapons were created one at a time from start to finish, usually by a blacksmith, and each weapon was unique. By creating interchangeable parts, not only did Eli Whitney make weapons that were easier to repair through replaceable component standardization, but he also laid the fundamental groundwork for mass manufacturing strategies to come (such as the moving assembly line).

In software engineering, writing the same code multiple times throughout your program is comparable to building a weapon from scratch each time in terms of each method's relative lack of productivity. In addition to the productivity loss of writing the same code twice, by writing duplicative code, you've also introduced multiple points of failure and maintenance rather than a single accountable piece of code. In contrast, if you "Don't Repeat Yourself" or ensure that you are writing DRY code, this is analogous to instead using an already mass produced interchangeable part to assemble that weapon. Thus, it could be said that the invention of interchangeable parts was the catalyst for modularity in manufacturing.

© Jason Lee Hodges 2019
J. L. Hodges, *Software Engineering from Scratch*,
https://doi.org/10.1007/978-1-4842-5206-2_8

In the previous chapter, you were introduced to functions as an idiom of creating modularity in your code. In this chapter, you will be introduced to another strategy for modularity known as classes.

Encapsulation

Classes are essentially custom data types in your code that capture or encapsulate certain values and functionality into a single namespace. Just like a String type has certain properties about it (like its length and its values at certain indexes) and operations that can be performed on it (like concatenation or interpolation), a class or custom type can be defined with properties and methods. A property or field is simply a variable that is contained within the class, and a method is simply a function contained within the class. Properties and methods are considered members of a class. Given that, it could be said generically that a class is simply a collection of members.

To create your own class in Scala, you first use the `class` keyword followed by the name you want to give to your custom type. By convention, the name usually starts with an uppercase letter. After you define the name of the class, you provide parameter variables inside parentheses just like you would a function. These parameter variables will populate the properties of the class. Next, you define the body of the class, which usually contains some default behavior that you want to accomplish each time someone uses the class, as well as functions or methods and any additional properties that you want to be able to access within the encapsulation of the class. Listing 8-1 demonstrates a basic example of creating and using a class. Using a class is typically referred to as instantiating a class or constructing a new class.

Listing 8-1. Defining and constructing a Weapon class

examples.sc
```
class Weapon(weaponType: String = "Musket") {
    println(s"Construction of ${this.weaponType} completed.")
}

var musket = new Weapon()
for(i <- Range(1,10001)){
    new Weapon(s"Musket #${i}")
}
```

You'll notice that, just like in a function definition, when defining the parameters of the class, you can provide default values to their variables. By doing that, if the Weapon class is instantiated or constructed without any arguments passed to these parameters, it will default to the value provided in the definition. To construct or instantiate a class, you use the new keyword followed by the name of the class with parentheses that contain the arguments you want to pass to the class. If you execute the code in Listing 8-1, you will see that the first instantiation of the Weapon class defaults to printing out the word "Musket" as its weapon type since no argument is passed to the weaponType parameter. After that, the for loop constructs 10,000 instances of the Weapon class and passes in the i variable to the weaponType parameter to denote in which iteration of the loop the weapon was constructed.

You might have noticed in the println function of the class body in this example that the weaponType variable was accessed using a this keyword. The this keyword is not necessary in this case but was provided to demonstrate a key point. In classes, when you provide arguments to parameter variables, they are assigned to the newly constructed instance of the class as a property, and the this keyword is simply referring to the individual instance of the class that was constructed. This default assignment functionality happens in what is known as the primary constructor method. The primary constructor method is a default function

131

that is built into the creation of a class that takes any arguments passed to parameters and assigns them as properties of the instance of the class. After the primary constructor method is finished executing, Scala will then execute the body of the code that immediately follows the class definition. This execution is known as the secondary constructor method since it executes each time a class is instantiated. In other languages, there is typically only one constructor method, and it is usually accessed by defining a method in the class with a special keyword.

Once you have constructed a new instance of a class, you now have an encapsulated namespace for calling properties and methods of the class. That being said, one of the main benefits of encapsulation is that you as the developer can obfuscate parts of the functionality of the class away from whoever is using it (abstraction). In the case of a String type, when the string is constructed, it assigns a value to the length property without us needing to know how it calculated the length. That property is available to us as the developer by typing .length after the string to access the length property. So, now that we have created our own type, let's access the single property of the Weapon class in Listing 8-2.

Listing 8-2. Attempting to access a property of the Weapon class

examples.sc

```
...
println(musket.weaponType)
```

Terminal Output

```
examples.sc: error: value weaponType is not a member of this.
Weapon
println(musket.weaponType)
                  ^
one error found
```

Unfortunately, when trying to access the property of the instance of our class, we encounter an error suggesting that the field we are attempting to access is not a member of the class that was instantiated. This is because, by default, all properties of the class are considered private unless explicitly deemed public for developer use, further providing obfuscation capabilities to the developer who defines the class. You can change the property to be public for use by adding a variable assignment keyword before the parameter in the primary constructor (either var if the value needs to change at any point during its lifespan or val if it can remain immutable). By adding the variable assignment keyword in the parameter definition of the primary constructor, you are telling the class that the parameter needs to be assigned to an instance variable of the class (otherwise known as a property or field). But, why would a developer want to keep some properties private and other properties public? In some cases, when you define a class, you will want to control the developer experience (DX) of the downstream developers who will be using your class. Perhaps you don't ever want them accessing a property directly, or perhaps you want to control how the property is stored in the instance variable. In these scenarios, a best practice is to use methods known in programming as getters and setters. Listing 8-3 demonstrates how to make an instance variable public for use as well as examples of getters and setters.

Listing 8-3. Demonstration of public and private variables in a class

```
class Weapon(var weaponType: String = "Musket", barrelLength:
Int) {
    private var length = s"${barrelLength} inches"

    def getBarrelLength(): String = {
        return s"The barrell is ${this.length} long"
    }
    def setBarrelLength(length: Int){
        this.length = s"${length} inches"
    }
}
```

```
var musket = new Weapon("Musket", 36)
println(musket.weaponType)
println(musket.getBarrelLength)

musket.weaponType = "Big Musket"
musket.setBarrelLength(40)

println(musket.weaponType)
println(musket.getBarrelLength)
```

Terminal Output
```
Musket
The barrell is 36 inches long
Big Musket
The barrell is 40 inches long
```

Notice that the secondary constructor sets a new instance variable, length, in addition to the parameters defined in the primary constructor. This variable is preceded by the private keyword to keep it protected from developer access similar to the default behavior for the barrelLength parameter in the primary constructor. The secondary constructor takes whatever argument was provided to the barrelLength parameter and stores it as a string along with its unit of measurement (inches). After the secondary constructor, two methods are defined to access and modify the barrelLength property, getBarrelLength and setBarrellLength. These are examples of a getter method and a setter method. The getter method returns a string that provides a message that we have tailored to ensure a good downstream developer experience. The setter method ensures that any integer passed into the setBarrelLength method gets stored in our private length variable as a string with a unit of measurement just as the secondary constructor did upon the creation of the instance of the class. We can therefore ensure that any time the property is accessed via the getter, it will always have a unit of measurement attached to it. Many languages require the use of getters and setters and do not allow for direct access to properties of a class. This can lead to an awfully verbose set of unnecessary boilerplate code if you don't need to control the experience behind getting and setting variables. Thus, in Scala, it is a best practice to only follow the getter and setter pattern when necessary and to protect your variables when necessary. Otherwise, you can stick to Scala shorthand to allow the downstream developers to access the properties of the class directly.

Object Reference

It's important to understand that class encapsulation creates an instantiated object that is not accessible from other objects but *can* be referenced from other variables. It is possible to store a newly instantiated class of type Weapon in one variable and then set another variable equal to the first variable. Now, two variables are both pointing to the same instantiated Weapon object in memory. This is known as object reference. Either variable can access the getter and setter methods of the underlying object to modify them, and the other variable will have access to the changes created by the original variable. However, if another object is created and stored in its own new variable, access to its getter and setter methods will not modify anything about the original object. Listing 8-4 demonstrates this object reference functionality using the Weapon class defined in Listing 8-3.

Listing 8-4. Demonstration of object reference functionality

```
var johnsMusket = new Weapon("Musket", 36)
var janesMusket = johnsMusket
var jimsMusket = new Weapon("Heavy Musket", 42)

janesMusket.setBarrelLength(40)
```

```
jimsMusket.setBarrelLength(45)
println(johnsMusket.getBarrelLength)
println(jimsMusket.getBarrelLength)

janesMusket = jimsMusket
janesMusket.weaponType = "Jim and Jane's Musket"
println(jimsMusket.weaponType)
println(johnsMusket.weaponType)
```

Terminal Output
```
The barrell is 40 inches long
The barrell is 45 inches long
Jim and Jane's Musket
Musket
```

Notice in this example that John's musket was originally instantiated with a length of 36 inches. Then the variable janesMusket is assigned to John's musket. Both johnsMusket and janesMusket are referencing the same object in the computer's memory. Separately, Jim has a musket instantiated with the weapon type of "Heavy Musket" and a length of 42 inches. Once all of the variables have been assigned to reference an object, janesMusket calls the setter method to change the barrel length on the object that it references and jimsMusket does the same. Next, the barrel length of johnsMusket and jimsMusket are printed to the terminal. Notice that when janesMusket made a call to the setter method, it changed the value of the barrel length of John's musket from 36 inches to 40 inches. When jimsMusket made a call to its setter method, it changed its barrel length from 42 inches to 45 inches but did not impact Jane or John's musket at all.

After those two print statements occur, the program reassigns janesMusket to the object referenced by the jimsMusket variable. Now, both janesMusket and jimsMusket are pointing to the same object in memory, and only the variable johnsMusket has access to the object that represented John's musket. The janesMusket variable then makes a direct call to set the weaponType of the object it references to "Jim and Jane's Musket." Then we print out the weaponType of jimsMusket to verify that the change to the janesMusket weaponType actually changed the weaponType of their shared object. Next, we print out the weapon type of John's musket to ensure that the changes to Jane and Jim's weapon type do not impact John's musket.

If, for some reason, you wanted to reassign the johnsMusket variable to either jimsMusket or janesMusket, then all three variables would be pointed to the same object in memory. At that point, the object that was originally instantiated to represent John's musket now has no variable reference and your program will no longer be able to access it anywhere. In order to free up memory, Scala will then collect that non-referenceable object and delete it in a process known as garbage collection.

It is important to have a thorough understanding of object reference because it is possible to have a class that is instantiated with arguments that are references to other instantiated classes. You could think of this as a kind of nesting of classes. Understanding that a referenced object can be modified from another part of your program and would therefor update the properties of a nested class might make you think twice about whether or not you should protect the properties of that nested class instead of allowing them to stay public.

Also, when comparing equality between two instantiated objects, the expression will only validate to true if the objects are the exact same reference in memory. If you wish to customize the way Scala compares two similar objects of the same class type, you can instead override the built-in equals method of the class. Listing 8-5 demonstrates the override of this built-in equals method as well as object reference comparison.

Listing 8-5. Comparing equality between instantiated class objects

examples.sc

```
class Weapon(var weaponType: String = "Musket", barrelLength:
Int) {
    private var length = s"${barrelLength} inches"

    def getBarrelLength(): String = {
        return s"The barrell is ${this.length} long"
    }
    def setBarrelLength(length: Int){
        this.length = s"${length} inches"
    }

    override def equals(comparableObject: Any): Boolean = {
        return (comparableObject.asInstanceOf[Weapon].
        weaponType == this.weaponType && comparableObject.
        asInstanceOf[Weapon].getBarrelLength == this.
        getBarrelLength)
    }
}

var weapon1: Weapon = new Weapon("Rifle",50)
var weapon2 = new Weapon("Rifle",50)
println(weapon1 == weapon2)
```

In this example, if you comment out the override of the default equals method, the print statement will print false because weapon1 and weapon2 do not point to the same object in memory. However, by overriding the default equals method, we can check each individual property of the class for equality and return an overall true or false if all the properties of the object are the same. You'll notice that the method signature requires an Any type for the comparableObject parameter. The parameter can be named anything you like, but in order to explicitly override the built-in equals method, the type of the method signature needs to match exactly (so it needs to take in an Any type and return a Boolean). Due to that, in the body of the method, we have to explicitly cast the comparableObject to a Weapon type using the .asInstanceOf method in order to access the getter and setter methods and the weaponType instance property. Because the weaponType of both instantiated objects is "Rifle" and they both have a barrelLength of 50, our override equals method will now return true when comparing equality for these two objects.

You might also notice that in this example when instantiating weapon1, the type of the variable that it is stored in is explicitly set to a Weapon type. This was done for the sake of example; however, it is typically considered redundant to specify the custom type that you are instantiating when you store a new class object in a variable. You can simply let Scala implicitly assign the variable to the class type as shown in the assignment to weapon2. Worthy to note that you could also have explicitly assigned the variable an AnyRef type as all custom types or classes are sub-types of the AnyRef type.

Up to this point, we have been printing out properties of the class object. However, what would happen if you tried to print out the object itself? What might you expect to see in the terminal? Perhaps you would only see the name of the variable or perhaps the properties of the class. But, what if the class only has methods and no properties? Listing 8-6 demonstrates the output of that operation using the weapon1 object created in Listing 8-5.

Listing 8-6. Printing an instantiated class object

examples.sc

```
...
println(weapon1)
```

Terminal Output

```
Main$$anon$1$Weapon@4d591d15
```

Just like a class has a built-in equals method, it also has a built-in
.toString method that is invoked implicitly when passing the object to
the println function. The built-in .toString method prints out some
information about the call site of the object, its type, and its location in
memory. But, most likely this is not what you want when using a print
in most cases. So, just like the equals method, you can override the
.toString to do whatever you need to do with it. Listing 8-7 shows an
override method that can be added to the Weapon class definition and an
example of what it would look like when printed to the terminal.

Listing 8-7. Overriding the default toString method of a class

examples.sc

```
...
override def toString(): String = {
        return s"Weapon(type: ${this.weaponType},
        length: ${this.length})"
    }
...

var weapon1: Weapon = new Weapon("Rifle",50)
println(weapon1)
```

Terminal Output
```
Weapon(type: Rifle, length: 50 inches)
```

It should be pretty obvious that this overridden .toString method is
now much more usable. It gives us the type of the variable as well as values
for each of its parameters in a customized way that we defined.

EXERCISE 8-1

Create your own custom class that represents a Date object. Your Date class will need to contain a property for month, day, and year. Also, add a method to subtract a day from the date and another method to add a day to the date. As you create your class, consider the following:

1. How will you represent months? Will they be numbers or strings?

2. Will your properties be public or private?

3. When adding a day to a date, how will the method behave if the date currently represents the last day of the month? What if it is the last day of the year?

4. How will the subtract day method behave if the date represents the first day of a month or year?

5. What format will be displayed on the terminal when printing your date? How might you provide a configuration option to allow the developer to specify what format they prefer?

6. How will you ensure that the developer passes the correct values to each property? What error messaging could you provide to the developer in the case that they get it wrong?

Case Classes

At this point, our class has gotten relatively big. It has a getter and setter, a private variable, and two overridden methods. You might wonder if you will need to put this much work into every single class that you create, especially if they will all need the exact same type of functionality. After all, isn't it a fundamental rule of coding not to repeat yourself? Some languages do in fact require that you write all of this boilerplate code for every class. However, in Scala there is a shortcut known as a case class. Case classes are often used as models to represent data in your program (perhaps coming from a database) and are really useful when you need more convenient functionality by default without having to write it yourself.

By adding the case modifier keyword in front of your class definition, it automatically sets all parameters to public variables (without requiring a var or val keyword), defines an equals method similar to what we just wrote, and provides a more useful toString method. If you need to explicitly set something to private or override one of the built-in methods, you still can, but the case class simply attempts to eliminate unnecessary boilerplate code from your program. Listing 8-8 illustrates the conversion of our Weapon class to a simple case class with no getter or setter to intercept any functionality of the instance properties of the object.

Listing 8-8. Example of a case class

```
case class Weapon(weaponType: String = "Musket", length: Int)

var weapon1 = new Weapon("Rifle",50)
var weapon2 = new Weapon("Rifle",50)
var weapon3 = new Weapon("Musket",32)
println(weapon1)
println(weapon1 == weapon2)
println(weapon2 == weapon3)
println(weapon2.weaponType)
println(weapon3.length)
```

Terminal Output
```
Weapon(Rifle,50)
true
false
Rifle
32
```

Notice that because there was no functionality that had to be explicitly written or overridden in this class, there is no body to the class, making its definition extremely concise. This is really useful when you need a quick inline object in a piece of code. Just as expected, the toString method prints out a string similar to what we had written in our override method, and the equals method works exactly the same as when we compared each individual property of the class. We also can access the individual properties of the class directly without a getter or a setter and without providing a variable keyword in the primary constructor. Hopefully by walking you through the verbosity that many other languages encounter, you can fully appreciate all of the functionality wrapped up out of the box in a simple case keyword provided right before the class keyword in your class definition.

EXERCISE 8-2

1. Write a case class that represents a character in a movie. The properties of the class might be the name of the character, their height, and perhaps a catch phrase that they are famous for.

2. Unlike our Weapon object, case classes can have bodies if they need to. Create a body for your movie character and define a method that will return the catch phrase in all caps when invoked.

3. Experiment with constructing a few instances of your case class. Access its properties directly, compare the instances for equality, and print out the objects to the terminal to see how they behave.

Companion Objects

A companion object in Scala is a simple data structure that encapsulates members, similar to a class, but the object does not need to first be instantiated and stored in a variable to use it. The companion object is required to have the same name of the normal class that it is a "companion" to and will then have access to the private members of that class. Accessible members of a class that is not first instantiated in many other languages are known as static members, and they are typically encapsulated into a class to organize the namespace of their functionality rather than to be used for unique instantiation.

To create a companion object, you first use the object keyword followed by the name of the class that the companion object is attached to. Then you define a scope or body of the companion object that contains members just like a class. Listing 8-9 provides an example of a companion object that is paired with our Weapon class.

Listing 8-9. Demonstration of a companion object for using "static" members

exmaples.sc
```
case class Weapon(weaponType: String = Weapon.default_weapon,
length: Int)

object Weapon {
    val unit_of_measurement = "inches"
    val default_weapon = "Musket"
    def useWeapon(weapon: Weapon){
        println(s"Using weapon ${weapon}")
    }
}
```

```
println(Weapon.unit_of_measurement)
println(Weapon.default_weapon)
Weapon.useWeapon(new Weapon("Big" + Weapon.default_weapon, 40))
```

Terminal Output

```
inches
Musket
Using weapon Weapon(BigMusket,40)
```

In this example, notice that in order to print out the default weapon and the unit of measure, we did not need to first instantiate a Weapon object with the new keyword. We simply referenced the member directly from the definition of the companion object by calling Weapon.unit_of_measurement and Weapon.default_weapon. You might have also noticed that the static member default_weapon was used in the class's primary constructor as well to provide a default value in case no argument is passed to the weaponType parameter. This eliminates the need to keep both references updated if you decided to change what the default weapon should be. However, in order to pass an actual Weapon data type to the useWeapon method, we did need to instantiate a new Weapon inline to pass as an argument. That newly instantiated weapon is now an instance of the Weapon case class and uses its conveniently built-in toString method when the useWeapon static method passes it to the println function.

Application

Now that you've learned how to create classes, lets modify our Nebula Operating System with some additional commands that can take advantage of this new functionality. Just like any basic operating system, our shell should have the ability to make basic text files. We can represent text files in our system as a case class that contains two members: a title and text body. Listing 8-10 provides an example of two new commands that we will need to add to our pattern matching scenarios in order to create new text files and to list out text files that have already been created. Those two commands will call two additional functions that are also provided in this listing along with the definition for the case class we will be using and a variable that will store a list of the saved files.

Listing 8-10. Additional commands added to the Nebula OS shell to create and list out basic text files

nebula.sc

```
...
case c if c.contains("make") => createTextFile(c)
case c if c.contains("show") => showTextFiles()
...

case class TextFile(title: String, text: String)
var files = new scala.collection.mutable.ListBuffer[TextFile]()

def createTextFile(userInput: String) {
    var tokens = userInput.split("/")
    try{
        files += new TextFile(tokens(1).trim, tokens(2).trim)
    }
    catch {
        case _: Throwable =>  println("An error occurred trying
        to create a text file.")
    }
}

def showTextFiles(){
    for(i <- Range(0,files.length)){
        println(files(i))
    }
}
```

Terminal Output
```
Welcome to the Nebula Operating System (NOS)! Version 1.0.4
NOS> make/Star/A star is born.
NOS> show
TextFile(Star,A star is born.)
NOS>
```

It is important to remember how pattern matching works when adding these commands into your pattern scenarios. Because your text files may contain + or - characters, you may want to ensure that these new commands are added before the add command and the subtraction command patterns so that those commands do not inadvertently try to call their subsequent functions instead of calling the new function to create a text file. You'll notice that the command to create a new text file, make, requires you to separate the user input of the title and the text body by a forward slash. This is used as the delimiter for our tokens in this example so that spaces can be used in the text body. In a more complicated system, you would also want to allow the user to be able to use forward slash characters in their text body. However, for the sake of simplicity in this example, we can consider it a forbidden character as it will split the text body into separate index positions of the token list in the createTextFile function.

Note that the files variable is initialized as an empty list that will contain objects of our custom type TextFile. The createTextFile function simply takes the index position of the title of the file (the next value passed after the make keyword) and the text body (the value passed after the title of the file) and instantiates a new TextFile object that it then adds to the files list after trimming any unnecessary whitespace. If the function is unable to properly parse the command, it will handle the error and print a message to the screen just as it did when we created the addCommand function. Once the file has been added to the list of files, you can show all the available files created in our operating system using the show command, which simply loops through our list and prints out each object. Because the objects are instances of a case class, it can use the built-in toString method to print a readable object to the screen.

EXERCISE 8-3

See if you can extend the Nebula OS script to edit an existing text file. You may need to loop through all the objects in the files list to check for the title of the file in order to modify it. Consider the following:

1. What types of commands will you need to add to make this usable?

2. What kind of parsing tokenization will you use to allow for editing the file?

3. Will the user be able to preview what the existing text of the file is when editing?

4. What additional functions will need to be added for the commands to utilize?

Summary

In this chapter, you learned that a class can encapsulate functions and variables (known as methods and properties respectively) as members of the class. You learned how to define a new class and how to reference it with variables. Next, you were introduced to some of the default behavior of accessing the public and private members of a class and how to modify that behavior. After which you were shown the shorthand version of that behavior modification using case classes. From there, you were introduced to companion objects and their use for accessing members of a class without first creating an instance of a class. Finally, we applied the use of a case class to our example command-line operating system. This OS script is now starting to get quite large and will continue to grow larger as we add more commands, classes, and functions. In the next chapter, you will be introduced to a new method of breaking up your scripts into modules to help organize your code.

CHAPTER 9

Dependency Management

With regard to the subject of mechanical engineering, there are six simple machines that are considered the building blocks from which all more complex machines are composed. These include the lever, the wheel and axle, the pulley, the incline plane, the wedge, and the screw. It is fascinating to know that even the most complicated of our modern machines, like cars, robots, or even computers themselves, are made up of such simple concepts. But, just like in mechanical engineering, there are a finite amount of fundamental components in software engineering that compose all programs and programming languages. These include variables, expressions, conditionals, loops, functions, and classes – all of which have been covered in this book up to this point. Given that you now know all of the fundamental pieces of programming in Scala, you would be justified in feeling confident enough to build any program you wish with the knowledge you already have.

However, as your programs begin to increase in size and complexity, it becomes important to organize your code into separate files and folders for further abstraction and/or modularity and to help facilitate collaboration. In this chapter, you will expand your knowledge of the Scala object which you were briefly introduced to when learning about classes. You will also be introduced to a method of organizing objects into a larger

© Jason Lee Hodges 2019
J. L. Hodges, *Software Engineering from Scratch*,
https://doi.org/10.1007/978-1-4842-5206-2_9

encapsulation mechanism known as packages. Finally, you will learn how to reference members between packages and objects through the use of imports. That being said, cross file referencing is not possible in Scala without first compiling your code, so let's first take a brief look at the Scala compiler.

Compiler

Up to this point, all the code that has been written in this book would be considered interpreted code. Interpreted code is code that can be written and rewritten several times and is only translated for the computer to understand at the time that it is run. Whether it is coded from the REPL or written iteratively from a Scala script file, interpreted code is seen by many as a really great paradigm for rapid application development, proof-of-concept prototyping, or smaller utility type programs that help with task automation processes.

As your programs become larger and more complex, the need to separate them into isolated files for organization and collaboration becomes increasingly apparent. In Scala, in order to separate a project into multiple files, you must first compile the code. Compiled code is translated into machine code at compile time rather than when the program is run. Compilation is an extra step that must take place before you can run your code. Compiled code is generally considered much faster than interpreted code because (among other things) it is translated ahead of time rather than at runtime. Additionally, when working on a large project with multiple files split out, only the files that are changed will need to be re-compiled, thus providing added productivity when prepping a code base to run. Conversely, all interpreted code is translated into machine code every time you run it. Examples of interpreted languages include Python, JavaScript, and Ruby, whereas examples of compiled languages include C, C++, C#, Rust, and Java. While there are varying implementations of all of these languages that can blur the lines between compiled and interpreted, Scala is one of the very few languages that comes with both an interpreted option and a compiled option out of the box, thus allowing you to easily learn both.

So how does compilation work for Scala? You might recall that when you installed Scala, you first had to ensure that you had a version of the Java SDK installed already. Scala, when compiled, is translated down to what is called Java Byte Code. Java Byte Code is code that has been compiled to be translated, not by an actual computer but by a virtual computer known as the Java Virtual Machine or JVM. That virtual machine is installed and running on any machine that you want to run your code on as a prerequisite. The reason Scala is compiled to Java is because so much work has been put into the JVM so that it will work on any computer. One of the biggest selling points for writing Java code in its infancy was that you could write code once and execute it on any machine because there was a JVM version for every type of computer out there. Conversely, other languages required you to have a very specific compiler to translate your code depending on what kind of machine you would be executing your code on and you would need to test and troubleshoot your code on each compiler for compatibility. You might see how that could get tedious.

By compiling Scala code down to Java code, not only are you able to leverage the work of the JVM, but you also get access to the entire Java community of code if you choose to collaborate with Java developers. Once compiled, Scala and Java code operate exactly the same so there is often really good interoperability between the two languages. When compiled, both Java and Scala code are transformed into files called `.class` files. From there, the .class files can be run by either Java or Scala. The command to compile a Scala file is `scalac` followed by the Scala file name (the "c" at the end of Scala standing for "compile"). This will create a `.class` file of the same file name in the same directory as the scala file that you are compiling (unless you are compiling a package – more on that later in the chapter). From there, you can execute the compiled code using the command `scala` followed by the name of the class file omitting the .class extension.

Note   You cannot compile a Scala script file unless your code is wrapped in either a class or an object. You were briefly introduced to the object type in Scala in the previous chapter when the topic of the companion object was covered. However, an object in Scala can also be a stand-alone structure that can be used to encapsulate code on its own.

Scala Object

The basic object in Scala is a structure that allows code to be encapsulated without the need to instantiate it like a class. It is often useful to use a simple object when creating your first compiled program because you can wrap your entire program in a single object with very minimal boilerplate code. Listing 9-1 demonstrates how you might create a simple "Hello World" program in Scala, wrap it in an object, compile it, and then execute it.

Listing 9-1. A compiled "Hello World" program wrapped in an object

examples.sc
```
object examples extends App {
        println("Hello World")
}
```

Terminal Output
```
> scalac examples.sc
> scala examples
Hello World!
```

You'll notice that, just like the companion object, in order to create a basic object in Scala, you use the `object` keyword followed by the name of the object. In order to make your code executable after compilation, you also add the keywords `extends App`. This allows Scala to know that when your code is executed using the `scala examples` command, all of the code within the body of the object should be called as if it were running a function. If you did not add the extends App keywords and you called the `scala examples` command, the JVM would not find an entry point to start running your code and it would throw an error. This will become more apparent once you've started separating your code into several files.

You may have also noticed that when you ran `scalac examples.sc`, it created a file called `examples.class` in the same directory as your `examples.sc` file. The `examples.class` file is your compiled code. By calling `scala examples` and omitting the `.class` extension, you are telling Scala implicitly to run an already compiled `.class` file (regardless of whether it was originally written in Scala or Java). The behavior of the directory that your files compile to is altered slightly, however, when you are compiling files that belong to a package.

Packages

Packages are a great way to organize code under a single namespace across multiple files. Files that all belong to the same package have access to the members of the other files within the package. This allows you to break up your code into multiple files without needing to worry about rewriting pieces of common code across those files. All you need to do to group Scala class files together as a package is to include the `package` keyword followed by the common package name that you choose to use at the top of each of your files. Listing 9-2 demonstrates the creation of two Scala files grouped in the same package that have access to each other's members.

Listing 9-2. Examples of referencing and compiling multiple files from the same package

messenger.scala

```
package examples

object messenger extends App {
    println(messages.hello)
}
```

messages.scala

```
package examples

object messages {
    var hello = "Hello World!"
    var question = "How are you?"
    var farewell = "Regards."
}
```

Terminal Output

```
> scalac messenger.scala messages.scala
> scala examples.messenger
Hello World!
```

You might notice that the extension for the files in this example is no longer a .sc extension but rather a .scala extension. Since these files are not going to be interpreted but rather always compiled, it is better to use the .scala file extension, which is equivalent to the Java .java extension and is meant for objects and classes, rather than the Scala script extension.

The two files in this example both start with a declaration that they belong to the package "examples." This gives them access to each other's members implicitly. Thus, when the messenger file wants to access a member of the messages object, it can do so as if the code were written in the same file. You'll notice that only the messenger object uses the extends

App keywords as that is the entry point for our now multi-file program. We haven't declared anything to happen in the messages file, so its purpose is simply to exist as a reference for our main program, `messenger`, to make a call to one of its members. Once both files have been written, they are compiled at the same time using the command `scalac messenger.scala messages.scala` which creates a package directory that contains the compiled class files for both files. If you make a change to one of these files and not the other and need to re-compile, you only need to include the name of the changed file after your `scalac` command. To execute our program, we simply call the main entry point file from its package directory using the same dot notation that you would use to access the member of a class or object. The command `scala examples.messenger` looks in the package `examples` for the `messenger` object and executes it. This prints out the message "Hello World!" which is a string member that exists in the messages object.

Imports

There will be times in the development and organization of a program that you do not wish for all of the files or objects that you create to live in the same package. Perhaps they need to be logically divided or sub-divided into different package names to make it easier for collaborating developers to understand how to obtain or navigate to the appropriate piece of code that they wish to reference. Or perhaps you've created a utility that might be really useful in other projects so you want to abstract it out into its own package for later use. In this scenario, in order to reference a member of an object that lives in a different package, you can explicitly import that member or package into your code using the `import` keyword. Listing 9-3 demonstrates an explicit import.

Listing 9-3. Explicitly importing a stringWrapper object to the messenger app

messenger.scala
```
import stringWrapper._

package examples {

    object messenger extends App {
        println(stringWrapper.userMessage("John Doe",
        messages.hello))
    }

}
```

stringWrapper.scala
```
object stringWrapper {
    def userMessage(userName: String, message: String):
    String = {
        return s"${userName} says: ${message}"
    }
}
```

Terminal Output
```
> scalac messenger.scala stringWrapper.scala
> scala examples.messenger
John Doe says: Hello World!
```

In this example, we are importing all of the members of the stringWrapper object into the messenger.scala file. This is denoted by the underscore wildcard after the stringWrapper import statement. If you only wanted to import a single method from the object, you would explicitly add the method name instead of the underscore. If you wanted to import multiple methods but not all methods, you would list them inside curly braces after the import statement. Listing 9-4 shows an example of this. The `stringWrapper` class in this example simply takes a username and a message and returns a string that wraps those two parameters so that the downstream consumer of this wrapper knows who was providing the message (like the signature of an email or the user icon in a chat or comment box). You can see how this `stringWrapper` might be useful in more than one program which is why you might not want to keep it exclusively in the `examples` package.

Listing 9-4. Example of explicitly importing multiple methods from an object

```
import objectname.{method1, method2, method3}
```

You will also notice from the example in Listing 9-3 that the `examples` package now adds curly braces around the `messenger` object to denote the package scope is separate from the import. It's worthy to note that just like the scope of a function or a conditional branch, packages can have nested scopes of sub-packages if you wish, denoted by nesting curly braces and additional `package` keywords.

If you still do not have the full understanding of why you would explicitly import objects rather than keeping everything in the same package, a great example would be to look at some of the functionality that can be imported from the Scala standard library. You've seen examples of these Scala standard library features in some of the example code thus far in the book because your Scala programs have implicit access to their methods as long as you reference the entire package namespace. However, your code can be dramatically abbreviated by importing the Scala Standard Library package you want to use at the top of your files instead of referencing the entire package name inline with your code.

Standard Library

You may have noticed in previous chapters that sometimes we used classes or data types from the Scala standard library that have really long namespaces. While this is fine if you only need to type the entire namespace once, it gets exceptionally verbose if you need to repeat that code all throughout your program. In this scenario, you can simply add an import statement to the top of your file and you then have access to that module namespace anywhere within the scope of the program that you have imported the module in to. In the chapter on expressions, there were several methods that were used as part of the Scala Math package that could have been cleaned up. Also, in the previous chapter, our Nebula Operating System example used a ListBuffer from the Scala standard library as a means for storing any files that might be added dynamically by the user during runtime. Listing 9-5 provides an illustration on how those packages could be imported using our examples object.

Listing 9-5. An example of importing the math package and the ListBuffer class from the Scala Standard Library

examples.scala
```scala
import math._
import scala.collection.mutable.ListBuffer

object examples extends App {
    println(pow(3,2))
    println(round(2.45))

    var splitList = "apples, oranges, bananas".split(",")
    var fruit = new ListBuffer[String]
    for(i <- Range(0,splitList.length)){
        fruit += splitList(i)
    }
```

```
    println(fruit)
}
```

Terminal Output

```
9.0
2
ListBuffer(apples, oranges, bananas)
```

Notice that in the body of the examples object that you no longer have to explicitly type out math.pow or math.round, you simply have direct access to the methods of the math package since you have imported all the methods of that package using the underscore wildcard. The same is true for the ListBuffer class. While this example is somewhat futile in terms of the end results of the list of fruit since it simply moves the strings from one type of list to another, more mutable, type of list, it does serve to provide an example of how to import and use a ListBuffer without needing to explicitly type out the entire namespace each time you use it.

Note   It is possible to run into method name collisions if you attempt to import methods from multiple packages with the same name. If this occurs in your code, you can alias a particular method using the arrow operator encapsulated in curly braces (i.e., Math.{pow => power}).

EXERCISE 9-1

1. Go to www.scala-lang.org/api/current to browse the list of Scala standard library classes, objects, and methods. See if you can use any of these in your current code to simplify any of the code you have already written.

2. For all code examples you have followed up to this point, go back and remove any explicitly typed out namespaces and instead import the method or object you need at the top of your file.

Application

Now that you have seen how to split code into several files for further modularity and organization, let's apply that knowledge to our Nebula operating system shell. We'll start by defining a package at the top of our main script called os.nebula. It is a best practice to use package names that coincide with top-level web domains that you own so that when the broader community uses your code, they will not encounter any namespace collisions. For example, if you owned the top-level domain www.ilovescala.com, the standard convention would be to use the package name com.ilovescala.mypackagename. In this case since we are just creating example code that will not be used by other developers, we can resign to simply using our os.nebula namespace with no concern for collisions.

Next, let's create two additional files. One called TextFile.scala and another called Utilities.scala. It is a best practice when organizing your code to put individual classes, whether they be case classes or otherwise, into their own files. Typically, classes that model data (like our TextFile case class) are often organized into a sub-folder called "Models," but we will just keep everything at the top level for now for the sake of simplicity. In both of these files, add the package name at the top so that members can be shared between these files. Now we can move our case class declaration into the TextFile.scala file. Listing 9-6 demonstrates this move.

Listing 9-6. Isolating the TextFile case class into its own file

TextFile.scala
```
package os.nebula

case class TextFile(title: String, text: String)
```

Next, we can move all of our command functions into our Utilities. scala file. They will need to be wrapped in a basic object so that they can be compiled and called statically. Let's call that object Utilities. Back in your main script, any reference to these functions needs to have the "Utilities" object name prepended so that our Scala file knows that it needs to look in that object to find them. Listing 9-7 shows an example of this new Utilities.scala file.

Listing 9-7. Utilities.scala file that contains all of the command functions

Utilities.scala
```
package os.nebula

object Utilities {
    def addCommand(userInput: String) {
        ...
    }

    var files = new scala.collection.mutable.ListBuffer[TextFile]()

    def createTextFile(userInput: String) {
        ...
    }

    def showTextFiles(){
        ...
    }
}
```

163

Finally, we need to wrap our main script in an object that extends App so that Scala knows that it is the entry point for our program. Listing 9-8 demonstrates this as well as the addition of the Utilities object name to our function calls. Once these files have all been created, you will need to compile them all using the command scalac nebula.scala TextFile. scala Utilities.scala.

Listing 9-8. Wrapping the main script in an object that extends App

nebula.scala

```scala
package os.nebula {

    object nebula extends App {
        println("Welcome to the Nebula Operating System (NOS)!
        Version 1.0.5")
        var command = ""
        do {
            command = readLine("NOS> ")
            command match {
                case c if c.contains("make") => Utilities.
                createTextFile(c)
                case c if c.contains("show") => Utilities.
                showTextFiles()
                case c if c.contains("+") => Utilities.
                addCommand(c)
                case c if c.contains("-") =>
                println(s"Subtraction command: ${command}")
                case c if c.equalsIgnoreCase("help") =>
                println("Help Command")
                case c if c.equalsIgnoreCase("shutdown") =>
                println("Shutting down...")
```

```
        case _ => println(s"${command} is not a known
        command.")
      }
    }
    while (!command.equalsIgnoreCase("shutdown"))
  }
}
```

EXERCISE 9-2

Now that all of the files have been separated, run your nebula program with the command scala os.nebula.nebula (the package name followed by the object name that extends App). Test to ensure everything works the same as it did previously.

Try to identify opportunities to further abstract this program into separate files for better organization. See if you can figure out how to create sub-directories to organize these files in.

In addition to organizing your code, the added knowledge of understanding imports and the power of compiling your code to Java provide new possibilities to our Nebula terminal. Let's create a new command that writes an actual text (.txt) file using an import from the Java standard library. Listing 9-9 details the implementation of this endeavor. We could technically replace our createTextFile function with this new function; however, it is a good example of other Scala functionality so we will leave it in for the time being.

Listing 9-9. Implementing a write command that leverages the Java standard library

nebula.scala

```scala
package os.nebula {

    object nebula extends App {
        println("Welcome to the Nebula Operating System (NOS)!
        Version 1.0.5")
        var command = ""
        do {
            command = readLine("NOS> ")
            command match {
                case c if c.contains("write") => Utilities.
                write(c)
                ...
            }
        }
        while (!command.equalsIgnoreCase("shutdown"))
    }
}
```

Utilities.scala

```scala
import java.io.PrintWriter
package os.nebula {
    object Utilities {
        ...

        def write(userInput: String){
            var tokens = userInput.split(" ")
            println("[Enter the text you wish to write to your
            new file below]")
            var textBody = readLine()
```

```scala
    try{
        new PrintWriter(s"${tokens(1).trim}.txt") {
        write(textBody); close }
        println("[Saving File...]")
    }
    catch {
        case _: Throwable =>  println("An error
        occurred trying to write a text file.")
    }
    }
}
```

Notice that in the first line of the Utilites.scala file, we are importing the java.io.PrintWriter function that allows us to write actual files to the operating system that our shell will be running on. We also added a write command to the list of commands that the shell can take as user input in the main nebula.scala file. This new command provides a new user experience that differs from our original make command. Instead of having the function parse the user input by splitting the command on a forward slash, it assumes that there will be no spaces in the file name and therefore only takes the command name and the file name as the original input. Then, once the function has kicked off, it prompts the user on a separate line to provide the text input that they wish to add to their .txt file. The user then enters the text they want to provide and hits enter. This then incites the program to save the text file and let the user know that the file is saving. The input from the second user prompt is stored in the textBody variable and passed into the PrintWriter function that we imported from Java. The PrintWriter then does the actual work of saving the .txt file to the file system of the computer.

Remember to compile your nebula.scala file and the Utilities. scala file again and then re-run your shell to test it out. You'll notice that when you successfully run this command, a new text file with the name you provided will be written to the same directory that your shell is being run from. Listing 9-10 provides an example of how you would implement another function to list out all text files that have been created in this same directory.

Listing 9-10. An implementation of a List command to list out all text files in the current directory

```
def list(){
    import java.io.File
    var dir = new File("./").listFiles
    for(file <- Range(0,dir.length)){
        if(dir(file).getName.contains("txt")){
            println(dir(file))
        }
    }
}
```

Notice that imports can occur within the scope of functions in Scala as demonstrated by the import of the `java.io.File` class in this list function. This import is only accessible within the body of the function. If you tried to access the File class outside of this function, you would get an error. This is exceptionally useful when you do run into namespace collisions, particularly between the Scala standard library and the Java standard library, and you want to limit the scope of your import to avoid the collision.

EXERCISE 9-3

---

1. See if you can identify other functionality from either the Scala standard library or the Java standard library that you can add to your shell. Perhaps you can wrap the Math library to provide additional functionality for arithmetic operations.

2. Try to add a command to edit an existing text file in your
    operating system. What will the user experience be like? Is
    it easier to do this given functionality from the Java standard
    library?

Summary

In this chapter, you learned about splicing your Scala code into individual files while still maintaining continuity between them using packages. You also learned how to import compiled objects for methods that do not exist in your package. Building on that knowledge, you were shown how to import methods and classes from both the Scala and the Java standard libraries. All of this knowledge allows you to now organize your code for easier digestion which will, in turn, facilitate more productive collaboration. In the next chapter, you will be introduced to several programming paradigms that will build off of the fact that you can now separate your code into different files.

CHAPTER 10

Programming Paradigms

The radical, young, and dynamic sport of mixed martial arts has seen an incredible boom in popularity over the last few decades, rivaling classical combat sports such as boxing. There have even been recent attempts to feature star athletes from both MMA and boxing in head-to-head competition to determine the relative athleticism of both sports. Regardless of the outcomes and subsequent conclusions derived about the superiority of either sport or its athletes in such attempts, it is clear to most that in a real combat scenario – one free of gloves, a ring, and a referee – the probabilistic advantage would lie with the athlete who can more readily respond to a wider variety of attacks.

Bruce Lee, a famous martial artist and Hollywood film star, has at different times been attributed the title of the "Father of Mixed Martial Arts." He founded a methodology, or paradigm, known as "Jeet Kune Do," or "The Way of the Intercepting Fist," in 1967 that sought to do away with the stringent nature of traditional martial arts styles and patterns. He vehemently rejected this paradigm being classified as "his own style" as, in his mind, it was really the absence of style. He believed that the classical styles were too rigid and unrealistic in real combat and that by combining the strengths of different styles and removing any unnecessary movements from them, a martial artist would be free to react

© Jason Lee Hodges 2019
J. L. Hodges, *Software Engineering from Scratch*,
https://doi.org/10.1007/978-1-4842-5206-2_10

to the spontaneity of combat in an efficient manner. Alternatively, if an athlete were to stick to only a single paradigm, for example, Fujian White Crane or Black Tiger Fist, they may be bound by the patterns they know and are familiar with, which might leave them vulnerable to the known exploitations of that style.

In a similar vein of thought, it has been said that "When all you have is a hammer, everything looks like a nail." Meaning that if you are only familiar with a single paradigm, you may inadvertently apply it to everything with a confirmation bias that deems it correct even if there is a better way. It is thus an easy leap in logic to suggest that at least being familiar with multiple paradigms is important in assessing a wide variety potential solutions to problems. Said another way, if you have multiple tools in your tool belt, you will be best equipped to know which tool to use for each problem. When assessing software engineering paradigms, it's imperative to remember to use the best tool for the job.

The three main programming paradigms in software engineering include procedural programming, object-oriented programming, and functional programming. All three paradigms have their strengths and weaknesses, along with their fanatical zealots who will blindly defend them to their retirement. However, it is important to understand them all to form a personal understanding for when they are best used and which you prefer when tackling a particular engineering problem.

The main reason Scala is used in this book is to be able to demonstrate multiple paradigms in a single language. Hopefully by learning each paradigm in Scala, you will be best equipped to draw from the strengths of each while sloughing the unnecessary from your repertoire. If, by the end of this chapter, you decide to subscribe to a multi-paradigm approach to software engineering, it would not be incorrect to classify yourself as a disciple of Jeet Kune Do – the style free of styles.

Procedural Programming

Go (or Golang) is a programming language designed by Google in 2007 with a goal of introducing a language that was simple, hyperproductive, and high performance primarily for systems administrators working on servers that hosted web applications. This resulted in a language that is primarily procedural in nature. Procedural programming is a linear idiom wherein a developer writes a consecutive sequence of code statements that are executed a line at a time, one after the other, in a top-down approach, similar to following a simple cooking recipe. This top-down approach is known as hierarchical decomposition. Decomposition, in this context, is used in the same modular sense as described when referring to abstraction. However, in this context it allows for composing modules in a strictly linear or structured fashion. Procedural programming can thus be categorized as a subset or an implementation of structured programming, which is a construct that enforces logical structure within a program. An example of this logical structure is demonstrated in Listing 10-1.

Listing 10-1. A demonstration of structured procedural programming

examples.sc
```
// non-structured
def isMMA(fightingType: String): Boolean = {
    if(fightingType == "boxing"){
        return false
    }
    if(fightingType == "Tai Chi"){
        return false
    }
    if(fightingType == "Jeet Kune Do"){
        return true
    }
```

```scala
    return false
}

// structured
def isMMA(fightingType: String): Boolean = {
    if(fightingType == "boxing"){
        false
    }
    else if(fightingType == "Tai Chi"){
        false
    }
    else if(fightingType == "Jeet Kune Do"){
        true
    }
    else {
        false
    }
}
```

You'll notice the two functions in this listing are almost identical, but one is labeled with a comment suggesting that it is structured and the other is not. So what is the difference? In the structured version of this function, there is only one logical branch in which this function can terminate. Each of the branches is mutually exclusive – there will always be a single entry point and a single exit point. Because of this, coupled with the capability of functions in Scala to imply the return value based on the last line in a function, the return keyword can be eliminated from the structured function. However, the unstructured function does not have an exclusive path that could be executed – each of the if statements could evaluate to false and it will kick out of those branches which requires it to return a fallback or default value outside of a conditional branch. Thus, the non-structured function must explicitly provide a return statement for each condition. It's worthy to note that the non-structured style of this particular function is typically more popular in practice; however, it is logically less structured in a strict and disciplined sense of programming.

Thus far, most of the programming you've seen in this book would be considered procedural programming, especially any programs that were written as scripts or directly in the REPL. The benefit of writing in a procedural fashion is that it is often very easy to follow and clear to read. Thinking of things in chronological sequences tends to be more natural and intuitive, which is why most introductory programming examples are written in a procedural style. Keeping programs simple and intuitive enables long-term maintainability and collaboration among peers. Procedural programs also tend to be really lightweight programs with less compile time and runtime overhead simply due to the nature of what you can do procedurally. A common theme among procedural programmers is to create a program that only does one thing and does it really well, which coincides directly with the concept of modularity. Also, because of its simplicity, procedural programming often requires less coordination regarding overall architecture and integration with other programs. This makes debugging a procedural program much easier since you can step through each line of a program individually to determine the source of any problems without dealing with a spiderweb of dependencies or non-intuitive branching.

That being said, in order to do anything interesting with a procedural program, it often requires the mutation of application state. Application state is the value of all variables at different times throughout the runtime execution of a particular program. Many procedural programs will initialize variables at the beginning of the program and then change them as the program moves from one line to the next as needed. If the procedural program were to crash during runtime and needed to be started over, the application state would be set back to its initialized state rather than the state that was changed or mutated throughout the course of its previous execution.

A good example of application state is demonstrated in our Nebula OS script. At the beginning of our program, after we print out our welcome message, we initialize the variable command to an empty string. Then we execute a continuous loop that takes in user input, mutates the command variable, and performs a pattern matching action based on the new application state. If we shut down our Nebula shell and start it over, we now have an application state wherein command is set back to an empty string.

As procedural programs grow in size and complexity, it becomes difficult to hold application state in a global context, meaning all the variables are accessible in the same global namespace. Eventually you might run into a place where you want two variables of the same name to have different contexts. This is called a namespace collision. When running into namespace collisions, you will often see developers unintentionally updating the application state of a variable that they were not aware existed somewhere else in the procedure. Then, later on in the program when the program tries to access the state of the unintentionally mutated variable, the procedure will run into runtime semantic errors. This is the danger of mutation. Both the object-oriented programming and functional programming paradigms attempt to remedy this danger through encapsulation and "pure" functions, respectively. It is worthy to note that larger, more complex programs that primarily use object-oriented or functional styles can still have aspects of procedural programming laced throughout them. If you encounter a program that seems unnecessarily complex, consider how you might be able to safely refactor a piece of it into a simple, linear procedure.

Object-Oriented Programming

Java, the language for which the JVM was developed, is a pure object-oriented programming language that was created by Sun Microsystems in 1995. Object-oriented programming is a paradigm whose primary purpose is to provide a strategy to deal with complexity, as opposed to procedural programming which requires simplicity. In the object-oriented paradigm, all aspects of a program use classes defined to instantiate objects. Nothing in traditional object-oriented programming, including programs written in Java, can exist outside of some form of object. As you know, objects create encapsulations that guard protected variables and provide a namespace for public variables which directly combats namespace collisions. However, object-oriented programming takes the capabilities of classes further by introducing the concepts of inheritance, polymorphism, interfaces, and abstract classes. To understand the benefits of object-oriented programming, we must dive into the details of each of these topics individually.

Inheritance

Prior to object-oriented programming, when executing a method on a data type, the programmer would be forced to write an exhaustive pattern matching statement to determine what type the method was being applied to and then perform the specific implementation of that type's method. For example, if the developer were trying to call a "print" method, they must first check the data type that "print" was being applied to and call the specific implementation of print. That print implementation might be the same for an integer or a double but might be different for a string. As more data types and methods were added to a program, the dependency complexity for this type of exhaustive checking became exponential, leading to unscalable maintainability problems.

In object-oriented programming, in order to tackle this complexity, it was determined that each data type should define the possible methods that can be applied to it within the object itself. This reduced the complexity dramatically as all methods are encapsulated within a single module of code. The downside to this methodology was that each new data type required the developer to re-implement every single method, which violated the DRY principle in scenarios where two data types might share the same implementation of a method. To combat this, object-oriented programming includes the notion of inheritance.

Just like data types in scala have super-types, classes can also have superclasses that they inherit from. This inheritance relationship takes all of the methods and properties of the parent class and gives the child class access to them. Thus, two classes who share an implementation of the same method can both access that method without having to write the method twice. This inheritance model lends itself really well to modeling simulations of real-world objects. A good example of this is video game simulations. Listing 10-2 demonstrates an example of Scala's inheritance syntax between two similar weapons in a combat video game.

Listing 10-2. Demonstration of inheritance

```scala
package CombatGame
class Fighter (var hp: Int = 20) {
    def reduceHP(damage: Int) {
        this.hp -= damage
    }
}

package CombatGame
class Sword (val length: Int = 10, val attackDamage: Int = 5) {
    def attack(opponent: Fighter){
        opponent.reduceHP(attackDamage)
    }
}

package CombatGame
class Knife(override val length: Int = 3, override val
attackDamage: Int = 2) extends Sword(length, attackDamage)
```

You'll notice in this example that the extends keyword defines the inheritance relationship between the Knife class and the Sword class. You've seen an example of this inheritance relationship before by using the extends App syntax to inherit the default entry point functionality of the App class. In this example, the Knife class does not need to define the length property, the attackDamage property, or the attack method but has access to all three. However, the Knife class in this example provides its own parameter list that allows it to override the constructor of the superclass (the Sword class) to set its own length and attackDamage property defaults and allows the user to set separate values for the Knife if desired using the override keyword preceding the parameter declarations. If these values are not presented at the time of instantiation, they will default to 3 and 2 for a Knife and 10 and 5 for a Sword. If you do not provide a parameter list for the child or sub-class when defining the sub-class, (the Knife class in this example), it will always inherit the default properties of the Sword, 10 and 5.

What is not demonstrated here is the ability for you to add additional properties and methods to this child class to extend the functionality of the parent class. Perhaps, in our make believe combat game, this particular Knife is magical and can heal our allies. Listing 10-3 demonstrates how you might update the Knife class to account for this while still maintaining the advantage of inheriting the normal behavior of a blade-like weapon from the Sword class.

Listing 10-3. Refactor Knife class to add additional functionality that the Sword class does not have

```
package CombatGame
class Knife(override val length: Int = 3, override val
attackDamage: Int = 2, val healPower: Int = 5)
    extends Sword(length, attackDamage) {
        def heal(ally: Fighter) {
            ally.hp += healPower
        }
    }
```

If you wish, you can also override methods from a superclass by simply preceding the definition of the method with the override keyword. This is particularly useful when you want to inherit several methods from a parent class but need to change just one or two of them. When you find yourself overriding everything about a parent class, you may realize that it would be better to simply rewrite a new class from scratch rather than extend anything at all (and perhaps what you really want is an interface which will be covered later in this section). Hopefully, given this demonstration of inheritance, you can see how object-oriented programming allows for productive, non-repeating code.

Polymorphism

Given that you can create classes that inherit from other classes, let's assume that you want to genericize your Sword and Knife classes and have them both inherit from a base Weapon class. The Weapon class can then have several classes that inherit from it – perhaps a Projectile class and a Blade class. From there you can add functionality to each of those subclasses that are specific to their classification. Figure 10-1 demonstrates what this might look like from a relationship perspective.

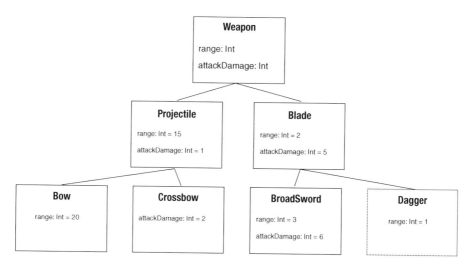

Figure 10-1. *Demonstration of a polymorphic inheritance model wherein each class inherits the properties and methods of its parent or superclass with its own overridden defaults where necessary*

Now that you have all of these defined, let's assume you want to create a property on your Fighter class to allow you to give the fighter a weapon. Since all of these Weapon types are now available and they have been written in such a way so that you don't have to repeat any code, how can you add a property with a defined type to your Fighter class? You might assume that you have to explicitly provide a specific type upfront, therefore limiting the Fighter class to only one weapon type. Your intuition might lead you to believe that you should create a class for each fighter depending on what type of Weapon you want them to have and have those classes inherit from the base Fighter class. These new classes might be called something like SwordFighter, KnifeFighter, CrossbowFighter, Archer, etc. The SwordFighter class might have a constructor method like SwordFighter(var weapon: BroadSword, var hp: Int = 20). However, polymorphism provides you a mechanism that prevents you from having to do this.

Polymorphism literally means "having many forms." You've already seen an example of polymorphism in the Scala type system. You've seen how you can define a variable to accept an AnyVal type and then you can assign any value that inherits from the AnyVal type. In a similar way, in our example you can provide the Fighter class a property with a Weapon type and assign it a value that is of any of the class types that inherit from the Weapon type. Listing 10-4 provides examples of this functionality along with some of the classes defined in Figure 10-1.

Listing 10-4. Demonstration of polymorphic inheritance by providing a Weapon type as a property to the Fighter class and then assigning sub-classes to that property during instantiation

Weapon.scala
```scala
package CombatGame
class Weapon (val range: Int, val attackDamage: Int) {
    def attack(opponent: Fighter){
        opponent.reduceHP(attackDamage)
    }
}
```

Blade.scala
```scala
package CombatGame
class Blade (override val range: Int = 2, override val
attackDamage: Int = 5)
    extends Weapon(range, attackDamage)
```

BroadSword.scala
```scala
package CombatGame
class BroadSword(override val range: Int = 3, override val
attackDamage: Int = 6)
    extends Blade(range)
```

Dagger.scala

```scala
package CombatGame
class Dagger(override val range: Int = 1) extends Blade(range)
```

Fighter.scala

```scala
package CombatGame
class Fighter (var weapon: Weapon, var hp: Int = 20) {
    def reduceHP(damage: Int) {
        this.hp -= damage
    }

    def attack(opponent: Fighter){
        weapon.attack(opponent)
    }
}
```

run.scala

```scala
package CombatGame
object run extends App {
    val Thief = new Fighter(new Dagger())
    val Knight = new Fighter(new BroadSword())

    Thief.attack(Knight)
    Knight.attack(Thief)
    println(Thief.hp, Knight.hp)
}
```

There's a lot going on in this code, most of which is simply defining the inheritance model between the different weapons. Luckily they follow the branch on the right side of the inheritance tree demonstrated in Figure 10-1 so you can refer back to that if you get lost. The three main things to notice in this code (besides the inheritance model and the overridden defaults between weapons) are

1) The Fighter class has been given a property weapon that has a type of Weapon.

2) The Fighter class has been given an attack method that wraps the attack method from whichever Weapon was provided to the fighter during instantiation.

3) There is a main scala class that extends App as an entry point to our program so we can run it and demonstrate how these scala classes can interact with one another.

Note   In scenarios where you have created a lot of new Scala classes that all need to be compiled, you can compile them using the command scalac *.scala.

This command utilizes the asterisk character which the compiler will treat like a wildcard. The compiler will search for every file with a .scala extension in the current directory and compile them all which prevents you from having to type out each class name individually.

Remember to compile your code, then type scala CombatGame.run (which is a reference to the run.scala class that was defined to extend the App object) to run the main application. The main program will create two new fighters, Thief and Knight, and assign them weapons upon their construction, a Dagger and a BroadSword respectively. Next, we call the attack method for both Fighters and pass their opponent to the method. Finally, we print their hp property (the number of hit points the fighter has left which is defaulted to 20 in the Fighter class constructor) to see how they have been impacted by the attacks. The println method will print out (14,15) to show that the Thief has 14 hit points left and the Knight has 15 hit points left. This is because the BroadSword deals 6 damage, since it overrides the default Blade damage of 5, and the Dagger only deals 5, since it inherits its damage dealt directly from the Blade class.

The key takeaway from this example is that you did not need to provide a specific Weapon type to the Fighter class constructor. By giving it the generic Weapon type, the fighter can take any weapon that extends the Weapon class. Thus the fighter can wield a weapon "in many forms." As you can see, polymorphism, in addition to inheritance, also prevents you from having to repeat code throughout your project leading to massive productivity gains.

Interfaces and Abstract Classes

You might notice from the example in the previous section that the Weapon class and its corresponding sub-categorization classes, Blade and Projectile, can also be instantiated and passed to the Fighter class. From a software design perspective, this doesn't make a lot of sense since those classes were simply designed as a method of categorizing like functionality. Interfaces and abstract classes allow for defining classes like these categorization classes that can be created for architectural design without allowing them to be instantiated.

If we add the abstract keyword in front of our Weapon class and our Blade class and then try to instantiate a new Blade, we will get an error as demonstrated in Listing 10-5. The key value in abstract classes is the ability to create a partial base class like Weapon or Blade that tells your collaborating developers that they can extend the functionality and obtain polymorphism without ever needing to fully define a concrete class.

Listing 10-5. Adding the abstract keyword in front of a class prevents it from being instantiated

Weapon.scala
```scala
package CombatGame
abstract class Weapon (val range: Int, val attackDamage: Int) {
    def attack(opponent: Fighter){
```

```
        opponent.reduceHP(attackDamage)
    }
}
```

Blade.scala
```
package CombatGame
abstract class Blade (override val range: Int = 2, override val
attackDamage: Int = 5)
    extends Weapon(range, attackDamage)
```

run.scala
```
package CombatGame
object run extends App {
    val Thief = new Fighter(new Dagger())
    val Knight = new Fighter(new BroadSword())

    Thief.attack(Knight)
    Knight.attack(Thief)
    println(Thief.hp, Knight.hp)

    new Blade();
}
```

Compilation Output
```
run.scala:10: error: class Blade is abstract; cannot be
instantiated
    new Blade();
    ^
one error found
```

It is worthy to note that a concrete class (a class that is not abstract and has an actual implementation that can be instantiated) can only extend one abstract class. An abstract class can also contain abstract methods. Abstract methods are methods that define the method name arguments that the sub-class will inherit but omit the actual implementation logic that lives in the body or scope of the method. It is up to the inheriting sub-class to fill in the implementation details of the abstract method. Listing 10-6 illustrates this by abstracting the attack method out of the Weapon class, forcing the Blade class to either implement it or delegate it to its sub-classes.

Listing 10-6. Illustration of an abstract method

Weapon.scala

```
package CombatGame
abstract class Weapon (val range: Int, val attackDamage: Int) {
    def attack(opponent: Fighter)
}
```

Blade.scala

```
package CombatGame
abstract class Blade (override val range: Int = 2, override val
attackDamage: Int = 5)
    extends Weapon(range, attackDamage) {
    def attack(opponent: Fighter){
        opponent.reduceHP(attackDamage)
    }
}
```

Notice that the attack method in the Weapon abstract class does not contain a body with implementation details and the Blade class implements it instead. If the Blade class did not implement the attack method and you tried to compile this project, the compiler would fail and provide an error suggesting that the Dagger and BroadSword classes need to be abstract since they don't implement the attack method either. If you did make those two classes abstract, then you would not be able to instantiate them and the run Scala object would fail. Hence, when extending abstract classes it is important to ensure that all abstract methods are implemented by the sub-classes.

It might not be overly intuitive as to why you would use abstract methods. However, it might become clearer when trying to create design specifications for a large project that you are trying to architect but not necessarily implement all by yourself. You could create abstract classes with several abstract methods, therefore defining a contract between collaborating developers that must be fulfilled in order to extend your class. By defining that contract, the compiler guarantees that any class that extends your abstract class, and therefore can be categorized as your generic polymorphic type, has all of the methods that you deem necessary for your software architecture.

Taking that abstraction one step further, if your abstract class exclusively has abstract methods and no constructor, it can be deemed an interface. An interface is simply a contract of properties and methods that can be implemented by a collaborating developer with no implementation details of its own at all. The Weapon abstract class in our example might be a good candidate for this. We want our Blade abstract class and Projectile abstract class to be classified as a Weapon, but the Weapon class itself does not necessarily need to provide any implementation details – it can delegate that to the abstract classes. Listing 10-7 demonstrates how we might refactor the Weapon class to be an interface which uses the Scala keyword trait.

Listing 10-7. Using a Scala trait as an interface

Weapon.scala
```
package CombatGame
trait Weapon {
    val range: Int;
    val attackDamage: Int;
    def attack(opponent: Fighter)
}
```

Blade.scala

```scala
package CombatGame
abstract class Blade (override val range: Int = 2, override val
attackDamage: Int = 5)
extends Weapon
{
    def attack(opponent: Fighter){
        opponent.reduceHP(attackDamage)
    }
}
```

In this example, we've eliminated the primary constructor method from the Weapon class and changed its defining keyword from abstract class to trait. Now we have a contract of methods and properties that any extending sub-class has to fulfill. Since the Weapon class no longer has a constructor, we removed the call to the Weapon superclass constructor in the Blade abstract class. If you run this code, you will see that everything works as it did before, but now there are strict controls around what can be instantiated and what should not be instantiated. It is worthy to note that in the object-oriented paradigm, a class can implement multiple interfaces (unlike abstract classes in which a class can only extend one). In Scala, when implementing more than one trait, the first trait uses the extends keyword and subsequent traits use the with keyword. Listing 10-8 provides a mock demonstration of this syntax.

Listing 10-8. Syntax for a class implementing multiple traits

```scala
class Projectile extends Weapon with ArrowTrait with
QuiverTrait {
    ... implementation details
}
```

Traits in Scala are an example of the interface paradigm that is common in object-oriented programming. Interestingly, they have additional functionality in Scala that is not present in other languages. Traits in Scala can also be extended by static objects or added to an instance of an object at its instantiation. Because of this, traits don't comply with the strict definition of an object-oriented interface. They can provide static blocks of code that exist outside of methods and properties that will be executed whenever the extending object is instantiated. This falls outside of the scope of the object-oriented programming pattern but is a worthy topic for further investigation if you find yourself needing such functionality.

EXERCISE 10-1

Implement the left branch of the Weapon inheritance tree model represented in Figure 10-1. Use an abstract class for the Projectile class that extends the Weapon Trait.

Try implementing class-specific functionality for the Crossbow and Bow classes.

As you can see, object-oriented programming allows for organizational and architectural design patterns to wrangle the complexity of large code bases. It provides a good method for classifying the real world around us using interfaces and abstract classes that can be extended. Its polymorphism enables a rich customizable type system that gives you the capability to add generic types to your class properties and static variables all while providing strategies to minimize code duplication.

However, there are typically two disadvantages associated with object-oriented programming. The first is that it is often known to be overly verbose. As you could tell in the examples in this section, it took a lot of different files to demonstrate the functionality (and these were very basic examples). The second is that it requires a lot of upfront planning and very thoughtful architectural considerations. When deciding whether or not to use object-oriented programming, consider the size and complexity of the project and weigh that against the opportunity cost of upfront planning and extra code that needs to be written. You will find that for smaller projects, the time savings may often favor procedural programming. However, a good compromise between the two paradigms might be the functional programming paradigm, if you feel comfortable with its style.

Functional Programming

Haskell, Clojure, and early forms of JavaScript are great examples of common languages which follow the functional programming paradigm. It could be said that these languages aim to provide a solution to complexity, much like object-oriented languages, but in a concise and less error-prone way. After all, Steve Jobs once said at a visiting lecture at MIT that the easiest code to maintain and debug is the code you don't have to write. So how, then, does functional programming tackle complexity without adding more code to write? The early pioneers of functional programming turned to math to answer that question.

Functional programming is a paradigm whose roots date back to the concepts of lambda calculus in the 1930s. In this paradigm, the entire program is written as a series of inputs and outputs to mathematical functions, and all variables and data structures are immutable by nature. By approaching programming in this way, entire applications can be written in mathematical-like expressions, similar to what you were introduced to in the expressions chapter. If you can recall back to that chapter, there was not yet any notion of state that could be mutated, simply expressions that evaluated to an explicit result.

Expanding upon the thought of immutability, the main objective of functional programming is to minimize (or eliminate entirely) "side effects." A "side effect," in programming, is an action that mutates the existing state of the application, whether that be changing a variable or a piece of a data structure stored in memory. The motivation behind removing side effects is to eliminate errors in your code. If, for example, multiple functions within a code base are accessing a global variable and one of those functions mutates the variable without the other function knowing about the change, it could create some runtime semantic errors. This is especially true for multi-threaded or parallel process applications which could be touching the application state in an unpredictable order. In these types of applications, their processes are essentially racing to the variables in order to obtain their values before the other process has a chance to mutate it. This is known as a "race condition" and is extremely vulnerable to errors in your code. Functional programming combats race conditions through the use of "pure functions."

A function is said to be a "pure function" if, and only if, it takes in inputs and returns an output without mutating application state in the process. Pure functions are guaranteed to always return the same result for the same inputs. This is known as referential transparency. As a counterexample of a pure function, in Listing 10-7 in the previous section, refer to the attack method of the Blade class. That method takes a Fighter as an input and then directly mutates the state of that fighter's hit points by reducing that property's value by the number represented by the weapon's attackDamage property. The act of changing the hit points within the function is the side effect.

When attempting to write a program in the functional programming paradigm, there are a few red flags or "code smells" to look out for. If you answer yes to any of these questions, you are likely mutating state within your application and should consider going back and refactoring your code:

1. Does your program have functions which take no input parameters?

2. Does your program have functions with no return type?

3. Does your program explicitly import mutable data structures?

4. Do you find yourself using a lot of variables defined with the var assignment keyword rather than val assignment keyword?

After reading this list, you might be asking yourself, "If I can't mutate the state of the application in any way, how am I supposed to get anything done?" It does take a bit of getting used to, but you will find after working within a functional programming paradigm that there are a lot of beneficial patterns you can follow. One such pattern is the replication of data. Within many functions, instead of mutating the state of an input parameter, you can simply replicate the input with a slight change and then return the copy of the input. By doing so, you have allowed the original input to remain unchanged in case it needs to be accessed by other parts of the application, but you have allowed the part of the program trying to access the changed state to use a copy of what it was after. Listing 10-9 represents an example of this pattern.

Listing 10-9. Representation of duplicating an object rather than mutating it in the functional programming paradigm

```
package CombatGame
object funcs extends App {
    def attack(opponent: Fighter, damage: Int): Fighter = {
        return new Fighter(opponent.weapon, opponent.hp -
        damage)
    }
}
```

As you can see in this example, rather than directly accessing and changing the hp property of the opponent parameter in this attack function, we instead instantiate a new Fighter object, passing in the existing weapon as a parameter to the new object's constructor as well as the existing hp minus the amount of damage that you would like to apply. This guarantees that the Fighter that was passed into the function does not have any side effects applied to it but still allows the developer who calls this function to have access to a Fighter whose hit points have been reduced by the appropriate damage. That developer may assign the return object to a variable that used to hold the previous fighter object, thus mutating state which violates the pure functional nature of the application, but at least this function is now considered a pure function.

It is worthy to note that sometimes writing a completely functional program in Scala or any other functional language can sometimes be really difficult to accomplish. Oftentimes you will notice that applications written in functional languages tend to be written almost entirely of pure functions at its core with minor side effects sprinkled at the fringes of the program – often to read or write data to and from files and/or databases or to print messages to the user via the user interface. You will also find that there are some use cases that simply require mutable variables or data structures. This tends to be acceptable if they are limited to a very controlled scope within a function that only your function can access and mutate. As long as your function maintains referential transparency, it is okay to occasionally use mutable variables and data structures. However, as you are starting out with functional programming, try to not use them at all so that you can get used to the pattern.

Higher-Order Functions

One of the benefits of writing applications in the functional programming style is that it affords you the opportunity to write extremely rich expressions. By doing so, oftentimes you will see functional programs that lack any procedural style whatsoever. What that means is that you will not see any for loops, very few conditional branches, and few if any try/catch blocks or null handlers. In order to accomplish the same things as procedural programming through expressions, the functional paradigm turns to higher-order functions.

A higher-order function, in its most basic form, is simply a function that either takes another function as its input or returns a function (or both). For example, let's assume we want to create a function that can repeat an action a set number of times. This might be useful if we are performing some sort of test and we want to automate the creation of some dummy data. Your procedural intuition might lead you toward the use of a loop to accomplish this. However, a loop is not an expression. If we want to limit ourselves to a simple expression so that we can conform to the functional style, we might write a repeat function like the one outlined in Listing 10-10.

Listing 10-10. A higher-order function repeat that takes a function to be repeated as one of its inputs

```
def repeat(n: Int, iter: Int = 0)(func: => Unit){
    if(iter < n) {
        func
        repeat(n, iter + 1)(func)
    }
}
val dagger = new Dagger()
repeat(3){ println(dagger.attackDamage) }
```

Terminal Output
```
5
5
5
```

This `repeat` function actually demonstrates two useful principles of functional programming. First, notice that it takes a second set of parameters: the function to be repeated. You use this higher-order function by calling `repeat` with the parameter for n, representing the number of times you want the function to repeat, followed by curly braces and then the function that you want to call. The second thing to notice in this higher-order function is that it calls itself. In the implementation details for this function, you will notice that it has a second parameter (`iter`) in the first set of parentheses that we did not pass an argument for since it has a default value of zero. However, in the body of the function, the code checks to see if the `iter` value is less than the number of times we are meant to repeat the function. If it is less, it calls the function (`func`) and then calls itself, but it increments the `iter` parameter this time. This will cause the function to continue calling itself until the if condition becomes false. This if condition can be seen as the same type of conditional check as when terminating loops. Functions that call themselves are called recursive functions, and they are a common strategy in functional programming to eliminate the need to use loops. However, just like in a while loop, you must be careful to ensure that you have a base case condition that will eventually be satisfied to terminate the recursive calls or you will crash your program by trapping it in an infinite call stack of functions.

Writing higher-order functions can be somewhat mind-bending at times. Fortunately, most functional languages, Scala included, have a lot of really handy higher-order functions built into common data structures by default (mostly iterable data structures). These will be really useful to memorize to make your code more concise and eliminate the possibility for mutable errors. I recommend using them in your code even if you ultimately end up favoring a primarily object-oriented or procedural paradigm. Let's dive into each of them in detail.

Foreach

The foreach function is a function that can be applied to a collection of data. Often in functional programming, foreach is used as a replacement for the traditional loop or recursion when the loop or recursion is simply meant to continue looping until it reaches the end of a collection of data. It is worthy to note that unlike the rest of the higher-order functions that will be covered in this section, the foreach function is the only higher-order function that does not return anything. This function is meant to explicitly perform side effect actions. Listing 10-11 shows an example of this function.

Listing 10-11. An example of the foreach higher-order function

```
val data = List("Bruce Lee", "Chuck Norris", "Chuck Liddell",
"Ronda Rousey")
def printFighter(fighter: String): Unit = {
    println(fighter)
}
data.foreach(printFighter)
data.foreach(println)
data.foreach((fighter) => {
    println(fighter)
})
data.foreach(fighter => println(fighter))
```

In this example, we first define a collection of data: a list of MMA fighters. Next we define a function that can be passed to the higher-order foreach function. Then we call foreach on the data collection using simple dot notation. Each of these four methods of calling the foreach function results in the same action, each fighter's name being printed to the screen. However, each implementation is markedly different in its explicitness.

The first call passes a function that we have previously defined to the foreach function. The foreach will implicitly provide each individual iteration of its data as an argument to its fighter: String parameter. Then that parameter is passed to the println function. Alternatively, we could pass that data implicitly to the println function directly as demonstrated with the second call to foreach. In the third call to foreach, we provide it with what is called an anonymous function. An anonymous function is a function that does not use the def keyword and does not provide the function with a name for later use (hence anonymous). To create an anonymous function, you can provide a list of arguments in parentheses just as if you were creating a normal function (but without the def keyword or the name of the function) and then you let Scala know that you are creating an anonymous function by following the parentheses with an arrow operator, which is the equal sign followed by the greater than sign. After the arrow operator, you provide a function scope just as you would a normal function. The last call to foreach also uses an anonymous function but with shorthand syntax. If you do not need more than one parameter and you do not need more than one line of the function body, you can leave off the parentheses and the curly braces, and Scala will understand implicitly that you are still defining an anonymous function. Each of the remaining higher-order functions will use anonymous functions in any of these same formats.

Map

The map function is another higher-order function that can operate on a collection of data. When applying a map to a collection, it is often described as "mapping over" that collection. It is useful to map over a collection if you wish to change something about some or all of the items in the collection. Listing 10-12 provides an example of mapping over our list of MMA fighters.

Listing 10-12. Demonstration of a map higher-order function

```
val data = List("Bruce Lee", "Chuck Norris", "Chuck Liddell",
"Ronda Rousey")
val formattedData = data.map(fighter => fighter.toUpperCase)
println(formattedData)
```

Terminal Output
```
List(BRUCE LEE, CHUCK NORRIS, CHUCK LIDDELL, RONDA ROUSEY)
```

As you can see, the map function returns a new collection and stores it in the formattedData variable. The map function is passed an anonymous function as its input. That anonymous function takes one parameter, fighter, which represents each individual fighter in the list of fighters. Each fighter is transformed with a toUpperCase function and then added to the formattedData collection. Finally, we print out the formattedData variable to see the new collection transformed to have the fighters' names formatted with all uppercase letters.

FlatMap

The flatMap function operates very similar to a map function. It is used on a collection, takes an anonymous function, and returns a new collection. The difference is that the flatMap function can operate on data structures that are nested. The data variable in Listing 10-13 contains a list of lists. Each nested inner list contains both the fighter's name and their competition weight.

Listing 10-13. Demonstration of a FlatMap higher-order function

```
val data = List(List("Bruce Lee", 141), List("Chuck Norris",
170), List("Chuck Liddell", 205), List("Ronda Rousey", 134))
val flattenedData = data.flatMap(item => item)
println(flattenedData)
```

Terminal Output
List(Bruce Lee, 141, Chuck Norris, 170, Chuck Liddell, 205, Ronda Rousey, 134)

In this example, the flatMap takes in each item of each sub-list and returns it in a single flat list. The anonymous function takes in a single parameter, item, which represents each individual item of each sub-list. That item is then simply returned to the flat list contained in the variable flattenedData. We could have done any other transform we wanted to the individual item from the sub-lists; however, in this particular example, we are just returning it unaltered just to demonstrate that it comes back in a flattened state, which you can see in the final step where the flattenedData variable is printed to the terminal.

Filter

The filter function is similar to the map function; however, the anonymous function that is passed to filter must return a Boolean value. Any individual item that returns a true value during its iteration through the list will end up in the resulting new collection. Items whose iteration returns false will be excluded. Listing 10-14 shows an example of filtering our MMA fighters' list by fighters whose competition weight is greater than 140.

Listing 10-14. A demonstration of a Filter higher-order function

```
val data = List(List("Bruce Lee", 141), List("Chuck Norris",
170), List("Chuck Liddell", 205), List("Ronda Rousey", 134))
val filteredData = data.filter(item => item(1).
asInstanceOf[Int] > 140)
println(filteredData)
```

Terminal Output

```
List(List(Bruce Lee, 141), List(Chuck Norris, 170), List(Chuck
Liddell, 205))
```

As you can see from the final `println` function, the resulting `filteredData` collection contains all of the fighters from the original list except Ronda Rousey, whose competition weight, at 134, is less than the condition 140 that evaluates and returned a `Boolean`. In this example, since we did not define any types for our sub-lists and they contain mixed types, Scala implies that they are lists that contain `Any` types. Because of this, when evaluating the condition, we first pull out the index position from the list, (1) which is the second item in the list, and then cast it to an integer so that it can be correctly compared to the integer 140.

Find

The `find` function is very similar to the `filter` function. However, in the `find` function, the first item that returns a `Boolean` of true stops the iteration. Essentially this function attempts to find the first matching value and returns it in a single item list. If it does not find any matching values, it returns a value of `None`. Listing 10-15 demonstrates this functionality.

Listing 10-15. A demonstration of a Find higher-order function

```
val data = List(List("Bruce Lee", 141), List("Chuck Norris",
170), List("Chuck Liddell", 205), List("Ronda Rousey", 134))
val findData = data.find(item => item(0).toString.
contains("Chuck"))
println(findData)
```

Terminal Output

```
Some(List(Chuck Norris, 170))
```

As you can see in this example, the anonymous function defines a
single parameter item that represents each item in the list. Each individual
item is simply the sub-list at each index position. In order to access the
name of the MMA fighter within the sub-list, we access the first index
position (0) of the item that is currently being iterated on. Then, because it
is an Any type, we cast it to a string in order to have access to the `contains`
method. Then we check to see if the name contains the word "Chuck."
There are two sub-lists in our data list that contain the word "Chuck" in
their first index position. However, since "Chuck Norris" is encountered
first, that item is the only item returned to the final `findData` list, as you
can see from result of the `println` function.

Reduce

The `reduce` function is a bit of a shift from the previous higher-order
functions that you've encountered thus far. This function iterates over a
collection with two parameters passed to its anonymous function instead
of one. On the first iteration, the first parameter represents the first item
in the list and the second parameter represents the second item in the
list. Then, the anonymous function performs an operation using those
two parameters and returns a value. That return value is then fed back
into the anonymous function as the first parameter value and the second
parameter value is now the third item in the list. The same operation
defined in the body of the anonymous function is then performed on these
two parameter values and then returns another value. That return value is
again fed back into the anonymous function as the first parameter value
and the second parameter value is now the fourth item in the list and so
on until there are no more values in the list. You might be able to gather
that this type of higher-order function is really great for creating a running
total of data or other types of aggregations. Ultimately this function tends
to return one value as its final output. Listing 10-16 provides an illustration
of this concept.

Listing 10-16. A demonstration of a Reduce higher-order function

```
val data = List(List("Bruce Lee", 141), List("Chuck Norris",
170), List("Chuck Liddell", 205), List("Ronda Rousey", 134))
val reducedData = data.map(item => item(1).asInstanceOf[Int]).
reduce(_+_)
println(reducedData)
```

Terminal Output

650

   In this example, we are looking to find the total weight of all of the fighters in our data collection. To do that, first we map over the original collection and pull out just their weights by accessing the second index position (1) for each item (sub-list). After that map function is completed, we can chain on the reduce function. We can do this because we know that the expression data.map is evaluated to a new List that can also take higher-order functions. The reduce function in this example simply takes wildcards (_ + _) that suggest that whatever the two parameters that are being passed to it are, simply add them together and return their result. This can be written out in long form like so: (a, b) => a + b. Once we have reduced the weight data and print it out, you can see that it is the sum of all the weights with a value of 650.

Fold

The fold higher-order function works exactly like the reduce function except you can *seed* it with an initial start value. As you can see in Listing 10-17, the fold function call is followed by a set of parentheses that can take whatever start value you want your anonymous function to begin with instead of the first item of the collection.

Listing 10-17. A demonstration of a Fold higher-order function

```
val data = List(List("Bruce Lee", 141), List("Chuck Norris",
170),List("Chuck Liddell", 205), List("Ronda Rousey", 134))
val foldedData = data.map(item => item(1).asInstanceOf[Int]).
fold(100)(_+_)
println(foldedData)
```

Terminal Output

750

This fold function is seeded with the value 100. Thus, 100 is passed as the value to the first parameter in the anonymous function and the second value is populated with the first value from the collection. The value returned by that first operation (100 plus the first weight in the collection, 141, which equates to 241) is then passed back to the anonymous function as the first parameter value and the second parameter value is populated with the second item in the collection. You can see from the final result of the print function that by seeding this fold higher-order function with a value of 100, the result is 100 more than the result of the reduce higher-order function from the last section.

Zip

The zip function is not actually a higher-order function, but it is fun to talk about in conjunction with the higher-order functions as it performs a specific operation on collections that we can chain together along with other functions. The zip function is added to an existing collection and takes another collection as its argument. The collection taken as an argument should have the same length as the collection that zip is being called on. In doing so, zip returns a nested collection of tuples that zip the two collections together. Listing 10-18 shows an example of this by zipping together our MMA fighters together with their weights.

Listing 10-18. A demonstration of a Zip function

```
val namesData = List("Bruce Lee", "Chuck Norris", "Chuck
Liddell", "Ronda Rousey")
val weightData = List(141, 170, 205, 134)
val zippedData = namesData.zip(weightData)
println(zippedData)
```

Terminal Output

```
List((Bruce Lee,141), (Chuck Norris,170), (Chuck Liddell,205),
(Ronda Rousey,134))
```

Putting It All Together

Just as we chained together a map and a reduce function previously, you can chain together as many of these higher-order functions as you need to accomplish many number of things. We can do this because we know that each higher-order function (besides foreach) returns a new evaluated value that can then be operated on just like the examples of expression evaluation that was demonstrated earlier in the book. In this way, many functional programs are written exclusively in this expression syntax with little or no procedural notation at all. Listing 10-19 shows an example of how chaining together several higher-order functions can create extremely rich expressions. You'll notice that, by convention, this functional chaining separates each higher-order function onto its own line with aligned indentation.

Listing 10-19. An example of how functional programming can chain together higher-order functions to create rich expression. This example takes two lists and returns a single string that contains the names and weights of fighters whose names contain the string "Chuck"

```
val namesData = List("Bruce Lee", "Chuck Norris", "Chuck
Liddell", "Ronda Rousey")
val weightData = List(141, 170, 205, 134)
val data = namesData
    .zip(weightData)
    .filter(item => item._1.contains("Chuck"))
    .map(item => List(item._1, item._2))
    .flatMap(item => item)
    .reduce((item1, item2) => s"${item1} ${item2}")
println(data)
```

Terminal Output
```
Chuck Norris 170 Chuck Liddell 205
```

This example takes two lists, names and weights, and zips them together. Next it filters the resulting list by items whose first tuple value contains the string "Chuck." If we simplify the expression up to this point, we know that we should have a list of tuples that is of length two that contains the names and weights of both of the "Chuck" fighters. Next, we map over this new List and convert our tuples to Lists so that we can perform a flat map on them. After the `flatMap`, we should now have a flat collection of Any values that contains names and weights. Finally, we call a reduce function that constructs a single string with a space delimiter between values in our flat list. The resulting variable if this chained expression, data, then contains a single string, which when printed returns "Chuck Norris 170 Chuck Liddell 205" to the terminal.

EXERCISE 10-2

Go back to our Nebula OS model command-line shell and try to refactor any procedural code with functional code. If you open up the Utilities.scala file, the showTextFiles() and list() methods use procedural iteration that could be changed to higher-order functions.

As you might have gathered, it is often the goal of many in the functional programming paradigm to represent all aspects of the program in terms of mathematical formulas or expressions. While this creates safe and concise code, there are cases where it can become confusing and hard to follow. If you find an expression that is too long and hard to understand, try breaking it into smaller pieces and perhaps refactoring into a procedural style for parts of the program.

Summary

In this chapter, you learned about the three major programming paradigms: procedural programming, object-oriented programming, and functional programming. In procedural programming, you learned that the goal is to do one simple thing and to do it really well in an easy-to-follow linear format. In object-oriented programming, you learned how to tackle complexity with upfront planning and simulating the problem you are trying to tackle using objects that can inherit, take many forms, and be represented in an abstract way. In functional programming, you learned how to tackle complex problem sets using a series of chainable expressions with no side effects to eliminate the possibility of semantic errors in your code. This paradigm proved to be less verbose than its counterparts.

While each of these programming paradigms represented their own strengths and weaknesses, it is important that you understand that no single paradigm can be considered a silver bullet. When choosing a paradigm, ensure that you are using the right tool for the job rather than the paradigm you like the most or are most familiar with. Channel your inner Bruce Lee and find the strengths in each paradigm while minimizing their weaknesses. Finally, and probably most importantly, ensure that you are open-minded to other paradigms. Paradigm tolerance tends to be a hard thing to come by among software developers. Many choose a paradigm and never grow or adapt beyond it. The best software engineers are those who can see the advantages of each paradigm and can identify the best time to use each. It is worthy to note, also, that many languages are starting to fuse these paradigms together, so knowing them all will give you a leg up if you begin to learn those languages. Knowing all the paradigms and how to use them in Scala may also help you to convince your colleagues that they should be using Scala for all of their projects since they can accomplish all paradigms using this one powerfully flexible language.

CHAPTER 11

What Is Software Engineering?

It is my hope that what you have learned in this book so far will come of great use to you as you grow technically and pursue a career in software engineering. You've learned about expressions and variable assignments, data types, basic program control flow, functions, classes, and several programming paradigms. These concepts are all crucial in their relevance to the practical application of programming. But what is software engineering and how is it different from programming?

Software engineering is the practice of stringently applying quantitative and disciplinary principles and standards to the process of programming. This becomes exponentially important as the programs that you write increase in scale, complexity, and impact and collaboration becomes mandatory. In such scenarios, it is not enough to simply program or "code," instead you must *engineer*. This is an important distinction between a software engineer and a programmer in terms of career title.

Consider, for example, that you have been charged with the implementation of a system that could solve the problem of moving people between floors in a very large building. In this theoretical scenario, let's pretend that the elevator has not yet been invented, but you decide to take a shot at a similar solution. At first glance, an automated pulley system seems to be the obvious solution. Fulfilling that request seems fairly

J. L. Hodges, *Software Engineering from Scratch*,
https://doi.org/10.1007/978-1-4842-5206-2_11

simple, it requires only a passenger platform, an electric motor, a rope, and a pulley at the top and bottom of the potential floors that you want to move the platform between. So, you create this simple system, and you run it a few times to make sure it works and then open it up for others to use. It works beautifully and provides an amazing amount of efficiency for the building and its few tenants. However, tenants of other buildings start to obtain word of these efficiency gains and move into your building hoping to realize the same gains in their day-to-day operations. Suddenly, your elevator is being used by more and more passengers every day. It's also starting to take on more and more concurrent passengers as the building fills up with tenants and people begin to get impatient. In this theoretical scenario, it is easy to see in hindsight that the rope of the elevator is eventually going to break as it wears down and too many passengers crowd your platform. If such an event were to occur, it is likely that a lot of passengers would be injured.

Applying engineering principles to the design and implementation of this theoretical elevator would account for the potential problems encountered in this scenario. Instead of only seeing the obvious simple solution and diving straight into implementation, an engineer might have considered the cost of both materials and operating expenses, analyzed all the risks, thoroughly tested with different load capacities and construction materials, and designed fail-safe mechanisms (like brakes) in the event of an emergency. Once satisfied with the result, that engineer would have provided direct communication to the building administration about the weight limit and passenger capacity for safe use, posted documentation of those limits in the elevator itself, and ensured that the system was over-engineered to operate above those limits for a reasonable margin of safety in the event that they were breached. Obviously not every problem in software engineering is worth that much planning, testing, and effort. However, many problems intended to be solved by a software application tend to grow over time. The best thing to do when considering how much testing and architecture planning is required for a particular software problem is to consider the potential risks in the solution and measure their likelihood of occurrence vs. their impact. Figure 11-1 illustrates a grid that can plot these risks.

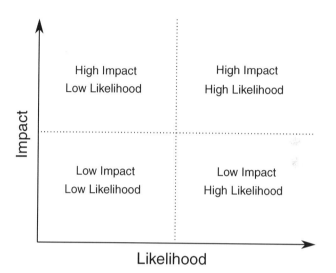

Figure 11-1. *An illustration of plotting risks in software design based on their relative likelihood of occurrence vs. their impact if they do occur. More architecture and testing should be applied to risks that end up in the top right quadrant*

It is fairly obvious to see that projects that fall in the top right quadrant require the strictest engineering practices. Examples of such projects might include creating the software that powers self-driving cars, the software behind robotic surgical equipment, the coordination software for air traffic control at airports, or the software that powers millions of dollars worth of trades on a stock exchange every day. What is less obvious is what the other three quadrants might contain. Some of the risks you are evaluating might have varying levels of importance relative to your perspective. Software that produces optimal driving routes to deliver pizza might have a high likelihood of producing less than optimal routes depending on traffic or weather conditions. However, the impact of these sub-optimal routes is low. No lives are at stake and only a minimal amount of transaction cost per delivery is on the line. But, if you have created a company whose sole business is to sell this routing service to pizza companies, you might not have a business if you continue to produce sub-optimal routes. So, do not take the evaluation of software risks lightly. Consider all possibilities and mitigate any significant risks with the following engineering strategies.

Efficiency and Optimization

The first engineering strategy to minimize risk in your software is to ensure that your programs are optimized for efficient performance. As your programs scale in size, complexity, and usage, how will your program respond? Determining how your program responds to scale is important in understanding its operating cost. Having the ability to measure the performance or the cost of a piece of software is often key in determining whether a business can be profitable or even possible. For example, if your software analyzes customer feedback to determine the sentiment of customer interactions with your product, is it possible to analyze every piece of feedback? How many computers or servers must your software run on in order to analyze each response? If your business grows and you continue to get more responses, will you have to buy more server space to run your software? If you do buy more computers, how much will it cost you each year to pay for the salaries and equipment to maintain these machines?

As you might have gathered from that example, the performance of your software can potentially be a big risk in creating and maintaining a viable software solution. So, how do you measure the performance of a program? Do you measure it in the time it takes to run? That would be a good first impression, but wouldn't the time it takes to run depend on the computer it is running on? In order to standardize performance measurement regardless of computer hardware, software engineers turn to a process of complexity analysis known as Big O notation for measuring algorithmic efficiency. An algorithm is simply a set of repeatable instruction to accomplish a particular task. Big O notations is said to measure the order of magnitude of complexity of a specific algorithm or set of operations. It is expressed in terms of n, which is the length of input data that the algorithm in question uses to accomplish its task. The more operations that occur on the data, the more complex the algorithm. Take the procedure in Listing 11-1 for example. In this simple algorithm, we simply wish to print out each item in a list to the screen.

Listing 11-1. A procedure that prints each item from a list to the terminal

```
val items = List("apples", "oranges", "bananas")
items.foreach(println)
```

In this procedure, we are performing an operation on every item in the list of length n. Thus the Big O notation of this algorithm is expressed as O(n) (which is pronounced "Oh of n," since it is a description of a function O with input n). Since we touch every item in the list, the computer performs the print function n times. This is known as linear complexity. As the list grows, so does the amount of work the program has to perform. If you were to plot such performance on a graph, it would look like Figure 11-2. As you can see, there is a 1 to 1 linear relationship between the amount of operations performed and the amount of data being put into the program.

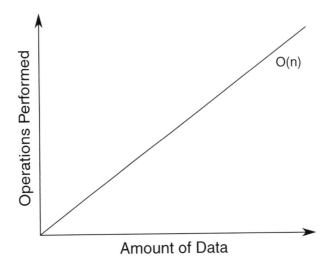

Figure 11-2. *A depiction of linear algorithmic complexity*

Some programs perform many more operations on their input data. If, for example, we transformed each item in our list of data to uppercase before we printed it to the screen, we would be performing two operations per item. This would be described as O(2n). However, in software engineering, we are often more concerned with how quickly the "operations performed" part of the graph grows rather than the minute specifics of each operation. What we actually care about is whether this program can be completed in seconds, minutes, hours, days, years, or even decades. The leaps between these types of measurements are known as orders of magnitude. When measuring algorithmic complexity, the order of magnitude is what is most important to measure. If it's in the range of seconds, I don't really care if it's 20 seconds or 30 seconds. That level of specificity is less useful to me because that can vary depending on the hardware and the type of input data. Thus, we tend to drop any coefficients in measurements like O(2n) and generalize them to O(n) because they are still linear in complexity (just with a slightly different slope). The order of magnitude measurement of an algorithm tells me whether it is worth pursuing for my solution or if I should try something else. Listing 11-2 provides another example of a procedure where we can measure Big O notation to see a different order of magnitude.

Listing 11-2. A procedure with exponential growth in algorithmic complexity

```
val items = List("apples","oranges","bananas","apples")

items.foreach(item => {
      var duplicateCount = -1
      items.foreach(innerItem = > {
           if(item == innerItem) {
                  duplicateCount += 1
           }
      }
      println(s"Duplicates of ${item}: ${duplicateCount}")
}
```

In this example, we loop through each item of the list and then check it against every other item in the list to see if there are any duplicates. If there are, we increment the duplicate count by one. The accumulator, duplicateCount, starts at −1 because we expect to always find the item in question in the list at least once (itself). If it is found again, we can consider it a duplicate. This procedure shows us an example of an algorithm that grows exponentially. As the items in the list grow bigger, we have to check each item against even more items in the list. This is expressed in Big O notation as $O(n^2)$. There are also algorithms that grow at factorial speed and some that grow with a half-life (logarithmic) speed. Finally, there are algorithms that, no matter how much data you throw at it, always just do one thing. This is known as constant complexity and is expressed as O(1). Figure 11-3 adds depictions of different growth rates, or orders of magnitude, to our linear complexity graph along with how they are expressed in Big O notation.

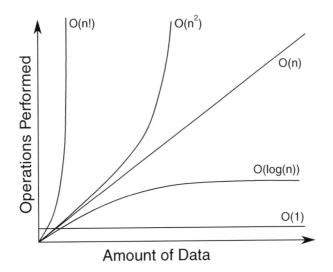

Figure 11-3. *Common orders of magnitude in Big O notation complexity analysis*

Understanding how to measure the algorithmic complexity of your programs is the first step in optimizing them. Of the algorithms depicted in this figure, algorithms with O(1) complexity are the fastest and O(n!) algorithms are the slowest. In the coming chapters, you are going to see examples of data structures and algorithms that you might end up using in many of your programs. These will be demonstrated along with their Big O notation that you should seek to memorize in order to be best equipped to optimize your code and reduce the risk of creating slow or cost-prohibitive programs.

EXERCISE 11-1

For each of the following code snippets, determine the algorithmic complexity using Big O notation given the list of input items from Listing 11-2.

1. `println(items(1))`

2. `val longFruit = items.filter(fruit => fruit == "bananas")`

3. `items.map(fruit => fruit.toUpperCase()).find(fruit => fruit.length == 6)`

Testing

The next engineering strategy to apply to your projects is meticulous testing through automated test scripts. Automated testing can help you determine if there are bugs in your code by ensuring that you not only know the outcome of the "golden path," or the expected normal path of your program, but also the outcome of some of the unexpected edge cases. For example, what happens when you don't provide your program with any data? What happens if you overload it with data? What happens if you give it unrecognizable special characters? In addition to the benefits of this exhaustive edge case exploration, testing can help you identify quickly if making changes to one part of your code breaks any other part of your code. By maintaining thorough test coverage, you can feel confident that when you ship your large-scale project, all of it will work as expected.

There are a couple of common types of tests typically used within the software engineering industry. The first is what is known as a unit test. A unit test is a small test script that tests the outcome of one function (or one small block of code) within your program. A unit test relies on the code being tested to have no external dependencies, like network or database connections or calls to other functions. Unit tests work really well with pure functions since giving it a certain input should always yield the same output. The other type of common test is known as an integration test. Integration tests typically aim to determine how different parts of your program interact with one another. For example, by making a call to one function, how does that impact the state of your entire application? These are typically much more complicated to write and maintain over time and are usually much less performant.

For the purpose of simplicity, we are going to focus on demonstrating only unit tests in this section and we will be using our NebulaOS project as an example. However, it does require some additional tooling that you will find convenient for other parts of your development experience. Unit tests can be written as simply plain functions; however, there are really good testing suites maintained by the Scala community. One such suite is called ScalaTest. In order for you to use ScalaTest as a dependency in your project, you will need to download a dependency management and project build tool called SBT (Simple Build Tool). In addition to enabling you to pull down ScalaTest from a remote repository to use in your project, this tool will allow you to pull down any external, third-party library that you want as long as you know where it is stored and what it is called. You can download or look at the documentation for SBT at `www.scala-sbt.org`. However, if you are using VS Code, you can simply install the SBT plugin. Figure 11-4 provides a screenshot of where to find the plugin. You will want to download the SBT plugin provided by Lightbend, the official company that backs the Scala language.

Figure 11-4. *A screenshot depicting where to download the Simple Build Tool (SBT) for Scala from the VS Code Extension Marketplace*

From your terminal, type `sbt sbtVersion` to verify that you have SBT installed correctly. If it returns a version number, then it has been successfully added to your computer. If you receive an error, go to the SBT web site and follow the installation instructions for your operating system. You may prefer to download SBT outside of the VS Code Extension Marketplace if you are having trouble. If you are certain that you have installed SBT correctly but you are still getting errors from the command line, you may need to add the `sbt` command to your environment variables (Windows) or PATH (Mac or Linux). Refer to the "Installing Everything You Need" chapter for more instructions on how to accomplish that.

Once you have the SBT plugin installed, you can open up a terminal, ensure that you are in your project directory, and then type `sbt` to initialize the Simple Build Tool's interactive shell (which is not unlike our Nebula OS shell). From this shell, several built-in SBT commands are available. One of which is a simple `compile` command that can replace the `scalac` command when inside the SBT shell (also known as a command runner). The two commands we will be using for our unit testing are the `test` command and the `testQuick` command. The first command looks through all of our project files and finds any unit tests we have written and executes them one time, printing the results of the tests to the screen. The second command does the same thing but in "watch" mode, meaning it executes the test and then listens for any changes to your files. In the event that you save one of your files, it immediately executes all of your tests again and continues in a loop until we tell it to stop.

Tip   Have you gotten tired of compiling all of your changes after each save of your program's files? SBT provides you with a `~compile` command that will run in your terminal while you are coding, listen for any changes when you save your `.scala` files, and auto-compile any changed files for you. You might also consider adding the Scala (sbt) plugin provided by Lightbend as well. It is a language server that provides auto-completion and error highlighting when running the `~compile` command.

In order for SBT to find your test files, you must organize your tests into a very specific folder structure that the command runner is expecting. From the base of your project folder, create the following folder structure: src ➤ test ➤ scala. From within that new scala folder, you can create as many test files as you like. Common convention is to make a test file for each `.scala` file that you create in your project. Most projects have a mirroring folder structure in src ➤ main ➤ scala so that it is easy to map back which test files belong to a corresponding production file. For the sake of convention, let's move our NebulaOS project files into that main ➤ scala folder. Create a new test file in your test ➤ scala folder called utilities.spec.scala. We will create tests in this file that will call the functions we have defined in our main ➤ scala ➤ Utilities.scala file. Programming convention dictates that developers typically add either a `.spec` or a `.test` before the file extension to allow others to easily identify this file as a test file. In our utilities.spec.scala file, add the following lines from Listing 11-3.

Listing 11-3. Initial scaffolding for a test file

utilties.spec.scala

```
import org.scalatest._
package os.nebula {

}
```

build.sbt

```
libraryDependencies += "org.scalatest" %% "scalatest" % "3.0.5"
% "test"
```

The first line in this test script imports all the assets from the ScalaTest module. However, we have not yet declared ScalaTest as a dependency. In the root of your project folder, create a file named build.sbt. In that file, add the line denoted under the build.sbt file from Listing 11-3. This tells SBT to find you the external dependency for ScalaTest and bring it into your project automatically. From your terminal, type in sbt to start up the command runner. Once it is running and awaiting commands, type in compile to compile your project. If your project compiles successfully, you will receive a success response. This tells you that SBT successfully fetched and installed ScalaTest from a remote repository on the Internet for us to use in our project. Now that we can use ScalaTest, let's write some unit tests. Listing 11-4 provides a simple example of a unit test.

Listing 11-4. A simple example of a unit test

```
import org.scalatest._
package os.nebula {

    class UtilitiesSpec extends FunSpec {
        describe("When calling the add command") {
            describe("and passing 2 + 2") {
                it("should equal 4") {
                    assertResult(4){ 2 + 2 }
```

```
                }
            }
        }
    }
}
```

After importing our dependency and declaring our package, we create class that extends ScalaTest's FunSpec, which is simply a style of testing that we now have access to within our test file. ScalaTest provides several different styles to choose from, but this style will be very familiar to those who are used to Ruby's Rspec or JavaScript's Mocha testing suites. It allows us to write our tests in a flowing natural language fashion where we can describe the expected behavior of the program. Each individual unit test in our program is called using the it function which is wrapped in a describe block which organizes our unit tests by a description we provide to it. Within the body of the it function, we define an assertion. In this example, we are asserting that the result we expect should be 4 from the function we are testing, 2 + 2.

After adding this test to our test file, from your sbt command runner, type test to run all the tests in our project. The command runner should return a result with the number of tests that were run, how many passed, and how many failed. In this simple scenario, you should have had 1 test pass because 2 + 2 evaluated to 4 as our assertResult function expected. Let's swap out 2 + 2 for our Utilities.addComand() function to see if we get the same result (provided in Listing 11-5).

Listing 11-5. Testing the Utilities.addCommand function

```
describe("When calling the add command") {
    describe("and passing 2 + 2") {
        it("should equal 4") {
            assertResult(4){ Utilities.addCommand("2 + 2") }
```

```
      }
   }
}
```

Once you've modified your test to use the addCommand from our Utilities file, you can run your test again. This time, use the testQuick command to allow SBT to listen for changes to our test files. You should have received a response from the test runner similar to Listing 11-6 which tells us that our test has failed. The test failed in this case because, even though our function takes a string with addition commands, parses them, and adds them together, the final step in our addCommand function is to print the result to the screen rather than return the result. You can see that the assertion is expecting 4 but got a Unit value instead (which is the result of a function that returns nothing). This is an example of a side effect that makes a function difficult to test. If we refactor our program to return the result of adding the numbers together and pull the print function out of the addCommand function and add it into the pattern matching expression in our nebula.scala file, our test will now pass.

Listing 11-6. An example of the message returned when a test fails

```
[info] UtilitiesSpec:
[info] When calling the add command
[info]   and passing 2 + 2
[info]   - should equal 4 *** FAILED ***
[info]     Expected 4, but got <(), the Unit value> (utilities.
            spec.scala:18)
```

For additional information about writing tests using ScalaTest, including how to create setup and tear down functions that run before and after each test and the different possible assertions that you can call, visit the official documentation at www.scalatest.org.

EXERCISE 11-2

For each function in the `Utilities.scala` file in our Nebula project

1. Ensure that the function is pure and returns a value that can be tested.

2. Refactor the `nebula.scala` file to print the result of the functions from the command pattern matching expression.

3. Write a test for each function and ensure it passes.

Architecture Planning

The next risk you should seek to mitigate in your software engineering endeavors is the risk of uncoordinated or unorganized code among collaborating engineers due to lack of planning. You want to ensure that no matter how many engineers are working on your project, or who they are, what is written in your project is consistent, readable, and reusable throughout your code base. Oftentimes, this requires either a product manager, a software architect, or both to coordinate with a team to ensure that all code written by the team conforms to a set of quality and consistency guidelines. Architects or product managers also might provide a pre-ordained plan for how to tackle the project in question.

In the previous chapter, you saw a basic diagram for how one might describe relationships between classes, abstract classes, and interfaces. A similar, but more formally specified, graphical representation of a project might be formulated by an architect using what is known as Unified Modeling Language (UML). Having a UML diagram in advance of the start of a project allows all engineers to know what code they should be writing and provides a single unified plan of attack for the overall software implementation. By defining your software in terms of UML ahead of time, it makes it easy for engineers to divide the work based on the boxes in the diagram knowing that, when completed, their piece of the puzzle will most definitely fit nicely into the program as a whole as long as every other engineer stuck to the original specification. This allows for an engineer to write and test their code in a stand-alone, modular, and independent way without needing to wait for other engineers to complete their code as a precursor dependency to their task. This removes any bottlenecks in the engineering process and allows for maximum productivity. Figure 11-5 provides an example of a UML diagram for reference, although we will not be covering the formal specification in this book.

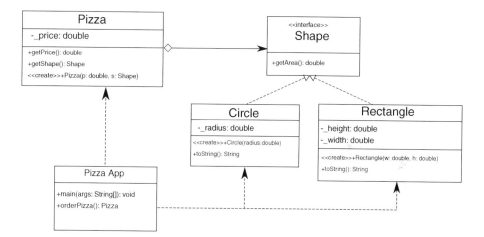

Figure 11-5. *An example of a UML diagram for reference. Notice the difference in lines and arrows. These each have specific meanings in the formal specification*

In addition to coordinating using a UML diagram, architects might also mandate that all engineers stick to a specific style guide. That style guide might include rules such as

1. Always specify a return statement, no implied returns.

2. Always specify types, no implied types.

3. Always use immutable variables and data structures.

4. Curly braces are to open on the same line as the definition of the scope and close on the same level of indentation as the first line with all lines in between indented at least one level further.

These style guides are obviously based on opinion rather than any hard fast rule, but often it's important for teams to agree upon them ahead of time in order to maintain a consistent code base. Code that does not follow the guidelines will still compile and run, so how might a team enforce such rules? With large, complicated systems, it is all but mandatory to have some form of version control system in place to keep track of changes to the software over time. Examples of such version control systems include Git and SVN (you might have heard of GitHub which contains cloud-hosted repositories of code that use the Git version control system). When making changes to code using a version control system, a team can put in place a mandatory peer review before allowing new code to be checked in to an existing project. It is during this peer review process that these style guides can be enforced for consistency. It is also a good opportunity to obtain feedback from peers among the team to ensure that your code is efficient and optimal, thus minimizing performance risk.

Software Deployment

The final risk to mitigate is the introduction of bugs into existing production software. For large enterprise software solutions that are deployed to a server farm for deployment, mitigating this risk involves using a specific deployment pattern to update production software over time without impacting existing users of that software. This pattern starts with testing code in a local or development environment, followed by a staging or quality assurance environment, and finalized by pushing to a production environment.

Local development environments are typically backed by databases with dummy data and partial code and services to minimize how much code a local computer might need to run (relative to the production server which might run a very large amount of code that could not be run completely on a local machine). The software engineer typically makes changes to this development environment, saves his or her changes in the version control system, and then passes the changes off to a peer for review. Once approved, the changes can then be sent to the staging environment for integration testing.

The staging environment is typically a mirror of the production environment. It has a separate database that is kept in sync with the production database to ensure a seamless experience when testing incoming changes from a development environment. The goal of the staging environment is to test the impact of changes from the development environment before they hit production. The staging environment, therefore, is used as a stop gap. If the development changes cause a negative effect on the staging environment, they can be rolled back to the previous version without ever affecting the production environment or the users that are using the production software. Typically, this step involves a quality assurance (QA) engineer who writes acceptance tests that must be satisfied before the staging environment can be promoted to production. These tests can be automated using software such as Selenium, but oftentimes they require manual testing as well. Once the QA engineer signs off, the software is then deployed to production.

For less critical software, deployment can follow a continuous integration process. Continuous integration (CI) is a deployment strategy wherein once a set of changes are checked in via the version control system, an automated process of tests kicks off to ensure the changes will not break any of the existing software. If all of the tests that have been set up in the CI test suite pass, the continuous integration system automatically deploys the new software to production. This type of deployment process is typically used for agile software development wherein teams are iterating rapidly on the software and need to deploy to production often.

Deciding which deployment process to choose typically involves understanding the risks and impacts to your software and business. Analyzing whether or not your software can be easily rolled back or backed up is an important consideration. Another is determining the amount of availability or uptime your software is required to have and whether there would be a significant impact to your business if your software were down for a particular amount of time due to maintenance or repairs during your deployment cycle. Understanding these principles along with fault tolerance, scalability, and distributed computing are all important in the modern era of software engineering.

EXERCISE 11-3

Look into additional information about the topics in this chapter:

1. Look up the formal specification of UML. Refactor the diagram of Weapon classes in the previous chapter using formal UML.

2. Look up different version control systems. Familiarize yourself with their commands and common usages.

3. Look up the various continuous integration systems and try to gain an understanding of how they are implemented. Examples of these systems are Jenkins, Circle CI, and Travis CI.

Summary

In this chapter, you learned that the difference between programming and software engineering is the amount of stringent process that surrounds engineering in order to ensure resilient and quality programs. Those processes included several key concepts. First, you were introduced to Big O notation as a means for measuring complexity. Next, you were given an introduction to unit testing as a strategy for ensuring edge cases and new code changes do not break your existing code. After that, you were introduced to architecture planning strategies that include UML diagramming, version control, style guides, and peer reviews. Finally, you were given an overview of the software deployment life cycle that is used to maintain and update production programs over time. In the next chapter, we will expound upon the engineering skills you learned in this chapter to dive deep into common data structures found in theoretical computer science to help optimize your programs.

CHAPTER 12

Data Structures

In the previous chapter, you learned that one of the essential strategies behind mitigating operational cost risk in your software is to optimize your code for performance efficiency. Imagine, for example, that you want to create a new social media company. Successful social media companies have potentially billions of users with complicated connections between the users. If you want people to use your service, you will need to ensure consistent uptime and that information on the network is retrieved in a responsive manner. This is an extremely difficult engineering challenge.

In order to ensure optimal experience in your software, you first need to determine how to measure the performance of a program using Big O notation. As you might recall, Big O notation is a measure of the order of magnitude of operations performed on an input data set of length n. In the case of a social media company, the input data will likely be either the number of connections in a particular user's network or the amount of activity in their feed. But the important thing to note is that performance is always measured based on an input data set, or group of data.

You were previously introduced to a variety of basic data types, of which included groups of data like Lists and Maps. Data structures are also groups of data that we can introduce to our programs in varying implementations in order to maximize the performance of our programs. Each of the following data structures, or groups of data, has very similar operations that can be performed on each of them. We will analyze each operation using Big O notation in order to compare and contrast their

© Jason Lee Hodges 2019
J. L. Hodges, *Software Engineering from Scratch*,
https://doi.org/10.1007/978-1-4842-5206-2_12

varying performance. Once you have a grasp on what each data structure can do, you can start to apply them to your software projects to optimize your program's algorithmic efficiency. Again, picking the right data structures could be the difference in determining whether your software is profitable or even possible.

Arrays

You were briefly introduced to the notion of an array in a previous chapter. Some languages consider lists and arrays to be synonymous, or at least, they abstract the implementation of this type of grouped data away from the user so they are not aware of the difference. But an array is a very particular arrangement of grouped data.

The traditional array is a group of data of a fixed size that must be determined upon its instantiation. It takes that predetermined size at instantiation and goes to the computer's memory and reserves consecutive memory locations. Upon construction, it places null values in those locations. Listing 12-1 demonstrates the instantiation of an array in Scala.

Listing 12-1. Instantiating an array in Scala

```
scala> val users: Array[String] = new Array(10)
users: Array[String] = Array(null, null, null, null, null,
null, null, null, null, null)

scala> users(0) = "me"

scala> users
res0: Array[String] = Array(me, null, null, null, null, null,
null, null, null, null)
```

It is important to identify the type of the array that you wish to instantiate; otherwise, Scala will imply that you want the array to be a group of data of type Nothing. This then means you cannot fill it with any data except nulls, which wouldn't be very useful. In this example, we told Scala that we want this array to contain 10 positions and that those positions would be filled with String type data.

Once you have initialized the array, you can fill it with data using the index accessor. In this example, we added a user, represented by the string "me", to the group's first position, index 0. Because a reference to the array was stored in the variable users, the computer was able to immediately find where this array was stored in memory. From there, the computer can add a number of memory location positions to the request to find the position you want to store the data in. In this example, we are asking the computer to store the value "me" in the starting memory position of the users array plus 0 positions. If we wanted to store a user at the end of the array, we would ask the computer to find the array's starting memory location plus 9 positions, or users(9). Because accessing memory in this way is just a simple arithmetic operation, finding or assigning data in an array is immediate. The computer doesn't have to look all over its memory to find where the data is stored; it has an instant reference point. Because the operation is immediate, no matter how big you decided the array should be, the assignment operation of an index position of an array is of constant algorithmic complexity, or O(1).

If you recall, O(1) complexity is the fastest we can hope to achieve in our software. So, if this is the fastest group of data, why don't we use it for everything? Well, what if you don't know how big your group of data is going to be? How could you possibly hope to guess? You might just try to instantiate an array so large that it would never be filled, but that would be a terrible waste memory. Not to mention, determining the length of data in your array would not be efficient. For example, determining the length of data in a full array is O(1) time since that information is decided upon instantiation. However, if you have an array of length 10,000 and it only has 100 actual items and the rest are null, you would have to traverse the entire array to determine the real length of the array. That would mean you would have to do 1 operation for each index position, which is considered O(n) time complexity.

So, it should be easy to see that the disadvantage of an array is that in order to realize its full benefits, you must know the size of data ahead of time. If your data grows too big for the array, you can always instantiate a new array with more positions and move all your items into the new array. However, that would require one assignment operation for each data point, which is O(n) time. So, in situations where you don't know the size of your group of data, or it needs to grow and shrink fairly dynamically, you might consider using a linked list.

Linked Lists

A linked list is a group of data that is not stored in contiguous memory. Conversely, each item in a linked list is stored separately as individual items with a reference pointer to the other items in the list. In a linked list, each item in the list is considered a node. The first node in a linked list is known as the head and the last node, or the node that points to no additional nodes, is known as the tail. The tail contains a reference pointer to null until a new item is added to the end of the list, at which point the previous tail now points to this new node and the new tail node now points to null. Figure 12-1 contains a visual representation of a linked list of nodes.

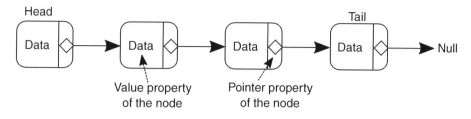

Figure 12-1. *Visual representation of a linked list of nodes*

Because each node in the list simply refers to another node, this data structure is free to grow and shrink as much as it wants without having to instantiate another data structure. It's also extremely efficient to insert nodes and delete nodes if you already have a reference to them in your program because all that is required is to change its reference pointer. For an insertion operation, if you have access to the two nodes between which you want to insert a new node, you simply follow these two steps:

1. Assign the reference pointer of the first node to the new node.

2. Assign the reference pointer of the new node to the second node.

In a full array, an insertion of this nature would require you to instantiate a new array, traverse the existing array to assign all its values to the new array, pause where the insertion should occur to insert the new value, and then continue on assigning its remaining values. Deletion on an array is the same procedure but simply in reverse. Insertion and deletion on an array, therefore, are of O(n) complexity. In a linked list that is free to grow and shrink, both insertion and deletion are simple operations of reassigning pointers. Therefore, insertion and deletion on linked lists are considered O(1) complexity operations. This is the major advantage of linked lists over arrays and is especially important when your data structures are required to maintain a certain order because adding new items to a list that needs to be sorted requires, by its nature, to insert new items in a specified order rather than at the end of the group of data.

The disadvantage of linked lists is that accessing an item in the list is O(n) complexity. Consider a linked list with ten nodes. If you want to access and use the seventh node in the list, you must first access the head and follow its reference pointer to the second node in the list. From the second node, you follow its reference pointer to the third node and so on until you reach the seventh node. In the best case scenario, the item you want to access is the head of the list and it only requires one operation. In the worst case scenario, the item you want to access is at the very end of the list and requires you to traverse the entire n length list, hence the O(n) complexity. We always measure the complexity of data structures based on the worst case scenario since we cannot rely on the best case when assessing risk in our software.

If you wanted to implement your own linked list in Scala, it would only require defining two classes, a LinkedList class and a Node class that the linked list could reference. An example of this implementation is demonstrated in Listing 12-2.

Listing 12-2. An implementation of a Linked List

LinkedList.scala
```scala
package data.structures

case class LinkedList[T](private val data: T, var head:
Node[T] = null) {
    head = new Node(data)

    def add(data: T) {
        val newNode = Node(data)
        if(this.head == null){
            this.head = newNode
        }
```

```
        else {
            var current = this.head
            while(current.next != null){
                current = current.next
            }
            current.next = newNode
        }
    }
}
```

Node.scala

```
package data.structures

case class Node[T](data: T, var next: Node[T] = null)
```

As you can see in this example, all that is required of the individual node in a linked list is to keep track of its own data value and the reference to the next node. This makes reassignment to its surrounding nodes a fairly trivial operation. You'll notice that we've created a method for adding data to the end of the linked list which requires traversal of the list to find the tail. This is an O(n) operation since it is seeking the last node. In an array, finding the last node would be an O(1) operation. Deciding whether to use a linked list or an array depends on what type of operations will be performed most frequently on the group of input data.

You might also notice some new syntax in this example. In both the LinkedList class and the Node class, there is a reference to a generic type [T]. A generic is a notation that allows you to let the downstream developer decide what type of data the linked list will use. If I were to instantiate this new linked list, I would assign it to a variable of type LinkedList[String] in order to tell the linked list that it expects all of its Nodes to contain String types in their data property.

It is worthy to note that you do not need to write your own linked list implementation for each project. Scala has built-in linked lists that you can use that are optimized for performance. The List data type that you were introduced to earlier in this book is an implementation of an immutable linked list. You can also use the mutable.LinkedList data structure from the scala.collection standard library if you need a mutable linked list.

EXERCISE 12-1

Consider the following scenarios. For each scenario, determine whether to use an array or a linked list data structure to optimize the performance of your program:

1. You are creating a program that keeps track of users in alphabetical order. More users are added to the group every hour.

2. You need to design a program that can list every tenth person from a list for statistical analysis on a regular basis.

Queues and Stacks

Queues and stacks are both specialized implementations of a linked list. The big difference that both of these share is that neither data structure allows for insertion. However, adding and removing items from a queue or a stack are both O(1) operations. Given this, these data structures might be considered fairly efficient, albeit limited.

You can think of a queue like a line for a ride at an amusement park. The first person in the line becomes the head of this bespoke linked list. As more people become interested in the ride, they begin to line up behind the head – first come, first serve. This is known as first in, first out or FIFO. No one is allowed to cut in the line to make their wait shorter; that would be considered rude. Hence, you cannot insert items into the middle of a queue. When someone reaches the front of the line and it is their turn to board the ride, they can then leave the queue which is known as dequeuing or being "popped" off the queue. An item can only be removed from the queue if it is in the head position. Thus, it could be said that, besides the other characteristics inherited from a linked list, there are three main attributes of a queue:

1. Items can only be added to the queue at the tail.

2. Items cannot be inserted into the queue.

3. Items can only be removed from the queue at the head.

Queues can be used for a variety of situations, most notably in algorithms regarding traversal of different data structures and in handling challenges associated with concurrency programming. In these scenarios, they are normally used as a temporary staging lists to handle items for short periods of time. Listing 12-3 provides an example of using a queue from the Scala mutable collections library.

Listing 12-3. Adding and removing items from a queue

```scala
scala> import scala.collection.mutable.Queue
import scala.collection.mutable.Queue

scala> val q = new Queue[String]
q: scala.collection.mutable.Queue[String] = Queue()

scala> q.enqueue("Lisa", "Dale", "Jared")

scala> q.length
res1: Int = 3

scala> val firstPerson = q.dequeue()
firstPerson: String = Lisa

scala> q.length
res2: Int = 2
```

As you can see from this example, to add items to a mutable queue in Scala, you use the enqueue method, and to remove items from the queue, you use the dequeue method. The dequeue method not only removes the item from the queue, but it also returns that item so that you can perform operations with it. You'll notice that we have stored the first item to be removed from this queue in the firstPerson variable. Just like a linked list, you can check the length at any point. Before the dequeuing operation occurs, the length is three and after it is two.

A stack data structure is much like a queue except it follows a last in, first out (LIFO) methodology. You can think of a stack structure like a stack of pancakes. As you add items to the stack, they always go on top. Likewise, items removed from the stack will always be removed from the top as well. The first item added to the stack, which is at the very bottom of the stack, will be the last item to be removed from the stack. Just like queues, stacks have three main characteristics:

1. Items can only be added to the stack at the head.

2. Items cannot be inserted into the stack.

3. Items can only be removed from the stack at the head.

Examples of usages for stacks include parsing tags in code like html or xml to ensure that each opening tag has a closing tag and that they are properly nested, adding instructions for execution to a computer processor, or keeping track of the history of visited web pages in the back button of a web browser. An example of using a stack from the Scala mutable collections library is demonstrated in Listing 12-4.

Listing 12-4. Adding and removing items from a stack

```
scala> import scala.collection.mutable.Stack
import scala.collection.mutable.Stack

scala> val history = new Stack[String]
history: scala.collection.mutable.Stack[String] = Stack()

scala> history.push("Google","Github","System76")
res4: history.type = Stack(System76, Github, Google)

scala> history.length
res5: Int = 3

scala> val lastViewed = history.pop()
lastViewed: String = System76

scala> history.length
res6: Int = 2
```

Just like the queue, you can add and remove items to and from the stack. When you add an item, you use the push method, and when you remove items, you use the pop method. Items that are popped off the stack are returned from the pop method so that you can use them in your program. In this case we have stored that item in the lastViewed variable for later reference. As you can see, the length of the stack before the pop operation was 3, and after the operation, it is now of length 2.

As you can see, arrays, linked lists, queues, and stacks all have their advantages and disadvantages when it comes to inserting, deleting, and accessing known items in the group of data. But what if you have no idea what values a group of data contains and you want to search for an arbitrary value? All of these data structures perform "search" operations in $O(n)$ time. Might we be able to improve upon that? If so, at what cost? Hash tables and trees may provide an answer to these questions.

Hash Table

A hash table is a data structure that uses a hashing function to determine the location of each item in the group of data. The hash function can have various implementations, ranging from extremely simple to increasingly complex. However, just like any function, a hashing function takes an input (the item to be added, removed, or looked up in the group of data) and returns a single output (the location of the item in the group).

By way of example, let's assume that we are creating a program that will need to store a list of friends in a group of data. We might start with a basic array with a predetermined length in which to store these friends. In our program, the need for a user to enter a search term to see if they can find a friend in the list is a basic requirement. Because this operation might be performed frequently, we want it to return a result in the most optimized time frame possible. In a basic array, the only way to know if the search term is contained in the list when searching is by iterating through each position in the array and checking if the search term matches the item in that position. This would be an O(n) operation as demonstrated in Listing 12-5.

Listing 12-5. An O(n) search operation on an array

```scala
val friends = Array("Jonathan", "Eric", "Jacob", "Kim", "Jeremy")

def search(input: String): Any = {
    friends.foreach(friend => {
        if(friend == input) {
            return friend
        }
    })
}

val result = search("Jeremy")
println(result)
```

In this example, the search term was contained in the very last position of the array, so the search function had to traverse the entire array to find it. This is less than ideal in an application that might need to scale to billions of searches. In order to optimize this search experience, we can add a hash function to our array, which allows us to determine whether any item exists in an array in O(1) time. The hash function demonstrated in Listing 12-6 is an extremely rudimentary modulo division implementation, which works for this simple example. However, production hash functions are typically much more complex.

Listing 12-6. Modulo division hashing function

```
def hash(item: String, group: Array[String]): Int = {
    return item.length % group.length
}

val hashIndex = hash("Jeremy", friends)
println(hashIndex)
```

Terminal Output
```
1
```

In this example, our hashing function takes the length of the input string, "Jeremy," and performs modulo division on it with the length of the array as the additional operand in the equation. The length of string "Jeremy," which is 6, divided by the length of the array, which is 5, is 1 with a remainder of 1. That remainder of 1 is returned by the hashing function and can be used as its index position. If we perform this hashing function on each item in the array before adding them to the array, we can ensure that simply by knowing what the item in the array is, we can determine its exact index location in O(1) time. Figure 12-2 illustrates this fact for each item in the group.

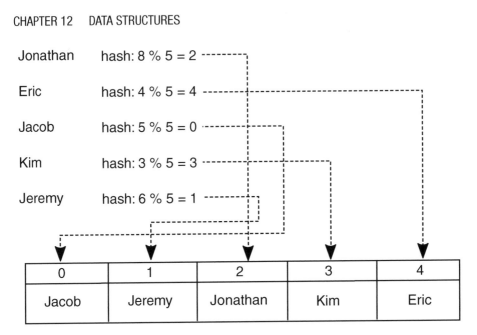

Figure 12-2. *Applying the modulo division hashing function to each item in a group of data with length 5 and then storing the item in the corresponding index position returned by the function*

By performing the hashing function on each item prior to adding it to the array, we will then have an optimized array for searching. Now, when a user types in a search term, we can perform the hashing function on the search term itself which will tell us which index position to look in to find the string in question. By avoiding the need to traverse the entire array, we have now optimized our search time to be O(1). Listing 12-7 provides a complete example of hashing items before insertion and upon searching.

Listing 12-7. Hashing items before insertion and upon searching for items

```
val friends: Array[String] = new Array(5)

def add(input:String, group: Array[String]) {
    group(hash(input, group)) = input
}
```

```
add("Jonathan", friends)
add("Eric", friends)
add("Jacob", friends)
add("Kim", friends)
add("Jeremy", friends)

def contains(input: String, group: Array[String]): Boolean = {
    if(group(hash(input, group)) == input){
        return true
    }

    return false
}

println(contains("Jeremy", friends))
println(contains("Bob", friends))
```

Terminal Output
```
true
false
```

As you can see, by inserting each friend into the array according to the result of their hash function, we can guarantee an O(1) operation when searching to see if the array "contains" a friend, as demonstrated by the contains function. In the second call to the contains function in this example, we perform the hash function on the input string "Bob" which evaluates to 3. We immediately check in the array at index 3 to see if Bob is there. Since that index position contains the value "Kim," we can automatically determine that "Bob" is not in the list of friends without needing to search the rest of the array.

You might notice that this methodology will not work if we are trying to add two friends whose names contain the same length of characters. If we wanted to add "Bob" to our list of friends, his hash code would be the index 3, which is already occupied by "Kim." In this situation we encounter what is called a hash collision. To deal with a hash collision, we can insert a list into the index position where the collision has occurred and store any name that has the same length of characters in that new inner list. So, index 3 would contain an inner list like so: List("Kim", "Bob"). Then when performing the contains function, we can iterate through each item in the list in that index position to see if the search term exists in the inner list. This is slightly less than O(1) time complexity since there is a bit of traversal going on within the inner list. However, it is more performant than traversing the entire array. More complicated hashing functions minimize the probability of hash code collisions.

It is important to note that, in order to ensure the uniqueness of hash code values, data structures that use hashes to store values must contain only unique values. You cannot store any duplicate data in hash tables. Also, given how the hash function determines where the data should be stored, it might be obvious to you that data stored via hashing cannot do so in any type of sorted order. If you attempt to sort a hashing table, you will forfeit the benefits of its O(1) search times.

In the Scala mutable collections library, you can see that the implementation of the HashTable is written as a Trait. Therefore, you cannot use a hash table directly in Scala. You can, however, decorate your own data structure with the HashTable trait if you desire. That being said, the HashTable is used in various implementations of both Maps and Sets, both of which have native Scala collections, which we will cover later in this chapter.

Trees

If you wish to have increased performance when searching for an item in a group of data but you must also mandate that the list maintain some kind of sorted order, a Binary Search Tree data structure might be what you are looking for. The binary search tree will not provide you the same O(1) time complexity achieved when searching for items in a hash table; however, it does allow for better than O(n) search time. There are many types of trees that can be used in software engineering, but the binary search tree is fairly common for searching items in sorted order.

Just as you would expect from the title, a binary tree is a tree in which every branch splits into two potential paths, left and right (hence binary). Like a linked list, the tree is composed of a set of nodes that reference each other. Unlike a linked list, the tree does not have a head but rather what is referred to as the root node. Every node, including the root node, has a property leftChild and rightChild in addition to a value property that contains the value of the item contained in that node. The left and right child properties are assigned to either other nodes or a null value. If both the leftChild and rightChild of a node are null, it is considered a leaf node. If either property points to another node, it is considered a branch node. Figure 12-3 provides an illustration of this data structure.

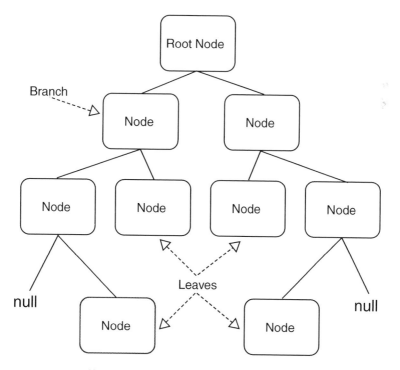

Figure 12-3. *An illustration of a Binary Search Tree data structure*

In order to allow for increased search performance, values inserted into the tree should do so in sorted order. At no point can a binary search tree ever be unsorted. When adding an item to the tree, if there are no items in the tree, then a root node is created and the value of the item is added to this root node. When the next item is added to the tree, if its value is less than the value of the root node, it is added as a node that the root's leftChild property points to. If its value is greater than the value of the root node, it is added as a node that the root's rightChild property points to. If leftChild or rightChild already have a node assigned to them, then the new item will be compared to the value of that node. The new item will continue to traverse the tree of nodes, comparing to the left and to the right, until it finds a null reference point to assign itself to. If the value of the node being inserted ends up being equal to the value of a node that already exists on the tree, then the new node will be ignored. Just like hash tables, the values in a tree must be unique in order to obtain the performance benefits that a tree can provide.

Note   There are edge cases in tree data structures where items being added to the list will already be in a sorted order. In this case, a straight-line tree will occur where either every leftChild or every rightChild is null which essentially creates a linked list, nullifying the benefits of the binary nature of the tree. In this case, many tree structures have built-in balancing algorithms that re-organize themselves to maintain performance. For further study, investigate red-black trees or weight balanced binary trees.

By assigning items to a binary search tree in this way, we can guarantee to find items in the group in less than O(n) time. Take Figure 12-4 for example, which contains a binary search tree of integer values. If we needed to know whether or not the number 5 existed in this tree, we would start by examining the root node. If the root node had a value equal to 5, we would return true and the search function would be done. If it does not equal 5, we check to see if 5 is larger or smaller than the value of the root node. Because it is smaller, we move to the left branch of the root node for further investigation. By doing this, we effectively eliminate half of the data structure that we would have otherwise needed to traverse in order to find the value we are looking for. After examining the next node, which contains a value of 3, we determine that 5 is larger than 3, and therefore we move to its right child node for further investigation, eliminated another half of the remaining values left to search. Each time we traverse through a level of the tree, we eliminate up to half of the potential values that we would have otherwise had to search in other data structures. This half-life type efficiency is what is known as logarithmic efficiency, or O(log(n)) time. Insertion, deletion, and searching in binary search trees are all performed in O(log(n)) time, which is not as good as O(1) time, but still exceptionally better than O(n) time.

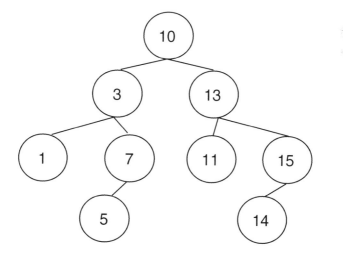

Figure 12-4. *Example of a Binary Search Tree with node values*

Just like hash tables, a tree is typically not used alone in Scala. In other words, like the hash table, a tree is an abstract data structure. Instead of using a tree on its own, its organizing principles are generally extended by either sets or maps. If you desire, you can also create your own data structures that extend the capabilities of a tree as well.

Sets

A set, in both mathematics and computer science, is a collection of items that are inherently unique or distinct, meaning that there are no duplicates. Sound familiar? One of the main side effects from the performance gains of both hash tables and trees is that the items contained within them must be unique. Thus, the abstraction of hash tables and trees can be applied to the Set data type.

In the Scala mutable collections library, the HashSet implements the characteristics of a hash table on a collection of unique items. Items can be added to the set, which are passed through the hashing function to assign them to their index position in the set. In the same vein, a HashSet has a contains method as one of its members. This method passes the item being searched for through the hashing function to look for corresponding matches in the set in O(1) time. The job of implementing a hashing function, deciding the size of the underlying hash table, and how to keep it efficiently balanced to minimize hash collisions is left up to Scala to implement for you. By using the built-in HashSet collection, you can be assured that these methods are implemented as efficiently as possible. An example of using the HashSet data structure in Scala is shown in Listing 12-8.

Listing 12-8. An example of using a HashSet from the Scala mutable collections library

```scala
import scala.collection.mutable.HashSet

val friends: HashSet[String] = new HashSet()

friends.add("Jonathan")
friends.add("Eric")
friends.add("Jacob")
friends.add("Kim")
friends.add("Jeremy")
friends.add("Bob")
friends.add("Eric")

println(friends)
println(friends.contains("Jeremy"))
println(friends.contains("Bob"))
```

Terminal Output
```
Set(Jeremy, Kim, Jacob, Bob, Jonathan, Eric)
true
true
```

Notice in this example that we've added two names to the set that have the same length, "Kim" and "Bob." The hashing function that the native HashSet implementation of Scala uses handles the hashing collision that we would have run into if we were using our own modulo division implementation of the hashing function. We also attempt to add in "Eric" to the set twice, which is ignored by the set as you can see when the final set is printed to the terminal. You might also notice that the order of the items the set ultimately prints is not the same order in which they were added. This is confirmation that they are being positioned according to the hashing function rather than according to the order in which they were inserted. Remember, data structures that implement hashes while gaining the O(1) access and searching performance cannot contain any type of sorted order.

If you wish to have a unique set of items that can maintain a sorted order, you can turn to the native TreeSet data structure from the Scala mutable collections library. Just like the HashSet, the TreeSet implements the features of the tree abstract data type for a set of values. By using the native Scala TreeSet, you can be assured that the ordering and balancing of the tree is implemented as efficiently as possible. An example of using the native TreeSet in Scala is provided in Listing 12-9.

Listing 12-9. An example of using a TreeSet from the Scala mutable collections library

```
import scala.collection.mutable.TreeSet

val numbers: TreeSet[Int] = new TreeSet()

numbers.add(1)
numbers.add(3)
numbers.add(13)
numbers.add(7)
numbers.add(5)
numbers.add(10)
numbers.add(14)
numbers.add(15)
numbers.add(11)
numbers.add(10)

println(numbers)
println(numbers.contains(5))
```

Terminal Output
```
TreeSet(1, 3, 5, 7, 10, 11, 13, 14, 15)
true
```

In this example, we add a collection of numbers to a set in random order. We also attempt to add the number 10 twice, which per the properties of a set is ignored. When printing out the resulting TreeSet, you can see that the items are stored in sorted order. Also, when printing whether or not the set of numbers contains the number 5, we receive a true value that was accessed in O(log(n)) time.

Maps

You've already been introduced to maps as basic data structures. Maps are collections of key/value pairs. In situations where you need key/value pairs but you want to obtain the performance gains of an abstract data structure, you can turn to the Scala mutable collections library for assistance. If you need maximum O(1) performance and order is not important, you can use the HashMap. If order is mandatory, then you can settle for the O(log(n)) performance of a TreeMap. Listing 12-10 provides an example of each.

Listing 12-10. Demonstration of a HashMap and a TreeMap from the Scala mutable collections library

```
import scala.collection.mutable.HashMap

val friends: HashMap[String, Int] = new HashMap()

friends.put("Jonathan", 32)
friends.put("Eric", 27)
friends.put("Jacob", 21)
friends.put("Kim", 42)
friends.put("Jeremy", 18)

println(friends)
println(friends.contains("Jeremy"))
```

```
import scala.collection.mutable.TreeMap

val ages: TreeMap[Int, String] = new TreeMap()

ages.put(32, "Jonathan")
ages.put(27, "Eric")
ages.put(21, "Jacob")
ages.put(42, "Kim")
ages.put(18, "Jeremy")

println(ages)
println(ages.contains(18))
```

Terminal Output
```
Map(Jacob -> 21, Kim -> 42, Eric -> 27, Jeremy -> 18,
Jonathan -> 32)
true
TreeMap(18 -> Jeremy, 21 -> Jacob, 27 -> Eric, 32 -> Jonathan,
42 -> Kim)
true
```

This example provides a collection of key/value pairs of the names and ages of the friends in our program. Notice in the terminal output that the items stored in the HashMap appear to be in no particular order. The contains method of the HashMap searches for any matching keys in O(1) time. Accessing an item by key in the HashMap will also occur in O(1) time since the key itself is stored based on the hashing function.

In the TreeMap output, you can see that the keys are stored in sorted order. Determining whether the age of a friend exists in the Map by key is performed in O(log(n)) time. Accessing any individual friend by key is also performed in O(log(n)) time as each friend is stored in the sorted tree structure.

EXERCISE 12-2

Based on the following scenarios, determine whether you should use a
HashSet, TreeSet, HashMap, or TreeMap:

1. Your program needs to access as quickly as possible the
   medical records of a patient by their id.

2. You have a program that generates error logs based on order of
   events, and you want to be able to search the logs for events or
   display them in order.

3. You want to create a search engine that indexes the entire
   Internet, and you should be able to search for the URL of each
   page as quickly as possible.

Performance Reference

If you forget the algorithmic efficiency for each data structure, they are
standardized across all languages, and you can find reference guides
all over the Internet to help guide you. In order to provide this same
convenient reference in this book, Table 12-1 provides the Big O notation
for the access, search, and insertion/deletion methods for each of the data
structures described in this chapter.

Table 12-1. *A reference guide of Big O algorithmic efficiency for each data structure*

Data Structure	Access	Search	Insertion/Deletion
Array	O(1)	O(n)	O(n)
Linked List	O(n)	O(n)	O(1)
Stack/Queue	O(1)	O(n)	O(1)
Hash Tables*+	O(1)	O(1)	O(1)
Trees*	O(log(n))	O(log(n))	O(log(n))

*Requires uniqueness
+Cannot be sorted

Summary

In this chapter, you learned how to optimize the performance of your programs by weighing the pros and cons of the different data structures that might impact your code. You learned that arrays are optimal for accessing items by index position but inflexible when it comes to inserting or deleting items. In order to gain efficiency in programs that need flexibility in that area, you learned that linked lists can grow and shrink with relative ease. From there, you were introduced to queues and stacks that are specialized implementations of the linked list. Finally, to gain performance in searching for items in a collection, you learned that Hashes and Trees can be applied to either Sets or Maps to give you optimal algorithmic efficiency.

CHAPTER 13

Algorithms

It must certainly be apparent to you by now that software engineering requires significantly more consideration than simply programming or, more idiomatically, "coding." In the previous chapter, you were introduced to an engineering strategy meant to help optimize the performance and minimize operational cost risk in your programs, which was that of determining the appropriate data structures to use for a given scenario. In this chapter, you will be introduced to a set of algorithms that will provide strategies to further optimize your code. An algorithm is a defined set of instructions meant to solve particular problems with contextually similar circumstances, agnostic of the programming language used to solve the problem. An example of a problem that could be solved with algorithms is the Rubik's Cube puzzle game. Given a particular combination of different colors on each side of the cube, a discrete set of steps can be enacted to solve part of the puzzle. With enough executed combinations of different algorithms to solve color patterns for either an individual side or a layer of the cube, you can solve the entire puzzle.

While the topic of algorithms is exceptionally large, increasingly complicated, and often considered one of the most difficult topics in computer science to learn, its importance cannot be overstated. Knowing some of the basic design principles of algorithms will help you to design your own algorithms in the future, to uncover solutions to previously unsolved problems, and to bring new knowledge to the world. New algorithms tend to become the basis for valuable intellectual property and

© Jason Lee Hodges 2019
J. L. Hodges, *Software Engineering from Scratch,*
https://doi.org/10.1007/978-1-4842-5206-2_13

advanced breakthroughs in technology. In addition to this, understanding existing algorithms will allow you to recognize when you should use previously discovered solutions to a problem rather than reinvent the proverbial wheel on your own. An exhaustive list of core algorithms will not be provided in this chapter, as that could instead be a book on its own. However, this chapter will provide you a solid basis of understanding that can ideally lead you toward a path of continued education on this topic.

In this chapter, we will continue to build out our model operating system. You will first be introduced to the performance tuning strategy of greedy algorithms demonstrated via a merge sort algorithm and a binary search algorithm to look for files in a folder. Afterward, in order to optimally search for files in an entire operating system of folders, you will learn about various graph traversal algorithms. Finally, you will be shown an optimization strategy known as dynamic programming which we will use to issue fuzzy match searching within our operating system.

Greedy Algorithms

Our model operating system has come a long way since we started developing a basic while loop. Let's imagine that its value has become clear to a group of power users and they have begun to use it at scale. They are starting to create hundreds or thousands of text files in the system, and their businesses have become dependent upon being able to access them dependably. As we know, scale challenges and their associated risks create unique engineering problems. As these power users begin to ask for new features in order to help them manage their files, and subsequently their businesses, we will need to keep the engineering principles we've learned thus far in mind.

The first request your users have asked for is the ability to sort the files in a directory. This will make it easier to navigate through the text files when they are printed to the screen via the "list" command. While it is likely that the underlying operating system that our Nebula shell is operating on already sorts the files in the directory by name, let's assume for the sake of example that they are always printed to the terminal in the order in which they were created. Given that information, the most basically intuitive, or "naive," way to sort these files might be to iterate through each file *i* and compare *i* to each file that comes before it. During that comparison, we would find the first file that should belong after *i*, insert *i* right before it, and then move on to the next iteration. This is an algorithm known as insertion sort and, in the worst case scenario, if the list were sorted in reverse order, each file would have to check every single item that comes before it. This results in exponential time complexity, or $O(n^2)$. Given that exponential time complexity is extremely slow, our users will likely not be very happy with that type of solution. Surely we can do better than this "brute force" approach.

The second request that your users have asked for is a way to search for an individual file based on an input keyword. This would make it easier to see if a file exists in a directory without having to scroll through a long list of files that have already been created. To accomplish this, we could implement a naive solution known as sequential search which performs a "brute force" check of every item in the directory one at a time. This approach would take $O(n)$ time which, albeit better than $O(n^2)$, is still pretty slow. How might we appease our users' requests in the most efficient manner possible?

Instead of using naive algorithms, let's instead use what is known as greedy algorithms to accomplish both of these requests. A greedy algorithm is an algorithm that, given a series of iterations, chooses the locally optimum solution at each iteration regardless of the effect that choice will have on the future outcome of the algorithm. An example of this might be that of a software engineer trying to maximize their total earnings over the course of their career. Let's assume, given that software engineers are in high demand, that they are recruited by a new firm every 2 years and that each new firm offers them a significant pay increase.

The software engineer would be left with the choice of either staying with their current firm or leaving to the new firm to accept the pay increase. A greedy algorithm would suggest that, for each iteration (every 2 years), the engineer should accept the locally optimal solution. Therefore, in order to maximize their career earnings, they must take the pay increase and leave their current firm every time they are offered more money to leave.

Given that the choices made in greedy algorithms are local and do not, by nature, need to consider every possible scenario and its effect on the future or overall outcome, these algorithms are extremely fast. This is the benefit that we are trying to take advantage of for our operating system. The downside is that in many scenarios, given that the algorithm doesn't consider every possible scenario like a naive or linear algorithm would, oftentimes greedy algorithms do not come up with correct solutions. For example, in the case of optimizing career earnings, an engineer might have received a larger pay increase by staying with their current employer before the next 2-year span because longevity in a firm tends to lead to better contextual knowledge and productivity. However, since the algorithm cannot consider all long-term possibilities, only the optimal choice for a local iteration, which in this case is the choice between more money and the same money, the greedy algorithm might not have maximized the career earnings of the engineer. However, for the problems we want to solve with our operating system, that of sorting and searching, there are greedy algorithms that we can use that have been proven to produce correct answers. In order to use greedy algorithms that yield correct results, they must contain two properties:

1. They must have a "Greedy Choice Property," meaning that making locally optimal choices derives a globally optimal solution.

2. They must have an optimal substructure, meaning the problem must be able to be broken into smaller sub-problems wherein the optimal solution can be found.

The algorithms that we are going to use that satisfy these two properties are the merge sort algorithm and binary search algorithm. Both of these algorithms employ a useful strategy known as "divide and conquer" in their implementations. The divide and conquer technique is considered an extremely efficient strategy for solving algorithmic problems and can be used when designing your own algorithms outside of the context of the two algorithms that we will use for sorting and searching.

Divide and Conquer

The divide and conquer strategy is one of dividing a problem into a series of smaller and smaller sub-problems with the intention of creating a sub-problem that is exceptionally simple or computationally inexpensive to solve. It typically involves defining a "base case" branch which is the most simplified version of the problem to be solved and then a separate branch that will further divide the problem into smaller problems if the problem provided does not meet the criteria of the base case branch. Implementations of divide and conquer algorithms often manifest themselves as recursive functions, which you were briefly introduced to in the chapter that contained the functional programming paradigm. Listing 13-1 provides an example of a function that prints the *nth* Fibonacci number in a Fibonacci sequence given an input number *n* using recursive divide and conquer. A Fibonacci number is a number that is derived by adding the two numbers that came before it in a sequence (i.e., 0, 1, 1, 2, 3, 5, 8, 13, 21, 34...).

Listing 13-1. A recursive divide and conquer algorithm that prints the nth Fibonacci number

```
def fibonacci(n: Int): Int = {
    if (n <= 1) n
    else (fibonacci(n-1) + fibonacci(n-2))
}
```

```
println(fibonacci(9))
```

Terminal Output

34

Note   Recall that recursion and recursive functions refer to a function that calls itself within the body of the function. Recursive functions often take the place of iterative loops in the functional programming paradigm. Recursive functions will continue to call themselves repeatedly until a set of criteria is met to keep the function from calling itself again.

In this example, we have defined a function with a conditional branch which checks for our base case, that of our input number having a value less than or equal to 1. As you might have noticed in the example Fibonacci sequence, if you think about the sequence of numbers as an array with starting index 0 and you try to access the 0 index or the 1 index, the number returned is the same number as the index. Because of that, our most simplified base case is that of returning n if n is 0 or 1 (less than or equal to one). If the input number is greater than 1, then you call the fibonacci function recursively twice substituting n for n-1 and n-2, respectively (which seeks to add the previous two numbers in the sequence). In our example, the input number is 9 and therefore the first thing that happens is our function calls itself twice and adds the results together fibonacci(8) + fibonacci(7). Because fibonacci of both 8 and 7 are not less than or equal to 1, they too must call themselves again twice: fibonacci(8) will call fibonacci(7) + fibonacci(6) and fibonacci(7) will call fibonacci(6) + fibonacci(5). These functions will continue to call themselves repeatedly, adding exponential function calls to the memory stack, until the base case is reached. Once the base case is reached and n is returned as either 0 or 1, each branch is able to start calculating actual values for their recursive call and it starts returning results up the function call chain. This recursive call nature is illustrated in Figure 13-1 for further clarity.

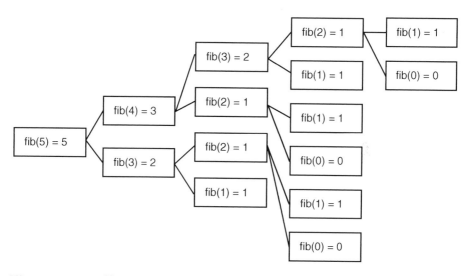

Figure 13-1. *Illustration of a recursive divide and conquer Fibonacci algorithm with input parameter 5 (for brevity)*

As you might have guessed, this implementation of a Fibonacci algorithm is not greedy. In fact, it has a time complexity of $O(2^n)$ which is the slowest program we have examined in this book so far. However, it is a great representation of how you can approach solving seemingly impossible problems by breaking them down into smaller and smaller sub-problems. Let's combine this divide and conquer strategy with the two properties of greedy algorithms to solve our users' requests for our model operating system.

Merge Sort

The first request from our users is to have the ability to sort the files in our operating system. Since we know that the insertion sort algorithm is not going to be fast enough to solve our users' needs, we must identify an algorithm that can sort the files in our operating system in faster than $O(n^2)$ time. Merge sort uses a divide and conquer method that will end up yielding $O(n*\log(n))$ time, which is relatively fast compared to the naive solution of insertion sort. What a merge sort attempts to do is take in two lists that are already sorted and merge them together, taking the lesser of the first values of the two lists as it builds up a list. This satisfies the "Greedy Choice" property of the greedy algorithm pattern since it can take the locally optimal choice (the lesser of the first values of the two lists) and it will result in a globally optimal result.

For example, assume we have two previously sorted lists of files with values "Alpha.txt", "Jason.txt", and "Zordon.txt" in the first list and "Billy.txt", "Kimberly.txt", "Tina.txt", and "Zack.txt" in the second list. The merge sort will examine the first item in both lists and determine that "Alpha.txt" should be added to its newly constructed list and not "Billy.txt". Then the merge sort will examine what remains of the two lists and compare "Billy.txt" to "Jason.txt", at which point it will add "Billy.txt" to its newly constructed list which now contains "Alpha.txt" and "Billy.txt" in sorted order. It will continue to examine both lists pulling the lesser value from the head of each list until an entirely new list is constructed in sorted order.

At this point, you might wonder how we can make the assumption that the two lists that are being merged are already in sorted order themselves. The answer to that comes from a recursive divide and conquer function. In our merge sort algorithm, we can continue to divide our list in half recursively until each list essentially contains only one item. This satisfies the optimal substructure property of the greedy algorithm pattern. In our example scenario, once the lists have been divided all the way down to their base case, we would have seven lists with only one item in each. From there, the recursive function that divided those lists will compare the two halves that it divided and merge them in sorted order.

Let's assume our function divided a list of "Kimberly.txt", "Tina.txt", "Zack.txt", and "Billy.txt" into two lists. The first list would contain "Kimberly.txt" and "Tina.txt", and the second list would contain "Zack.txt" and "Billy.txt". The next step would be to recursively divide each list again. At this point, we would have four separate lists with one item in each. The branch that divided "Kimberly.txt" and "Tina.txt" would merge those two individual lists back together. In this case, it would add "Kimberly.txt" into a newly created list and then "Tina.txt", which was the order it was already in. The branch that divided "Zack.txt" and "Billy.txt" would merge them back together selecting "Billy.txt" first and "Zack.txt" second. Then, the original function that divided our list into two lists of two items each will merge these two now sorted sub-lists. As you can see, by dividing our list into two halves repeatedly in a divide and conquer fashion, we can more easily sort small lists and merge them back up through a recursion chain until the entire list is sorted. Listing 13-2 provides a definition of two recursive functions, mergeSort and merge, that employ this merge sort algorithm.

Listing 13-2. Implementation of the merge sort algorithm

```
def mergeSort(files: ArrayBuffer[String]): ArrayBuffer[String] = {
    val midpoint = files.length / 2
    midpoint match {
        case 0 => files
        case _ =>
          val (left, right) = files.splitAt(midpoint)
          merge(mergeSort(left), mergeSort(right))
    }
}

def merge(left: ArrayBuffer[String], right:
ArrayBuffer[String]): ArrayBuffer[String] = {
    (left, right) match {
      case (_, r) if r.isEmpty => left
      case (l, _) if l.isEmpty => right
      case (_, _) =>
```

```
    if (left.head < right.head) ArrayBuffer(left.head) ++
    merge(left.tail, right)
    else ArrayBuffer(right.head) ++ merge(left, right.tail)
  }
}

val files = ArrayBuffer("Zordon.txt", "Jason.txt", "Billy.txt",
"Zack.txt", "Kimberly.txt", "Tina.txt", "Tommy.txt", "Alpha.txt")

val sortedFiles = mergeSort(files)
println(sortedFiles)
```

Terminal Output
```
ArrayBuffer(Alpha.txt, Billy.txt, Jason.txt, Kimberly.txt,
Tina.txt, Tommy.txt, Zack.txt, Zordon.txt)
```

In this example, instead of using a basic List data structure, the optimal data structure to use is an Array because we will need to continually access the midpoint of each list. To know the midpoint of a list, we must first determine its length, which takes $O(n)$ time in a List but $O(1)$ time for an Array. Using an array helps keep the operation cost of our algorithm down. You'll notice that we are actually using an ArrayBuffer from the scala mutable collections library. The ArrayBuffer collection implements various methods for us to help the array grow and shrink (via index copying to new lists) that we don't have to implement ourselves, for convenience.

In our first recursive function, mergeSort, we first check our base case, which is that of whether or not the midpoint is 0. The midpoint would be zero only if the length of the list were less than or equal to one, which would be the most basic list. In that scenario, we simply return the list as it is already sorted. If the midpoint of the list is anything besides zero, as denoted by the underscore operator, then we split the list into two lists, left and right, at its midpoint. From there, we call the merge function and pass a recursive call to mergeSort on the left list and a recursive call to mergeSort on the right list, which will continue to divide and merge all the way down to the base case.

The merge function is also a recursive function, but this one has two base cases. The first base case is a scenario that matches if the left list has values but the right list is empty. In this case, it simply returns the left list. The second base case is a scenario that matches if the right list has values but the left list is empty. In that case, the right list is returned. If both lists have values, then the heads of the two lists are compared. The head with the least value is added to a new ArrayBuffer and then that ArrayBuffer is added to the result of a recursive merge call on the remnants of the two lists. When all the recursive functions have been called down to their base cases, returned a value from the base case, and calculated back up the recursive chain, a new sorted ArrayBuffer will be returned in $O(n*\log(n))$ time. This should be fast enough to satisfy our users when using our file system.

Note   In many implementations of common data structures in the functional programming paradigm, including the ArrayBuffer, the tail of the data structure refers to every item of the list that is not the head rather than just the last item in the list.

To provide this functionality within our system, we can add the merge function and the mergeSort function to our Utilities.scala file for use in our Nebula OS and refactor our list function to take an optional argument if the user wants the list that is printed to be sorted. Because the operating system that our Nebula model shell is running on top of is already sorting the files alphabetically, let's flip the "less than" operator in our merge function to be a "greater than" operator to sort our list in descending order instead of ascending order. Next, let's add an extra argument to our call to the list function in our nebula.scala file that tells our function whether or not to sort the results. Listing 13-3 demonstrates these changes.

Listing 13-3. Refactoring the list function to sort the results

nebula.scala
```
...
case c if c.contains("list") => Utilities.list(c.
split(" ").lift(1))
...
```

Utilities.scala
```
...
def list(sort: Option[String]){
    val dir = new File("./").listFiles.map(file =>
    stripDir(file.toString))
    sort match {
        case Some(_) => {
            val sortedDir = mergeSort(ArrayBuffer(dir: _*))
            sortedDir.foreach(println)
        }
        case None => dir.foreach(println)
    }
 }
...
```

Now the command for list splits the user input and calls a `lift` function on the results to pull out the value at index 1, if it exists. The result of the `lift` function is an `Option` type. An `Option` in Scala is a data type that wraps the underlying data that you are interested in (in this case, we are using an Option that wraps a String) and will indicate to the code whether the data in question exists or not. If it does exist, it is said to be of type Some; otherwise, it is of type None. Some and None are both wrapped up within the type `Option`, and we can use a pattern match to pull out whether the underlying data actually exists.

In the method signature of our list function, we have added the parameter sort: Option[String]. This tells Scala that we are expecting an Option type to be passed to this function, and if any underlying data exists, it will be of type String. We then pattern match on the sort parameter. If the underlying data of the Option is of type Some, meaning it does contain data, then we want to take the contents of the directory, add them to an ArrayBuffer, and pass them to the mergeSort function. This will sort them in descending order and print them to the console. If the underlying data of the Option is of type None, then we just want to print each item in the directory in its existing order. We can test this command by typing the command list in our Nebula shell without any additional arguments to see the list printed normally or the command list sort (or any other additional argument) to see the list sorted in descending order.

EXERCISE 13-1

The example of merge sort provided was implemented in a completely recursive manor. In order to cognitively cement the concept of merge sort, try re-implementing the algorithm using a procedural paradigm.

Binary Search

The next request from the users of our model operating system is to be able to search for a file to see if it exists. We could simply check every file in the directory to see if it matches a given search term, but how might we use the concepts of greedy algorithms and divide and conquer to perform this operation in a more efficient manor? The binary search algorithm will improve the performance of a search function over a sequential search algorithm from O(n) time to O(log(n)) time.

Similar to the binary search tree data structure, the binary search algorithm attempts to divide a list in half and compare a given value to the midpoint of a list (rather than a root node or child nodes in a tree). If the midpoint is the value that you were looking for, then you've completed the operation. If not, then you check whether the value you are looking for is greater than or less than the midpoint. If it is less than the midpoint, then you take the left half of the list and divide it in half again and start the operation over again. If the value you are looking for is larger than the midpoint, you perform the same operations recursively on the right half of the list. In this way, you eliminate half the search space each time you iterate through the process. This is all predicated by the assumption that the list you are searching through is already sorted in ascending order. In your operating system, the files may be sorted by default, but if they are not, we can use the merge sort algorithm to sort them. Listing 13-4 provides an example implementation of a binary search algorithm added to our Utilities.scala file and a corresponding command added to the nebula.scala file.

Listing 13-4. Binary search algorithm implementation

Utilities.scala

```scala
def search(keyword: String, fileList: Option[Array[String]] =
None): String = {
    val files = fileList match {
        case Some(f) => f
        case None => mergeSort(ArrayBuffer(new File("./").
        listFiles.map(file => stripDir(file.toString)): _*))
    }
    val midpoint = files.length / 2
    return files.length match {
        case 1 => if(keyword == files(0)) files(0) else "No
        match found."
```

```scala
      case 2 => if(keyword == files(0)) files(0) else if
      (keyword == files(1)) files(1) else "No match found."
      case _ =>
         val (left, right) = files.splitAt(midpoint)
         if(keyword == files(midpoint)) files(midpoint)
         else if (keyword > files(midpoint)) search(keyword,
         Some(left))
         else search(keyword, Some(right))
   }
}
```

nebula.scala

```scala
...
case c if c.contains("search") => println(Utilities.
search(c.split(" ")(1)))
...
```

The input parameters to our search function are a keyword, which is the file that you are looking for, and optionally a file list (which is set to None by default), which is used during recursion but not for the initial call. The first thing our algorithm does is check to see if a file list was provided. If it is provided, then it sets the variable files to the provided value. If it is not provided, it initializes a new file list by pulling all of the files out of the current directory, adding them to an ArrayBuffer, and performing our mergeSort function on them. The result of the merge sort is then stored in the files variable. By performing the merge sort, we are satisfying the "Greedy Choice" property that allows us to choose a locally optimal path when we start dividing the list in half and searching through each half of the list. The fact that the sorted list can be continually divided and checked also inherently satisfies the optimal substructure property of the greedy algorithm requirements.

Next, the algorithm initializes a midpoint variable by performing integer division on the length of the list. This midpoint is used to check for values or continually divide the list in half, similar to how we used the midpoint in the merge sort algorithm. Finally, we perform a pattern match on the length of the file list that contains three cases. The first case is that the length of the `ArrayBuffer` is 1, in which case there is only one file to check the search keyword against. If that is the case, we perform the check, and if it matches, we return the value; otherwise, we return a message that says "No match found." The next case is if the file list length is 2. In this case, we can simply check both files to see if they match the search keyword or return our failure message otherwise.

The final case matches all other lengths of the list. In this scenario, we initialize a left variable and a right variable by splitting the file list in half at its midpoint. Next, we check to see if the file matches at the midpoint. If so, we return it. If not, we check to see if the search term is larger than the word contained at the midpoint. If it is larger, then we recursively perform the search on the left half of the list (since it is sorted in descending order) by passing the `keyword` back to `search` along with `Some(left)` as the parameter for the optional `fileList` argument. If it is smaller, then we recursively perform the search on the right half of the list instead. This will continue recursively, giving us a half-life characteristic of the search space each time, until either the keyword is found or the value "No match is found." is returned. A visual representation of this recursive strategy is provided in Figure 13-2.

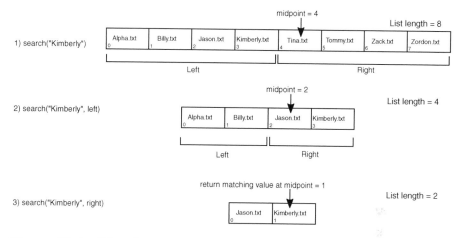

Figure 13-2. *Visual representation of recursive binary search*

In order to call this search function, we've added a command to our NebulaOS command list that checks if the user input contains the word "search." If it does, we split the input into an array and pull out the second position of that array (index 1) as the search keyword to pass to the search function. Thus, if our user provides in the input "search sample.txt", it will traverse all of the files in the directory, and if it finds a text file named "sample", it will print "sample.txt" to the terminal; otherwise, it will print "No match found."

This all works great if the users are happy to continue creating all of their files in a single directory. But at some point, for scalability's sake, they are going to want to organize their files a little better to make them easier to search. Let's take our operating system one step further and add the ability to create folders and navigate between them. Then we can put functions in place to search for files either within an individual directory or in the operating system as a whole. In order to do that, we must create a graph data structure to represent the folders in our operating system and implement graph traversal algorithms to search through them.

Graph Traversal Algorithms

In computer science, a graph is an abstract data type wherein a number of nodes are connected to various other nodes through what is known as edges. Our linked list data structure is an example of a graph that links each node in the list via a pointer that acts as the edge. In our linked list, each node only has one edge that connects to the next node in the list. Another example of a graph is our binary search tree data structure. In our binary search tree, each node contained two edges, one connecting to their left child and one connecting to their right child. However, in an abstract graph, each node can contain an infinite number of edges. Those edges can be either directed or undirected. Directed edges, such as the edges in our linked list and binary search tree implementations, are edges that only point to the next node in the graph but not back to their parent node. You can think of these as one-way streets. Undirected edges are edges that create a link between nodes wherein traversal can occur in either direction, like a two-way street. Some graphs can also contain circular references where a node has an edge that leads directly back to itself or indirectly back to itself through connections to other nodes. These are known as a cyclic graphs because they contain a cycle, or circular reference. Binary Search Trees and Linked Lists are considered directional acyclic graphs because their edges can only be traversed in one direction and they contain no cycles. Figure 13-3 provides an illustration of various graphs for reference.

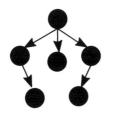

Directed Acyclic Graph

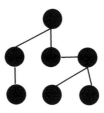

Undirected Acyclic Graph

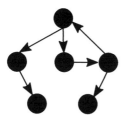

Directed Cyclic Graph

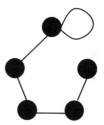

Undirected Cyclic Graph

Figure 13-3. *Various abstract graph data structures*

By creating a folder structure for our operating system, we are essentially deriving an undirected acyclic graph which contains a folder at each node and a reference to each sub-folder as its edges. Each node, therefore, would contain a list of file values as a property of the node. Once we have this mental model of our operating system, we can apply various graph traversal algorithms to satisfy the requirement of searching for files at either a global level or at the level of a given folder.

In order to set up a folder hierarchy in our operating system shell, we'll need to implement some commands to allow for the creation of and navigation through folders. Before we do that, however, we'll need to set up some infrastructure to let us know what the current directory is and where to start from when the shell originally boots up. Let's start by creating an actual folder in the base directory of our project called "root" that we can set as our origin folder when the application starts. After that we can define a variable called `curdir` in our `nebula.scala` file that keeps track of the

275

current directory that we are in as we navigate between folders. We'll set the curdir variable to "./root" by default. We'll also want to provide some feedback to the user as to which directory they are in as they navigate through the folders. To do that, we can create a variable called path that takes the curdir variable, which is a string, splits it into an array delimited by the slash, drops the first two items in that array (references to a period "." and our origin folder "root"), and then joins them back together as a string using the mkString method. This will give us a reference to each sub-folder that we are in that we can append to our original prompt message NOS> without having a reference to our root folder. Listing 13-5 shows an example of how this might be implemented.

Listing 13-5. Implementing infrastructure to keep track of current directory in the Nebula OS command line shell

nebula.scala

```scala
object nebula extends App {
    println("Welcome to the Nebula Operating System (NOS)!
    Version 1.1.1")
    var curdir = "./root"
    var command = ""
    do {
      val path = curdir.split("/").drop(2).mkString("/")
      command = readLine(if(path.length > 0) s"NOS/${path}> "
      else "NOS> ")
      command match {
          ...
      }
    }
    while (!command.equalsIgnoreCase("shutdown"))
    }
}
```

As you can see, when passing an argument to the readLine function to prompt the user for input, we can reference the path variable that was implemented to keep track of the directory path. If the path does not have a length greater than 0, then we must be in the root folder, and therefore our original prompt can be displayed as normal. If the path does have a length greater than 0, then we can append the path to the prompt to show the user what directory they are in and how they got there.

Now, let's implement a mkdir and cd command to allow our users to make new directories and navigate between them. The mkdir command will need to take an argument that contains the name of the folder that the user wishes to create. The cd command will need to take an argument that contains the name of the folder the user wishes to navigate to. Both commands will need to know what directory is currently assigned to curdir in order to properly function. Let's add these commands to our pattern matching expression as shown in Listing 13-6.

Listing 13-6. Addition of mkdir and cd commands to the pattern matching expression in the NebulaOS shell

```
...
case c if c.contains("mkdir") => Utilities.mkdir(curdir,
c.split(" ")(1))
case c if c.contains("cd") => curdir = Utilities.
changeDir(curdir, c.split(" ")(1))
...
```

Both of these commands contain references to functions in our Utilities module that we have not yet added. The Utilities.mkdir method is pretty simple to implement. It can simply append the name of the desired directory to the current directory and pass that derived path to Java's File API to create the folder. The cd command, on the other hand, sets the return value of the Utilities.changeDir function to the curdir variable that we initialized earlier. The changeDir function needs to be able do a couple of different things. First, if you pass it a string "..", the operating system should know that means you wish to navigate up one level. Second, if you pass it any value that is not the double period operator, it needs to check if the directory you want to navigate to exists. If the directory you are trying to navigate to doesn't exist in the current directory, or if you are trying to move up one directory and you are already in the root folder, the function should print a message suggesting that it can't find what you are looking for and simply return the curdir that was originally passed to it so that the directory of the operating system doesn't change at all. The implementation of these requirements is listed in Listing 13-7.

Listing 13-7. Implementation of the mkDir and changeDir functions, along with helper functions as necessary

```
def mkdir(curdir: String, dirname: String){
    println(s"[Creating Directory ${dirname}... ]")
    new File(s"${curdir}/${dirname}").mkdir()
}

def changeDir(curdir: String, newdir: String): String = {
    if(newdir == ".." && curdir != "./root") { return curdir.
    split("/").init.mkString("/") }
    if(dirExists(curdir, newdir)) { return s"${curdir}/
    ${newdir}" }
    else { println(s"[Directory ${newdir} not found... ]");
    return curdir}
}

def dirExists(curdir: String, newdir: String): Boolean = {
    var dir = new File(curdir).listFiles
    dir.foreach(item => if(stripDir(item.toString) == newdir)
    return true)
```

```
    return false
}

def stripDir(fileString: String): String = {
    val filename = fileString.split("/")
    return filename(filename.length - 1)
}
```

In this implementation, the changeDir function first checks if the passed-in argument is the double period operator and if the operating system is not currently in the root directory. If these conditions are true, it takes the curdir argument, splits it into an array, uses the init method to keep all items except that last item, and then joins the array back into a string separated by a slash. It then returns this newly constructed directory so that the operating system can set the curdir variable to the directory one level up from where it was before.

The next thing the changeDir function does, assuming the user did not pass in the double period operator, is check to see if the new directory the user requested exists. It does this by passing the curDir argument and the newDir argument to a helper function called dirExists. The dirExists function initializes an array of files and folders that exist in the directory referenced by curDir. Then it iterates through each of those files, passing those files to a stripDir helper function that removes the path prefix from the directory name and checks it against the newDir argument. If it finds a match at any point, it returns true; otherwise, it returns false. If the directory that the user is trying to navigate to exists, then it appends that directory to the current directory and returns that value to the operating system so that it can set the curdir variable to this new value. If it does not exist, it defaults to the final else condition which prints out the error message and returns the curdir that was originally passed into the function with no changes.

At this point, given that the infrastructure to support an undirected acyclic graph of folders is in place, we are ready to start adding the searching capabilities that our users will inevitably want to have. We can first start by adding the current directory as an argument to our search command. Listing 13-8 provides a description of the changes to allow this functionality.

Listing 13-8. Addition of the current directory as an argument to the search command

nebula.scala

```scala
...
case c if c.contains("search") => println(Utilities.
search(curdir, c.split(" ")(1)))
...
```

Utilities.scala

```scala
def search(curdir: String, keyword: String, fileList:
Option[ArrayBuffer[String]] = None): String = {
    val files = fileList match {
        case Some(f) => f
        case None => mergeSort(ArrayBuffer(new File(curdir).
         listFiles.map(file => stripDir(file.toString)): _*))
    }
    ...
            else if (keyword > files(midpoint)) search(curdir,
            keyword, Some(left))
            else search(curdir, keyword, Some(right))
    }
}
```

As you can see, a `curdir` parameter has been added to the method signature for the `search` function in the `Utilities.scala` file, and the `nebula.scala` file passes its `curdir` value as an argument to the `search` function. The search function now uses the `curdir` parameter to initialize the list of files in the None case, and it has to continue to pass that `curdir` parameter to itself as it iterates through recursive calls. Now that this is in place, users can search for files in their current directory. Next, we'll need to provide them the ability to search for a file in the entire graph of folders. There are two main algorithms that help us accomplish this, depth first search and breadth first search.

EXERCISE 13-2

By adding a current directory variable to the search function, we have given our users the ability to search for files locally within a given folder. They will want this same functionality applied to their `list` command and `write` command now that folders are available. Refactor the `list` command and the `write` command on your own to provide these features.

Depth First Search

Not all algorithms can be implemented in a greedy fashion. In the case of searching a graph for a value, it is not possible to use a divide and conquer strategy since the folders contain values independent of each other. Because of this, we are not able to sort the values in our graph to eliminate part of the search space as we traverse through the graph. Also, a graph similar to ours is not binary and therefore could have n number of child nodes for each node. This means that we cannot satisfy the optimal substructure or greedy choice properties required of greedy algorithms.

Because of this, we will need to resort to a more naive algorithm that checks every node for the values we are looking for. However, depending on the user's knowledge of their file structure, they might be able to optimize their search by choosing one of two graph traversal algorithms. The first algorithm is called depth first search.

The depth first search algorithm is a strategy wherein we traverse the nodes of a graph one branch at a time, checking every node until we hit the leaf and then returning back up the branch to check additional branches. This algorithm is impactful if you know that the value you are looking for is nested deep within many layers of nodes. If we do possess this knowledge, there's no reason to check the base of each branch in a broad sense before moving on to check the leaves as we know that would generate inefficiencies in our search. To further illustrate this point, consider the graph in Figure 13-4 and the order in which it visits each node.

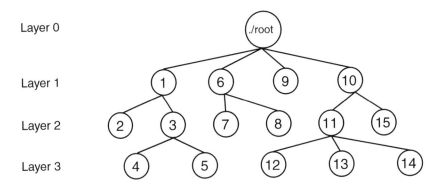

Figure 13-4. *A representation of the order in which nodes are visited in a depth first search algorithm*

As you can see from this depiction, we start with an entry point or a root node. In our case, the root node is our root directory. Along the left side of this illustration are labels that represent the layers of depth that our graph contains. In this instance, we have a graph that is three layers deep.

In a depth first search algorithm, we seek to search the deepest layer of an individual branch before moving on to the next branch. In this scenario, if you knew that the file you wanted to search for had a high probability of being found in layer 3, it would make no sense to explore all of layer 1 before moving on. Let's implement this algorithm in our operating system.

Listing 13-9. Implementation of depth first search algorithm

nebula.scala

```
...
case c if c.contains("search -dfs") => Utilities.
depthFirstSearch(c.split(" ")(2))
...
```

Utilities.scala

```
def depthFirstSearch(keyword: String) {
    val foldersToSearch: Stack[String] = Stack("./root")
    var folderFound = ""

    while (!foldersToSearch.isEmpty && folderFound.length == 0)
{
        val curSearchFolder = foldersToSearch.pop()
        if(search(curSearchFolder, keyword) == keyword) {
            folderFound = curSearchFolder
        }
        foldersToSearch.pushAll(extractFolders(curSearchFolder))
    }
    if(folderFound.length > 0) println(s"Found ${keyword} in
    ${folderFound}")
    else println("No match found using depth first search.")
}
```

```scala
def extractFolders(dir: String): Array[String] = {
    var directory = new File(dir).listFiles
    directory.filter(item => item.isDirectory()).map(d =>
    d.toString)
}
```

In Listing 13-9, we start by adding a search command with a -dfs parameter, signifying that the user wishes to use depth first search. Ensure that this command is placed before the original search command in our pattern matching expression so that it does not match the original search command first and ignore our depth first search command. This depth first search command should take a keyword in index position 2 after the command keyword and the -dfs parameter. Next, we define our depth first search function that is referenced in the command. The only argument it takes is the keyword to be searched for.

We start the algorithm by initializing a Stack data structure, imported from the `scala.collection.mutable` library, and adding the root directory to it. We call this stack `foldersToSearch`. Next we initialize a variable called `folderFound` which we set to an empty string for now. After that, we start a while loop that will kick off our graph traversal. That while loop is going to continue to iterate until the stack is empty or the `folderFound` variable contains a value. In the while loop, we first pop the first item off the stack and then pass that value to our binary search algorithm to search for the keyword in that directory. If the value is found, it is added to the `folderFound` variable and our algorithm is done. If it does not find the keyword in this root directory, it passes the node that was searched to a helper called `extractFolders`. This function checks all the contents of the given folder and pulls out only the items that are other folders or other nodes in the graph. Once extracted, these nodes are all pushed onto the stack for future investigation, keeping the stack from being empty and therefor ensuring that the while loop will continue to traverse nodes. The loop will continue to iterate until there are no more nodes to visit or until it finds the folder that contains the keyword. Once we break out of the loop, we print to the terminal where the keyword was found or that it was not found at all.

Note   If you recall, the binary search function makes a call to our merge sort function. Thus, both of these algorithms are employed each time a node is visited in these graph traversal algorithms. Because the graph traversal algorithms are not greedy, it is important that the algorithms that they depend on are performant since stacking algorithms on top of algorithms can add a lot of time complexity and potentially operational cost to our programs.

Breadth First Search

If you know that the keyword you are looking for is likely to be housed in a fairly shallow node in the graph, it is likely better to use a breadth first search algorithm. In contrast to the depth first search algorithm, breadth first search checks each node in a layer before moving on to the next layer. Figure 13-5 provides an illustration of the order in which nodes would be visited in breadth first traversal.

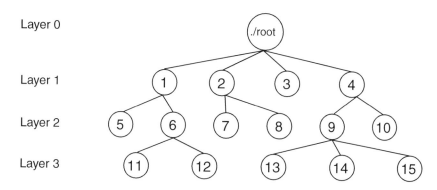

Figure 13-5. *A representation of the order in which nodes are visited in a breadth first search algorithm*

The implementation of a breadth first search algorithm is very similar to that of a depth first search algorithm. The main difference is in the data structure used to store the nodes to visit. Rather than using a Stack, breadth first search uses a Queue from the scala mutable collections library. This ensures that the first nodes that are added to the queue are visited first before moving on to more nodes. Each node that is visited adds its children, or sub-folders, to the end of the queue line rather than the front of the line like that of the stack data structure. By doing so, the queue ensures that entire layers are visited before moving on to the next layer. Listing 13-10 provides the details around this implementation.

Listing 13-10. Implementation of breadth first search algorithm

```
nebula.scala
...
case c if c.contains("search -bfs") => Utilities.
breadthFirstSearch(c.split(" ")(2))
...

Utilities.scala
def breadthFirstSearch(keyword: String) {
    val foldersToSearch: Queue[String] = Queue("./root")
    var folderFound = ""

    while (!foldersToSearch.isEmpty && folderFound.length == 0) {
        val curSearchFolder = foldersToSearch.dequeue()
        if(search(curSearchFolder, keyword) == keyword) {
            folderFound = curSearchFolder
        }
        foldersToSearch ++= extractFolders(curSearchFolder)
    }
```

```
    if(folderFound.length > 0) println(s"Found ${keyword} in
    ${folderFound}")
    else println("No match found using breadth first search.")
}
```

Our users now have the ability to create folders, navigate between them, add files to folders, search within a folder, and search globally using both depth first search and breadth first search. However, their search is still predicated on matching a keyword exactly. We could add in some logic to match on sub-strings rather than full strings, but that does not protect our user in the event that they made a small typo. How might we still return a matching result in the event our user made a mistake? To do that, we could introduce fuzzy matching using an algorithmic strategy known as dynamic programming.

Dynamic Programming

Dynamic programming is an algorithm design strategy that seeks to minimize the operational cost of exhaustive operations, such as the brute force searching in our graph traversal algorithms. It does this using a process known as memoization. Memoization refers to storing the values of previously solved solutions in a hash table during the execution of an algorithm. For example, Figure 13-1 depicted the recursive call chain that our Fibonacci function created while employing a recursive divide and conquer algorithm. If you notice, that recursion chain ends up calculating the same value several times throughout the lifespan of the algorithm. To optimize this, any time the function needed to calculate the *nth* Fibonacci number, it could first check a memoized hash table of known Fibonacci numbers. If the answer is not there, it can calculate it on its own and store the result in the hash table for future iteration to check. But if it is there, it does not need to re-calculate it. This will cut down the execution time of the algorithm significantly.

In our model operating system, we want to add a way for our users to search for files in graph nodes that don't exactly match the input keyword. This would allow for minor spelling differences in the input search term or if the files being searched for were unintentionally saved with a bad filename. One way to do this would be to calculate all the possible changes you could make to the input search term to make it match the file name in question and then return any file that takes less than a certain number of changes as a threshold. This type of calculation is known as an edit distance calculation, and the Levenshtein distance algorithm can help us determine the least amount of operations that could be performed on one string to turn it into another.

Levenshtein Distance

Given two strings to compare, the Levenshtein distance algorithm provides three operations to transform the first string into the second string: insertion, deletion, or replacement. Each operation that needs to be performed in the comparison incurs a cost that is counted. This dynamic programming algorithm tallies up all possible transformations to turn the first string into the second string and then returns a count of the minimum number of transformations required to satisfy the comparison.

For example, if the first string provided was "turn" and the second string provided was "turns," the minimum number of operations required to change the first string into the second string is 1: insertion of the letter "s" at the end of the first string. If the first string provided was "turns" and the second string provided was "torn," the minimum number of operations to ensure the words match would be 2: replacement of the "u" to be an "o" and deletion of the "s" at the end. Listing 13-11 provides an example of this algorithm written in a recursive fashion.

Listing 13-11. Levenshtein distance implementation function

```scala
def editDist(s1: String, s2: String): Int = {
    val memoizedCosts = Map[(Int, Int), Int]()

    def lev(s1_length: Int, s2_length: Int): Int = {
        memoizedCosts.getOrElseUpdate((s1_length, s2_length),
            (s1_length, s2_length) match {
            case (s1L, 0) => s1L
            case (0, s2L) => s2L
            case (s1L, s2L) =>
                List(
                    1 + lev(s1L - 1, s2L),
                    1 + lev(s1L, s2L - 1),
                    (if (s1(s1L - 1) != s2(s2L - 1)) 1 else 0) +
                    lev(s1L - 1, s2L - 1),
                ).min
        }
        )
    }

    lev(s1.length, s2.length)
    memoizedCosts(s1.length, s2.length)
}
```

In this example, the first thing that we do is initialize a hash map called memoizedCosts that will store the cost of operations for any two strings of given integer lengths. This satisfies the memoization property of the dynamic programming design pattern. Next, it creates an inner function that takes the length of the first string and the length of the second string as input parameters. The first thing the inner function does is check to see if it has already calculated a minimum cost for two strings of those lengths (with the characters defined at their given index position) that it has already stored in the hash table. If it has, then the inner function is complete. If it has not, then it must calculate the value and store it in the hash table. This is all wrapped in the getOrElseUpdate method call.

Next, the algorithm does a pattern match on the lengths of the strings which evaluates two base cases. First, a scenario wherein the first string has some length and the second string has length 0. The cost of transforming the second string of length 0 into the first string is the length of the first string since we will need to insert every character from the first string. Second, it performs this same logic but in reverse. After the base cases have been evaluated, in the event that both strings have some length, it initializes a list that contains three recursive function calls.

The first call represents a scenario wherein the last character position of the first string could be considered deleted. Such would be the only case if the first string were "turns" and the second string were "turn" and all we had to do was delete the last character in the first string. In that scenario, we count the cost (1) and then add in the cost of performing these evaluations on all the other characters in the remaining sub-string of string one and all the characters in string two.

The second call in the list represents a scenario where instead of deleting the last character position in the first string, we insert the last character in string two into the last position in string one. In that scenario, we now know that the last character from string two should now match, so we only need to finish comparing string one to a sub-string of all characters in string two except the last character. So we add one to a recursive call that removes one character length from string two.

The last recursive call checks to see if the last character positions in both strings actually match. If they do, the cost is zero, and if they don't, the cost of replacement is 1. Once we've determined what the cost will be for a replacement operation, we subtract one from the character lengths of both strings and advance it through recursion. In our Fibonacci recursive function, you were able to see how each iteration through the recursion split out two additional function calls into a tree that evaluated all the way down to the base case in each branch. In this edit distance algorithm, each of these recursive calls will make three additional recursive calls all the way down to their base cases. However, in many of those calls, the cost will have already been calculated and stored in the memoization table, thus speeding up the algorithm. This is the power of dynamic programming.

It is worthy to note that the unique part of this algorithm is that through each iteration, as it starts to return values up through the recursion chain, the whole function will only return the minimum cost evaluated for the three scenarios in the list. This is denoted by the call to the min method at the end of the list initialization. This demonstrates how useful dynamic programming can be in optimization problems that seek to find a min or max value from a set of scenarios. You will see these types of strategies employed in many algorithms that seek to find the shortest path between two nodes on a graph.

After defining the inner function, we actually call that inner function with the lengths of the two strings provided to the outer function. This call to the inner function builds up our memoization table. Once it has been built, we can access the key in that table that represents the lengths of the two strings that we are comparing to find the minimum edit cost of the two strings, and return that as the overall value of the outer function.

Given this useful functionality, instead of comparing equality in our three search functions, you can check to see if the edit distance of the search keyword and the file being evaluated falls below a certain threshold (you can decide whatever threshold you want that to be). In my case, I elected to check if the edit distance between the words was less than 2, meaning that there could only be at most a one-character difference between the words for my operating system to consider it a match. Now my users have a small margin for error in spelling differences when searching for files which adds a marginal level of convenience that hopefully contributes to the overall user experience of the application.

EXERCISE 13-3

Go back and refactor the three search functions in your operating system. Instead of checking the keyword against the files in the operating system for equality, try comparing their edit distance to a threshold number. If the edit distance falls below the threshold, return the file as a match.

Summary

In this chapter, the algorithm design strategies of divide and conquer, greedy algorithms, and dynamic programming laid the groundwork for your future exploration into the vast world of known algorithms. You were exposed to a few common algorithms, namely, merge sort, binary search, depth first search, breadth first search, and Levenshtein distance. Having a base understanding of known algorithms is important; however, knowing how to design your own algorithms can be just as useful in constructing large-scale software engineering projects. As you might have noticed, we layered each algorithm on top of the other in our operating system as we built up functionality. This demonstrates how important it is to ensure that each function is as efficient as possible because, when combined with other operations, things can start to get incredibly computationally costly. Knowing the right algorithm for the job and how much time complexity it adds to your program might be the difference in determining whether or not your project is probable or even possible.

CHAPTER 14

Design Patterns

The primary theme in software engineering is that of reuse over reiteration. You've seen this several times in this book already with the concepts of abstraction, modularity, inheritance, data structures, and algorithms. This same concept can be applied to software design. Design patterns are a set of best practices to use when encountering a specific problem in object-oriented software design. Similar to algorithms, these are proven solutions that should be reused in similar scenarios rather than being rewritten or rediscovered. Unlike algorithms, design patterns are typically not measured in terms of time complexity because their focus pertains more to writing code that can be easily understood, maintained, and decoupled from other parts of the code base.

There are three main categories of design patterns: creational, structural, and behavioral. In this chapter, you will be provided a description of the objective of each design pattern category, an example of a pattern for each category, and the names of a few additional patterns belonging to each category that you can research further on your own. Like algorithms, entire books have been written on the subject of design patterns. As such, this chapter will not provide an exhaustive list of patterns, but rather a solid foundation on which to build upon in the future.

© Jason Lee Hodges 2019
J. L. Hodges, *Software Engineering from Scratch*,
https://doi.org/10.1007/978-1-4842-5206-2_14

Creational Patterns

The objective of creational design patterns is to provide clean, idiomatic strategies for creating objects. Creational design patterns control the process of object creation by abstracting or decoupling the creation of the object away from the call site to reduce complexity in your software. Examples of creational design patterns include the builder pattern, the singleton pattern, the prototype pattern, and the factory pattern. We will explore the factory pattern in this chapter to further solidify the concept of creational design patterns.

The factory pattern is a design pattern that is used when you don't know what type of class object needs to be constructed at compile time. So, instead of instantiating a class at compile time, the class object you want to use during runtime will need to be dynamically generated. For example, say you are building a video game with a medieval theme. The very first thing you want your game to be able to do is allow the user to pick their character. The result of the user picking your character is the game building a class of that character's type. When designing your program, you do not know what your user is going to pick ahead of time. In this scenario, you can create a character factory to instantiate a class for you based on the user's selection. Listing 14-1 demonstrates this factory.

Listing 14-1. Demonstration of the factory design pattern

```
object CharacterFactory {
    abstract class Character {
        val weapon: String
        val hitpoints: Int
        val reach: Int
    }
```

```scala
    private case class Barbarian(
        weapon: String = "Long Sword",
        hitpoints: Int = 50,
        reach: Int = 5
    ) extends Character

    private case class Magician(
        weapon: String = "Staff",
        hitpoints: Int = 30,
        reach: Int = 15
    ) extends Character

    private case class Archer(
        weapon: String = "Bow",
        hitpoints: Int = 25,
        reach: Int = 30
    ) extends Character

    def apply(character: String): Character = {
        character match {
            case "Barbarian" => new Barbarian
            case "Magician" => new Magician
            case "Archer" => new Archer
            case _ => throw new Exception("Invalid Selection")
        }
    }
}

object main extends App {
    val choice = readLine("Choose your character: ")
    println(CharacterFactory(choice))
}
```

In this example, we've created an abstract class, `Character`, that each character type must extend. This is an important aspect of the factory pattern. In order to build a dynamic type, each class that the factory can generate must be a sub-type of a parent abstract class or interface. Because we want to ensure type safety within our software, the return type of the factory must be of this `Character` class, which therefore implies any class that the factory could build must extend the `Character` class.

After defining the parent abstract class, we next define three case classes that extend the `Character` class. These three case classes (Barbarian, Magician, Archer) are private classes, meaning they cannot be instantiated outside of our factory object. The case classes are each marked with default values for the properties they need to override in order to meet the requirements of extending the abstract class. By making them case classes, we have access to a `toString` method that will print these sub-classes in our program in a pre-formatted manner.

Finally, we define an apply function that acts as a constructor to our `CharacterFactory` object. That function takes a single parameter, `character`, which is of type `String`. The argument passed to that string parameter is then put through a pattern match which returns a newly constructed `Character` object that is of a dynamic sub-type depending on the input parameter of the method. Our `main` object, which extends `App` to be considered the entry point of our program, asks for a user's input and then makes a call to our character factory's apply method. The resulting dynamically generated character sub-type is then printed to the console using the built-in `toString` method of the case class.

This perfectly illustrates an example of abstracting the construction of a new object that is inherent in creational design patterns. Many creational design patterns follow similar steps to protect classes from direct instantiation. This helps remove the possibility of complex code implementations that need to keep track of several object types and how to construct them, allowing for a better developer experience downstream.

EXERCISE 14-1

For further study, look up the builder pattern, singleton pattern, and prototype pattern. Compare and contrast these patterns with the factory pattern.

Structural Patterns

The objective of structural design patterns is to efficiently simplify the composition of objects and their inheritance relationships with other objects. Examples of common structural design patterns include the composite pattern, the proxy patterns, the extensibility pattern, the bridge pattern, and the decorator pattern. We will drill into the decorator pattern to demonstrate the concept behind structural design patterns.

The decorator pattern is a common construct wherein an object is wrapped by another object in order to modify the structure of the original object. This provides a way to dynamically add functionality to an object without changing the underlying object. The benefit of this pattern is that the additional functionality is decoupled from the base class and can be reused to decorate many other classes of the same super-type as necessary. This decoupling allows the added functionality of the decorator to only be added to instantiated objects that are required to have this functionality, which differs from traditional inheritance wherein functionality or behavior added to the parent class will impact all instantiated sub-types of that parent.

As an example, suppose that you want to extend your medieval game to allow the user to select a bonus for the selected character to add to the character's inherent abilities. This type of dynamic selection needs to be applied to the character at runtime. In this scenario, you can define a wrapper class for each bonus that will not affect the code for each of the character classes that we've already built, but rather extend their capabilities. To do this, we must first define the wrapper classes and then use them in our apply constructor method. Listing 14-2 provides an example implementation of this scenario.

Listing 14-2. Example of the decorator design pattern

```
...

    def apply(character: String, bonus: String): Character =  {
        val selectedCharacter = character match {
            case "Barbarian" => new Barbarian
            case "Magician" => new Magician
            case "Archer" => new Archer
            case _ => throw new Exception("Invalid Selection")
        }

        return bonus match {
            case "Extra Health" => new ExtraHealth
            (selectedCharacter)
            case "Extra Range" => new ExtraRange
            (selectedCharacter)
            case _ => selectedCharacter
        }
    }

    private case class ExtraHealth(character: Character)
    extends Character {
        override val weapon = character.weapon
        override val hitpoints = character.hitpoints + 10
        override val reach = character.reach
```

```scala
        override def toString(): String = {
            return s"${character.getClass.getSimpleName}
            (${weapon},${hitpoints},${reach})"
        }
    }

    private case class ExtraRange(character: Character) extends
    Character {
        override val weapon = character.weapon
        override val hitpoints = character.hitpoints
        override val reach = character.reach + 10

        override def toString(): String = {
            return s"${character.getClass.getSimpleName}
            (${weapon},${hitpoints},${reach})"
        }
    }
}

object main extends App {
    val choice = readLine("Choose your character: ")
    val bonus = readLine("Choose bonus: ")
    println(CharacterFactory(choice, bonus))
}
```

In this example, we added two new wrapper classes which take in a character as an argument, the ExtraHealth class and the ExtraRange class. Both of these classes extend the parent Character class. At construction, these classes override the properties of the parent class to satisfy the requirement of extending it by copying the values of the character that was passed in as an argument. In the case of the ExtraHealth class, when copying the hitpoints property, it adds 10 points. In the case of the ExtraRange class, when copying the reach property, it adds 10 to the reach amount. In this way, these decorators have modified the object that was passed in as an argument without changing the underlying object.

If we tried to accomplish this same functionality without a decorator, we might try to override the default values of the character that the user picked. But in order to add 10 to the value, we would have to know what the default value is, which we won't know until after construction. We could get around this by creating a hash table of character types and their corresponding default values, but then every time we added a new character we would also have to update the table, which is less than ideal. We could instead try to modify the object after it has been constructed; however, in this case the properties of the object are immutable and can't be changed. Because of this, the decorator pattern is the most ideal way to add bonus functionality to the existing objects without modifying their underlying implementation.

Now, to use these decorators, in the apply constructor of the CharacterFactory object, we pull the dynamically constructed object out of our original pattern matching operation and capture it in a variable called selectedCharacter. From there, we do another pattern match that we return as the value for the overall constructor on a new parameter defined for the constructor named bonus. If the argument passed into the constructor matches one of the bonuses, then the selectedCharacter variable will be wrapped by the decorator in question and returned as a newly constructed object. If no matches occur, the selectedCharacter is returned with no decoration.

Finally, we add a line to our main object to read in a user selection for the bonus of their choice. After reading in their bonus selection, we pass that bonus as an argument to the bonus parameter in the apply constructor of the CharacterFactory object. When the resulting object is then printed to the terminal, if a correct bonus keyword was entered by the user, you will notice the corresponding property being modified. By walking through this example, you will notice that wrapping an object in another object is a great example of a structural design pattern meant to enhance the composition capabilities of our software.

EXERCISE 14-2

For further study on this category of design patterns, look up the composite pattern, extensibility pattern, and the bridge pattern. Compare and contrast these patterns with the decorator pattern.

Behavioral Patterns

The objective of behavioral design patterns is to identify common interactions between objects and abstract their behavior. In this way, these interactions can become more flexible among different types of objects. It also allows for these objects to be loosely coupled with an overall implementation which encourages modularity and reuse. Common behavioral patterns include the observer pattern, the strategy pattern, the visitor pattern, and the iterator pattern. Let's explore the iterator pattern in more detail.

The main goal of the iterator pattern is to provide a common interface for traversing different types of data collections. By creating this common interface, algorithms that use data collections can be decoupled from any particular collection type. This allows the algorithm to simply focus on its own implementation logic rather than collection specific logic, which provides the flexibility to use all collection types in that algorithm. Listing 14-3 provides an example of using an iterator in a function that is collection type agnostic.

Listing 14-3. Collection type agnostic iterator pattern

```
val charactersList = List("Barbarian", "Magician", "Archer")
val charactersArray = Array("Barbarian", "Magician", "Archer")
val charactersSet = Set("Barbarian", "Magician", "Archer")
val charactersMap = Map(1 -> "Barbarian", 2 -> "Magician", 3 ->
"Archer")

printAll(charactersList.iterator)
printAll(charactersArray.iterator)
printAll(charactersSet.iterator)
printAll(charactersMap.valuesIterator)

def printAll(group: Iterator[String]) {
    while (group.hasNext) {
        println(group.next())
    }
}
```

In this example, the printAll function defines an input parameter, group, which is of type Iterator[String]. This provides the flexibility to take in any collection that implements the iterator trait. The iterator trait, in Scala, is an interface that defines the methods that any collection should have in order to be considered an iterator. All iterators are required to have a hasNext method, which determines whether or not another item in the collection exists before we traverse to the next item. They also must contain a next() method which will actually traverse to the next item, if it exists. If you were defining your own custom collection and you wanted it to be able to be used by anyone implementing the iterator pattern, you would need to add the Iterator trait to your custom collection. All of the standard collections in Scala extend the iterator trait and therefore have iterator methods that can be called on them to return an iterator.

As you can see, we have defined four different collection types that each contain the same strings. If we were to write a function that printed each item in these collections, regardless of the collection type and without using higher-order functions, we wouldn't be able to. To loop over the items of an array or a list, you might choose to use the `length` property of the collection to construct the loop. For the set and map collections, you would need to use the `size` property instead. To access the items of the map, you would need to traverse its keys and pull out the values, whereas the other collections are simply index accessible. Instead, when passing these collections to the `printAll` function, we can access their iterator methods to change them to a common iterator that the function can use. Because of this, our function is now decoupled from the implementation details of the overall program, leaving it open for downstream developers to use whatever collection they like.

As you can see, the iterator pattern modifies the behavior of a collection and provides an abstract process for communication between objects, which is the overall goal of behavioral patterns in general. This should allow for a better downstream developer experience and future-proof your software from potential refactors due to collection-specific implementations.

EXERCISE 14-3

For further study on this category of design patterns, look up the observer pattern, the strategy pattern, and the visitor pattern. Compare and contrast these patterns with the iterator pattern.

Summary

In this chapter, you were introduced to the concept of design patterns which are used predominantly in the object-oriented programming paradigm. We broke down the design patterns into three main categories: creational, structural, and behavioral. Each had their own goal for making software easier to read, use, and maintain long term. If object-oriented program is a paradigm that resonates strongly with you, I encourage you to dig in and learn more about each of the patterns that were mentioned in this chapter.

CHAPTER 15

Further Study

You should be filled with great pride to have reached the culminating chapter of this book. However, you should also recognize that in doing so, you have not reached the end of your journey into the ever-expanding universe of computer science, but rather simply the end of the beginning. By reading this book, you have been introduced to many of the fundamental ideas and theories surrounding computer science and software engineering. However, it is imperative to understand that, though the core concepts have not changed in decades, software engineering is a rapidly evolving industry. New languages, frameworks, and conglomerations of paradigms and tools are being continually synthesized all the time. To be a successful software engineer, you must strive to keep up with these changes. Some of the most productive engineers are successful because they are chronic autodidacts or self-learners. In this final chapter, you will be introduced to several areas of specialty in software engineering that you can explore further on your own to deepen your understanding.

Database Administration

While you have been introduced to common data structures in which to store data during the execution of your software, you have not yet been exposed to where data is housed when your program is not running. In our model operating system, we briefly covered the idea that software can create text files and store them within a file system; however, most software application data is stored in databases.

A database is an organized collection of related data in a single system. Databases typically contain several tables which house rows of data with a consistent schema. A schema is a definition of the label, value, and type of data contained in each cell in a table in a database. For example, if you need to keep track of different users that have access to your software, you might house that data in a table that contains information about the user. That table will have several columns of information like the user's name, their email address, the number of times they have logged in, and the date they last logged in. The schema of that table would be a column named username which is of type string, a column named email which is also of type string, a column named logins which is of type integer, and a column named lastLogin which is a date type. Each row in this table would provide information matching this schema for every user that has access to your system.

Databases can contain several tables, that usually relate to each other in some way, that can be joined together via a query language. This query language is known as Structured Query Language or SQL. Database systems that allow for tables to be joined together in a related way are known as Relational Database Management Systems or RDBMS. Nearly all programming languages have database driver modules that can integrate directly with these database systems. This enables you to store your application data in an organized and efficient manner rather than writing them to disparate text files stored on a file system that are difficult and inefficient to search through and analyze. Common relational databases include MySQL, Oracle, and Postgres.

There are also databases that are not considered relational and do not store their data in tables. These are often referred to as non-relational databases or NoSQL databases. These databases organize data into collections rather than tables and contain unstructured documents of data rather than a schema-defined row. While this type of organization may be arguably harder to query and has no relational structure, it lauds the advantage of scalability and heavy access efficiency. It also is an extremely flexible paradigm as you don't need to plan and organize a schema for your data ahead of time; rather, each document can contain any label, value, and type that it needs to contain. Common non-relational databases include MongoDB and CouchDB.

Deciding whether you should use a relational database or a non-relational database is typically the decision of a database administrator. A database administrator is someone who specializes in databases and is tasked with architecting, maintaining, scaling, and querying databases on behalf of an organization. While this role typically does not involve writing any software, many companies rely heavily on database administrators to ensure that their software can query databases efficiently and reliably to power their application logic.

Data Engineering

Oftentimes, once software systems reach a certain critical scale, the data required to run an application, provide interactions between applications, or enable reporting for applications winds up being distributed among many data sources. In order to effectively use this data, someone must be well versed in the interaction of data between applications and how to effectively and efficiently transform data to match several schema or reporting requirements. A data engineer is a software engineer who specializes in accessing and transforming data to set up scalable and reliable data pipelines between applications.

A common theme in software engineering as of late is the idiom of "big data." Data engineers are skilled in sifting through this big data and formulating efficient structures and schedules to use this data to provide business value. For example, let's assume you are a data engineer tasked with understanding where to invest programmatic marketing spend for your company. Your directors don't want decisions surrounding where to invest their marketing dollars to be based on emotions or gut feelings, but rather well-informed data that can be parsed into a direct formula on how much money to allocate to each marketing option. Your marketing options include Google AdWords, Facebook Ads, Twitter Ads, and DoubleClick Ads, all of which are digital advertising platforms. You likely want to invest some of your ad spend in all of these platforms, but what is the most effective distribution? As a data engineer, you will need to programmatically connect to all of these systems, create new advertising campaigns, and continually monitor their results for adjustment.

When connecting to these different advertising systems, you will likely receive performance information about your campaigns in entirely different schemas for each system. How, then, will you objectively compare the results of campaigns across different systems? The job of the data engineer is to build reliable and consistently up-to-date data pipelines that can be transformed into an apples-to-apples comparison, regardless of the data schemas provided by the source system. However, oftentimes the data engineer is not charged with garnering insights from the data once it has been connected, collected, and normalized. In many organizations, that is the job of the data scientists.

Many of the common tools used by data engineers include Spark, Hadoop, and Airflow. Spark is a big data tool used for data transformation across a distributed network of server nodes that can scale to efficiently match the needs of the data transformation process depending on the size of the data. Spark has several language options for data engineers to choose from, but it was originally implemented using Scala. It is thus considered to contain several advantages when using Scala over other language implementations. Hadoop is also a distributed data transformation system that predates Spark. It is best known for its map reduce strategy which is closely related to the higher-order functions of map and reduce that were introduced in the functional programming paradigm section of this book. Airflow is a data pipeline scheduling platform that allows you to trigger data connection and transformation jobs in tandem. It also has built-in tools to allow for retrying jobs that have failed and reporting the status of all of the jobs in the data pipeline at any given time.

Data Science

Once data has been made available from the source application in a data pipeline, data scientists are often charged with obtaining insights from the data to drive business decisions. Oftentimes the hope is that these insights can include predictions about the future based on the data that has been gathered in the past. Recently, these predictive insights are gathered using machine learning and artificial intelligence algorithms that have become the main focus of data scientists' research. These algorithms rely heavily on proven statistical modeling techniques that have been around for decades. Unfortunately, these techniques could not be harnessed fully until the computing power was capable of handling the big data that is currently being produced in the industry.

In some specific situations, data scientists are not simply extracting insights from data but using the data to make programmatic decisions. For example, in the field of computer vision, data scientists use the data gathered from cameras to make decisions about how a robot should respond to a particular situation or whether a self-driving car should slow down or stop. These techniques are also used in the same manner to create facial recognition software. Recently, advances in data science have made it reasonably simple for computers to take audio data and transform that data into recognizable text. This can then be fed to software as input instructions. All of these amazing advancements in the field of computer science have been made possible by data science.

Data science is a very popular and rapidly growing field of computer science. To correctly harness it, understanding the concepts of database administration and data engineering are crucial along with specialized training in statistics and machine learning. The demand for great data scientist will only continue to grow in the near future as these skills become increasingly more valuable.

Embedded Systems

In conjunction with data science, another very popular topic in the software engineering industry currently is the "Internet of Things." The Internet of Things is a phrase used to describe the ever-increasing availability of connected smart devices. These might include devices such as a smart TV, a smart fridge, or home automation systems. All of these are made possible by embedded systems engineers.

An embedded system is a program that is developed and run directly on specific piece of hardware. Often this hardware is a micro-controller that is used to power specific functionality in a device. Examples of embedded systems include the software used to enable a printer to access information from a computer and print it to paper, the system embedded in a mouse that allows it to translate movement of a physical device into coordinates of a cursor on a monitor, or the monitor itself interpreting information from the computer and displaying it graphically. However, embedded systems are not limited to computer peripherals. Embedded systems are all around us. Behind every airplane, automobile, traffic light, drone, and robot is an embedded system.

Because embedded systems operate on small micro-controllers, they typically require software that is extremely efficient and extremely small in size. Because of this, many embedded systems are written in low-level software languages. These languages may include C, C++, or Rust. In many cases, embedded systems might even be written directly in assembly code depending on the constraints of the system.

If embedded systems interest you, a great place to start learning is by buying an inexpensive Raspberry Pi or Arduino board. A Raspberry Pi is a small computer that you can buy online that typically contains only a credit card size motherboard with common peripheral ports available to hookup monitors, keyboards, or a mouse. With this small motherboard, you can add on any electrical device you wish such as infrared sensors, microphones, or actuators. Using these basic add-ons, you can plug the Raspberry Pi into a monitor, load up its onboard operating system (usually a Linux variant called Raspbian), and write simple programs that interact directly with these hardware components. Similar components and do-it-yourself kits are available for Arduino chips; however, they do require a bit more knowledge of embedded systems and C++.

Distributed Systems

A distributed system can be defined as a network of computers working together as one system. To the user of this system, they are not aware that several computers are working together to power their requests. Said another way, the distribution of software across several node computers in the system is abstracted away from the user. Typically, distributed systems are used when software reaches a certain scale and cannot be reliably powered using a single computer.

Many of the topics surrounding software engineering in this book had to do with scalability and reliability. Distributed systems are usually deployed to accomplish these goals for our software. When a database reaches a certain size or requires the capacity for a very large number of concurrent queries, we often will replicate the database across computers to appease these requirements. The user querying the database will not be aware that the database has been replicated and distributed among many computing nodes, but their query performance will increase nonetheless.

The same is true for web sites on the Internet. Early web sites were powered off of single bare metal servers in the garage of start-up entrepreneurs. As their web sites grew, and increasingly more users would attempt to connect to their web site at the same time, a single server no longer could handle the network traffic. In this scenario, a user attempting to connect to an overwhelmed server might have to wait several minutes before the web site would respond or the web site would crash and not respond at all. To remedy this problem, a distributed systems expert might be called in to set up several servers for the web site. The software on the original server would be copied over to the additional servers, and a process would need to be put in place to keep the versions of the web site software in sync on each server. Additionally, extra software would need to be put in place that distributes the incoming user request among the servers to ensure that no individual server gets overwhelmed by requests. This process of distributing traffic is known as load balancing. Another problem that a distributed systems engineer would be faced with includes what to do when one of the computers in the distributed system crashes or fails to process an incoming request successfully. In this case, the distributed systems engineer might want to remove the failing node from the system and proxy the user's request to another node until the failing node can successfully be brought back online. This is what is known as fault tolerance in a distributed system.

These days, much of the work surrounding distributed systems for web sites is abstracted away by hosting providers that supply what is known as "Infrastructure as a Service" or IaaS. An IaaS provider, such as Amazon AWS or Google Cloud Engine, has several server farms all over the world that they can assign to customers who wish to host their web site software on the provider's hardware. The IaaS provider then provides a vast amount of configuration options available to the distributed systems engineer tasked with deploying the web site software onto the provider's servers. They can configure the load balancing settings, the security policies, the number of servers they wish to include in the distributed system, and many other options. Teams of distributed systems engineers who work with IaaS providers are typically referred to as "Cloud Operations" or CloudOps.

Much of the theory behind distributed systems requires deep knowledge of data structures and graph theories. If distributed systems is a topic that you are interested in, I recommend reading up on graph theory and understanding many of the algorithms related to this topic. Some of the algorithms you may want to consider include graph traversals and shortest path algorithms.

Web Development

Almost every piece of software written today interacts with the Internet in some way. The software written specifically for a web site or a native mobile application that is hosted on a server in the cloud is written by web developers. Typically, the work required to create a web site is divided into two sub-groups: front-end engineers and back-end engineers. Engineers who have expertise in both front-end and back-end technologies are known as full stack engineers.

A front-end engineer's primary responsibilities include writing the software that provides an interface for interacting directly with the user. This might include creating a navigation menu on a web site, a transition animation between pages, or interactive content on the body of the page. The technologies used on the front-end, at a very basic level, include HTML, CSS, and JavaScript. HTML, or hypertext markup language, is an XML notation variant that provides the structure of where elements of a web page belong. CSS, or cascading style sheets, provide information to the browser about how these elements should look (what color, how big, what spacing should exist, etc.). After these two structures have been defined for a web page, JavaScript (or ECMAScript as it is officially called) is written to create functionality on a web site. There are libraries in many languages, including Scala, that allow you to write web applications in your language of choice that compile down to JavaScript. The JavaScript for a web site is where the real software development occurs in front-end technologies.

A myriad of tools and frameworks have popped up to assist in front-end development, and understanding them and keeping up with them is key to being successful in this role. Common JavaScript frameworks include Angular, React, and Vue.js. Common CSS tool sets include pre-processors like Less and Sass. There are also tools such as Webpack, Gulp, and Grunt used for packaging the contents of your front-end code and minimizing them into smaller, more efficient code. If front-end engineering is of interest, you should also consider learning ECMAScript 6, or ES6, which is the latest syntax updates to the JavaScript language.

Back-end engineers typically handle any software application logic that needs to be realized across an entire web site or across both a web site and a mobile application. This usually includes APIs (application programming interfaces) that can be accessed using the HTTP protocol that your browser uses to load responses from web servers. These APIs might be responsible for tasks such as authentication, interacting with a database, or interacting with or extending the functionality of other web sites using their APIs. Back-end engineers can use just about any programming language they choose. Web frameworks exist for almost all languages to speed up the development of web-based software. For Scala, the two main web frameworks are Spring and Play.

Conclusion

As you can see, there are several unique and specific applications for software engineering skills in the industry. Deciding where to apply your engineering talent can be challenging, especially if your interest spans multiple topics. However, it is almost impossible to become an expert at everything. I would recommend picking a specific field of study and diving into it completely, becoming absolutely saturated by everything there is to know about it, before moving on to the next topic. This will prevent you from becoming the jack of all trades with no mastery in any field. Conversely, some of this might be outside of your control depending on whether you happen to get a job in a certain field or if there is no expertise in a given field and you are expected to fill the gap.

At the very least, hopefully by reading this book you have developed a base level of understanding of everything there is to explore in the world of software engineering. When you start to dive into other languages, you will notice that they all contain the same basic concepts of expressions, data types, control flow, functions, and classes. Also, the data structures and algorithms in this book should be applicable in any language, although the implementation details might vary depending on the primary paradigm of the language. By being exposed to all of the paradigms in one language, you have a unique opportunity to decide which you identify with the most and which you want to explore further in other languages.

I encourage you to continue learning and coding on a daily basis. It's important to seek out mentorship and a community of other engineers that you can rely on for support and motivation. If you want to be a successful engineer, you can never stop learning. The subject of software engineering is so vast that no one person can ever know it all. There is so much content out there that I expect you to be a student for life.

Index

A

Abstract class, 185
Abstract data structure, 250
Abstraction, 5, 20, 109
Accumulator pattern, 99
Acyclic graphs, 274
Algorithm, 213, 257
Anonymous function, 198
APIs, 314
Application state, 175
Argument, 115
Array, 232
Assemblers, 6
Assembling, 6
Assembly language, 6
Autodidacts, 305

B

Base case, 261
Big O notation, 213
Binary search tree, 246
Boolean, 60
Branching program, 88

C

Camel case, 110
Case class, 142

Classes, 130
CloudOps, 313
Code, 2
Code comment, 87
Code smell, 120, 192
Command runner, 219
Companion object, 144
Compiled, 6
Compiler, 6
Concatenation, 64
Concrete class, 186
Conditional statements, 88
Console, 21
Continuous integration (CI), 227
Creational design patterns, 294
CSS, 313
Cyclic graphs, 274

D

Database, 306
Database administrator, 307
Data engineer, 307
Data scientists, 309
Decomposition, 123
Depth first search, 282
Dequeuing, 239
Design patterns, 293
Destructured variables, 102

Developer experience (DX), 133
Directed edges, 274
Distributed system, 311
Divide and conquer, 261
Dynamically typed languages, 56
Dynamic programming, 287

E

Edges, 274
Embedded system, 310
Encapsulation, 130
Exception, 103
Expression, 32

F

Fault tolerance, 312
First in, first out, 238
Full stack engineers, 313
Functional programming, 191

G

Garbage collection, 137
Generic, 237
Getter, 133
Global variable, 99
Golden path, 217
Graph, 274
Graphical user interface (GUI), 20
Greedy algorithm, 259
Greedy Choice Property, 260

H

Hash collision, 246
Hashing function, 242
Hash table, 242
Head, 234
Hierarchical decomposition, 173
Higher-order function, 195
High-level language, 6
HTML, 313

I

Immutable operations, 65
Import, 157
Index, 34
Infrastructure as a Service
    (IaaS), 312
Input, 20
Input parameter, 23
Insertion sort, 259
Instantiation, 130
Integer division, 37
Integrated Development
    Environment (IDE), 33
Interfaces, 185, 188
Internet of Things, 310
Interpreted code, 33, 152
Interpreter, 33

J, K

JavaScript, 313
Java Virtual Machine (JVM), 153

L

Last in, first out (LIFO), 240
Lexeme, 27
Lexical analysis, 27
Linguistics, 28
Linked list, 234
Load balancing, 312
Local scope, 112
Loop, 95
Low-level language, 6

M

Members, 130
Memoization, 287
Method, 130
Modularity, 110, 123
Modulo, 44
Mutability, 50

N

Namespace collisions, 162, 176
Node, 234
NoSQL, 306
NTFS, 21

O

Object-oriented
        programming, 176
Object reference, 135
Operands, 35

Operator, 35
Optimal substructure, 260
Option, 268
Order of magnitude, 214
Output, 20

P

Packages, 155
Paradigm, 171
Pattern, 99
Polymorphism, 181
Pop, 239
Primary constructor method, 131
Primitive data type, 70
Procedural programming, 173
Program, 2
Property, 130
Pure function, 192

Q

Queue, 238

R

Race condition, 192
Recursive function, 196
Referential transparency, 192
Relational Database Management
        Systems (RDBMS), 306
Read, Evaluate, Print, Loop
        (REPL), 20

S

ScalaTest, 218

Schema, 306

Seed, 203

Selenium, 227

Semantics, 28

Sequential search, 259

Session, 34

Set, 250

Setters, 133

Side effect, 192

Simple Build Tool (SBT), 218

Software engineering, 209

Stack, 240

Static members, 144

Straight-line programs, 88

String interpolation, 74

Structural design patterns, 297

Structured Query Language (SQL), 306

Sub-type, 57

Superclasses, 178

Super-type, 57

Switch statement, 92

Syntax, 9, 28

T

Tail, 234

Ternary operator, 91

Tokenization, 105

Transistor, 3

Type casting, 59

Type class inheritance, 57

U, V

Unified Modeling Language (UML), 224

Unit test, 217

Unix file systems, 22

W, X, Y, Z

Web developers, 313

Printed in the United States
By Bookmasters